Cruising
Alaska

6th Edition

Cruising Alaska

6th Edition

A Traveler's Guide to Cruising Alaskan Waters & Discovering the Interior

Larry H. Ludmer

HUNTER

HUNTER PUBLISHING, INC.
130 Campus Drive, Edison, NJ 08818
732-225-1900; 800-255-0343; Fax 732-417-1744
www.hunterpublishing.com

Ulysses Travel Publications
4176 Saint-Denis, Montréal, Québec
Canada H2W 2M5
514-843-9882, ext. 2232; Fax 514-843-9448

The Boundary, Wheatley Road, Garsington
Oxford, OX44 9EJ England
01865-361122; Fax 01865-361133

Printed in the United States

ISBN 1-58843-510-5

© 2005 Larry H. Ludmer

Cover image: Glacier Bay © Jim Wark, AirPhoto
Index by Nancy Wolff, Wolff Indexing
Maps by Kim André © 2005 Hunter Publishing

4 5 6

Acknowledgments

The seemingly simple task of compiling the facts about cruise lines, their ships and destinations has become more and more difficult because of the sheer volume of choices. Any travel writer who wants to do the best by his readers must seek out the assistance of others to help amass this information. Ship facts and information on which ships have been assigned to cruising Alaskan routes were provided by the media relations staff of the cruise lines. It is important to note, however, that their role in providing information and/or services to me in no way affect what I have to say about a particular cruise line or ship. I am grateful to all public relations staff at the major cruise lines, but especially to Tori Benson, Susanne Ferrull and Marisa Cordola of Princess Cruises; Elizabeth Jakeway of Celebrity Cruises; Jaye Hilton of Royal Caribbean International; Irene Lui of Carnival Cruises; Heather Krasnow of Norwegian Cruise Line; and Susan Beresford, Hilda Cullen, Mary Schimmelman and Michele McCarthy of Holland America. All opinions expressed here are based on information gathered from a variety of objective sources and, most importantly, by firsthand experience.

www.hunterpublishing.com

 Hunter's full range of guides to all corners of the globe is featured on our exciting website. You'll find guidebooks to suit every type of traveler, no matter what their budget, lifestyle, or idea of fun.

Adventure Guides – There are now over 35 titles in this series, covering destinations from Costa Rica and the Yucatán to Tampa Bay & Florida's West Coast and the Alaska Highway. Complete with information on what to do, as well as where to stay and eat, *Adventure Guides* are tailor-made for the active traveler, with a focus on hiking, biking, canoeing, horseback riding, trekking, skiing, watersports, and all other kinds of fun.

Alive Guides – This ever-popular line of books takes a unique look at the best each destination offers: fine dining, jazz clubs, first-class class hotels and resorts. In-margin icons direct the reader at a glance. Top sellers include: *The Cayman Islands, St. Martin & St. Barts,* and *Aruba, Bonaire & Curaçao.*

Our *Romantic Weekends* guidebooks provide a series of escapes for couples of all ages and lifestyles. Unlike most "romantic" travel books, ours cover more than charming hotels and delightful restaurants, with a host of activities that you and your partner will remember forever.

One-of-a-kind travel books available from Hunter include *Best Dives of the Caribbean; The Virginia Handbook; Golf Resorts;* and many more.

Our website gives full descriptions for each book, along with reviewers' comments and a cover image. Books may be purchased on-line via our secure transaction facility.

Preface

The world of travel is a constantly changing landscape and cruising is no exception. In fact, the last couple of years have seen some particularly important developments as far as Alaskan cruising is concerned. Certainly the introduction of many spectacular new ships with an ever-greater number of amenities is among the most significant. Two other changes are reflected in the ports of embarkation and disembarkation. It was only a few years ago that almost all Alaskan-bound cruises left from Vancouver, Canada. While Vancouver is still a major gateway, you will now find just as many cruises departing from Seattle, Washington. At the other end, Anchorage used to be served by the port of Seward. Today, many Anchorage cruises dock at Whittier, which is closer to Anchorage. This change was brought about by the completion of a road tunnel from Whittier; the little town had been largely isolated before that. Finally, ports of call are being added. One cruise line has even introduced its own version of the "private island" so popular in Caribbean cruises. Here, it is Icy Strait Point, the former location of a fish cannery set in a glorious natural setting. Among the newest ports of call is Prince Rupert, British Columbia, and there could be others coming soon. So, read on in this completely revised edition and see what the cruise lines have to offer you.

Contents

Contents

Contents

Maps

The World of Alaska Cruising

*I*t wasn't long ago that cruising was an activity almost exclusively limited to people with lots of money to spend on their leisure time. While the number of people taking cruises has seen growth that's nothing short of dramatic over the past decade, it seems that a lot of people still think cruising is for the rich and famous. Indeed, cruise industry studies indicate that only about three percent of Americans have ever taken a cruise. If, after reading this book, you become one of the travelers who starts working that figure towards four percent or higher, then my objective will have been fulfilled.

Cruise Popularity

*C*ruising represents one of the fastest-growing segments of the travel industry, a trend that has seen gaining momentum in recent years. Preliminary figures show that during 2003 about 9.5 million people worldwide took a cruise. By far the largest segment of the cruising public resides in the United States. This figure was expected to take a huge leap – all the way to 10.5 million – in 2004, although final figures aren't yet in. But annual increases in the range of 15-20% are anticipated over the next few years. Although the Caribbean market dwarfs all other cruise market segments (in 2003 it represented more than 40% of all North American cruise passengers), Alaska is also a major market for cruise lines large and small. Approximately 776,000 people cruised to Alaska in 2003 (the last year for which full information was available at press time), but that number is estimated to have grown to as much as 850,000 in 2004.

There are many reasons why cruising has become so popular. Certainly one of the biggest factors is that today's cruise ships offer excellent value for whatever level of luxury your budget will bear. Cost factors will be explored in more detail later, but it will suffice to say that a typical week-long cruise to Alaska will cost you considerably less than the same period of time at a good resort hotel when all of the costs are calculated. Other things that attract people to cruising are the variety of activities available on these floating resorts, the fact that it is a comprehensive all-in-one vacation, and the romanticism and luxury associated with the experience. The ability to see several different and often exotic ports of call in a single vacation is also, no doubt, an important factor. Alaskan cruising has its own additional driving force – it's the easiest way to see many of the sights this state has to offer. And, if you let the cruise line handle all or most of your shore-based activities, the latter are accomplished without much of the hassle and uncertainty that can often accompany travel.

A trip to Alaska is, for many people, a once-in-a-lifetime experience and a cruise is without doubt one of the most extraordinary ways to go. It affords you the best scenery while floating on icy blue waters and gives you the opportunity to jump ship, hop on a flightseeing plane, and take a different look at the wonders that surround you. Once the cruise ends, many people continue their Alaskan experience either independently or with a cruise-line sponsored tour. While there are other ways to see Alaska besides traveling on big cruise ships, it is by far the most popular way to do so. So while we'll briefly explore some other means of seeing Alaska, most of the book will be devoted to what you'll encounter on one of the major cruise lines.

The increase in cruise ship capacity to Alaska is a result of both more ships and most of those ships being larger than in the past. This has, to some degree, helped keep costs down. On the other hand, many of the ships are now so large that they are unable to head into quite a few of the beautiful but smaller bays of the Inside Passage. Also, when a couple of mega-liners tie up at a small town such as Skagway, it can create a severe strain on the limited facilities of such communities. Shore excursions, however, can often take you to those places the big ships can't reach. The more adventurous individual might want to cruise on one of the many small ships that visit places the larger vessels can't venture into. There is a great choice for the consumer but, overall, I feel that a cruise on one of the larger ships is especially well suited to the first- or second-time visitor to Alaska.

A Brief Survey of Alaska

It is always helpful to have at least a basic understanding about places you are going to visit before you begin your journey. Such an understanding will enhance the experience for most visitors. In this section, you'll find basic information on the land and people of Alaska. For a more in-depth look at these aspects of the state, pay a visit to your local public library.

Alaska Facts

ENTERED UNION: January 3, 1959, the 49th state.

NICKNAME: The Last Frontier. Also known as the Great Land.

MOTTO: North to the Future.

AREA: 663,267 square miles, of which 571,951 square miles are land.

POPULATION: 643,786 (2002 U.S. census bureau estimate), the 47th most populous state.

POPULATION GROWTH: 1.6% from 2001 to 2002 (latest available figures).

POPULATION DENSITY: 1.1 persons per square mile (US average is 80 people per square mile).

HIGHEST POINT: Mount McKinley, 20,320 feet.

LOWEST POINT: Sea level

STATE BIRD: Willow ptarmigan

STATE TREE: Sitka spruce

MAJOR INDUSTRIES: Petroleum, tourism, fishing, mining and forestry products.

TOURISM INDUSTRY: Approximately $1.7 billion per year.

Geographically Speaking

*A*laska is far and away the largest state in the United States, dwarfing even mighty Texas by a margin of more than two-to-one. Its area is equal to one-fifth that of the entire Lower 48 states. One can cite endless statistics to impress you with its size and variety, but numbers cannot capture the beauty and magic of Alaska; it has to be visited in order to truly appreciate all of its outstanding features.

Alaska is shaped somewhat like a square except for two large projections (the Alaska Peninsula in the southwest and the panhandle which extends southeast from the corner of the "square" along the British Columbia border). Because of these projections, the maximum dimensions of the state are not

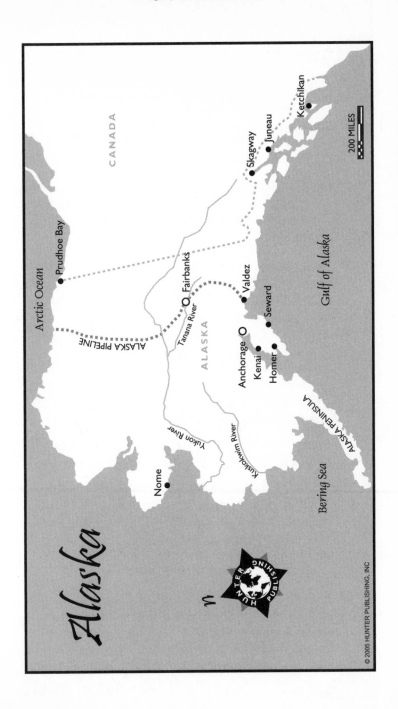

Alaska

CANADA

Arctic Ocean

Prudhoe Bay

Fairbanks

ALASKA PIPELINE

Tanana River

ALASKA

Valdez

Seward

Anchorage

Kenai

Homer

Gulf of Alaska

ALASKA PENINSULA

Yukon River

Kuskokwim River

Nome

Bering Sea

Skagway

Juneau

Ketchikan

200 MILES

HUNTER PUBLISHING

© 2005 HUNTER PUBLISHING, INC

5

square at all – about 1,100 miles from north to south and roughly 2,000 miles from east to west. The state has almost 7,000 miles of shoreline, with about 5,800 on the Pacific Ocean and the rest on the Arctic Ocean.

Regions

From a geologist's point of view, Alaska can be neatly divided into four regions stacked one on top of another in broad bands running from west to east. The regions are listed below, from north to south.

▶ Arctic Lowland (North Slope): In the extreme north and extending from the Arctic Ocean to the edge of the Brooks Range. The maximum elevation is only about 2,000 feet. It has extreme lengths of day and night depending on the season. The tundra landscape is known for its sparse vegetation and permanently frozen ground. Although it is the northernmost portion of the state, it is somewhat less cold than the interior due to the moderating influences of the Arctic Ocean.

▶ Brooks Range: A relatively narrow band of mountains with elevations less than 10,000 feet.

▶ Central Highlands & Basin (Yukon Plateaus): This is the largest region of the state as well as the coldest (although it has some of the highest summer temperatures). It has mountains large and small and notable valleys, including that of the Yukon River.

▶ Pacific Mountain Range: Covering the southern portion of the state, including the area around the Alaska Peninsula and the Gulf of Alaska as well as the Aleutians and the panhandle, this is the region of most interest to visitors. All cruise itineraries travel here, as do most of the major land excursions on cruise tours. This is the most physically diverse region of Alaska and the most beautiful. It has an abundance of magnificent snow- and ice-covered mountains, glaciers and fjords. The Boundary Range separates Alaska from Canada. On the water side is the famous Inside Passage, the sheltered waterway that is the main route for Alaskan cruises. It separates the mainland from the seemingly countless offshore islands of the Alexander Archipelago. The most heavily-visited region of Alaska lies along the long strip of coast from just beyond the Canadian border at Ketchikan north to Yakutat Bay and then west along the south coast bordering the Gulf of Alaska. Roads on the panhandle, where they exist at all, generally run for only a few miles in either direction of the major towns and then end. Boats are the primary means of getting from place to place. They serve as a lifeline to many of these remote communities. The other main touring area is also in the Pacific Mountain Range region and is an almost straight line that extends north from the city of Anchorage to Denali National Park. This area can be reached either by bus or car or via the Alaska Railroad.

Rivers & Mountains

Alaska has an abundance of great rivers. The most notable is the mostly broad 1,979-mile Yukon River (including a portion that is in Canada). Other significant rivers include the Susitna, Matanuska and Copper. As if the oceans and rivers weren't enough water, Alaska has thousands of lakes both large and small. But it is the mountains that are the most outstanding geographic feature. Over 16,000 of the state's peaks measure more than 14,000 feet above sea level, about the same number of 14,000-foot-plus mountains as in all of the Lower 48 states. (Actually, the highest in the Lower 48 is just under 14,500 feet, while all of Alaska's mountains in this size group are more than 14,500.) Of course, mountains in the panhandle/Inside Passage area are made all the more dramatic by their precipitous rise from the sea and stunning setting amid fjords and glaciers.

A Brief History

The native tribes of Alaska were never very numerous. Those that lived along the coast subsisted on fishing, while the interior tribes hunted. All carried on a varying degree of trade with one another and, although there were sporadic disputes between the tribes, things were generally peaceful because of their low numbers and the abundance of food (except for the even more isolated groups in the Arctic regions) and other resources. And with all that space available, one tribe didn't often encroach on another's territory.

The first Europeans to discover Alaska were Russians. This was natural considering how close Alaska is to Russia's eastern coast. Vitus Bering, a Dane sailing for Russia, made an expedition in 1741 to the southern coast. He returned to Russia with furs, and eager traders started operating in the Aleutians the following year. Kodiak Island was soon colonized. The Russian-American company was granted a monopoly over the fur trade in 1799. The company's first Chief Manager was Aleksandr Baranov. He founded two dozen trading outposts throughout southern Alaska and selected Sitka to be the main commercial center and *de facto* capital. By the end of the 18th century, other European countries and Americans were trying to get in on the lucrative fur trade, but the Russians remained in firm control. They also discovered that Alaska was rich in gold, copper and other resources, but their preoccupation with the fur trade meant they neglected these other potential sources of wealth. It was the British (who still owned Canada) and the Americans who became the beneficiaries of the mineral wealth. A decline in fur prices and fear of a British invasion (which was never really that likely) perked the Russian's interest in selling Alaska to the Americans as early as the 1850s. The process of completing the purchase was delayed by disinterest in Washington and the more pressing needs of the American Civil War, but William H. Seward finally completed the deal in 1867. Although it was called "Seward's Folly" at the time, at a cost of about two cents per acre it turned out to be one of the most brilliant real estate deals ever made.

The early years of United States ownership were mainly in name only as there were still many Russian business-people residing there and no real American authority except for a few Customs collectors. The Navy arrived in 1879 to keep law and order but it was not until 1884 that Congress saw fit to actually establish a civil administration. Salmon canning and other fishing operations were important by this time but the 1896 start of the Gold Rush was the first real key to Alaska's development. It was made a Territory in 1912. With the end of the Gold Rush era, the economy languished and the territory actually saw a decrease in population between 1910 and 1930. Public works programs as a result of the New Deal helped somewhat, but it was World War II and the obvious strategic value of Alaska's location that helped it reemerge as a viable place economically. The Japanese occupied two of the Aleutian Islands in 1942 and it was more than a year before they were retaken. During this time the government also built the Alaska Highway. In the early years of the Cold War Alaska became the home of the DEW (Distant Early Warning) Line. By this time the fishing industry was in decline, but forest products picked up the slack.

Alaska finally became a state in 1959. Tourism started to develop as an important industry shortly thereafter. Growth was slow overall and the Easter Sunday earthquake of 1964 that killed 131 people and did millions in property damage didn't help. But determined Alaskans pushed on. Their wait for a return to prosperity didn't take too long. Ranking in historic importance with the Gold Rush was the 1968 discovery of huge oil deposits on Alaska's North Slope. The economy grew by leaps and bounds during and after construction of the remarkable 800-mile Trans-Alaska Pipeline from Prudhoe Bay in the north to the port of Valdez in the south. The oil started to flow in 1977 and revenues to the state have been so great that each year every Alaskan citizen receives a dividend payment from the government. Not that the oil hasn't created some problems. The *Exxon Valdez* oil-spill incident is the most notable. As bad as it was, however, it was the lawyers and extreme environmentalists who made the biggest case out of it. Today, you won't see any damage. As far as the state treasury is concerned, oil production is already way down from its peak and the decline is likely to continue unless new sources are exploited. This would involve drilling for oil in the vast Arctic National Wildlife Refuge and it is one of the hottest political topics in Alaska and the nation's capital. It is likely to remain an issue for some time to come. Most Alaskans are for the development, but environmentalist opposition will probably keep this oil in the ground for the forseeable future.

People & Culture

*W*ith a population of less than three-quarters of a million, there is certainly plenty of elbow room for everyone. About 17% of the population is Native American. The single largest native group is the Inuit (referred to in the past as Eskimos, but that term is now politically incorrect and should be avoided). The Inuit number about half of all the Native Americans in Alaska. By the way, the native groups prefer to be called Native Alaskans.

Other significant native groups are the Aleuts, Tlingit and Haida of the coastal areas and the Athabaskans of the interior. These cultures might have died out as separate entities if it weren't for a recent interest in preserving their heritage. Thus, native languages are being taught to native children and pride in their culture is instilled. Tourism has actually had some benefit to preserving this culture because visitors are interested in seeing it and purchasing native crafts.

But most of the population is not Native Alaskan. It will probably still be quite a few years before a majority of Alaskans are Alaskan-born as the population was minuscule until after the discovery of oil on the North Slope. Alaskans are a hearty breed and fiercely individualistic. People who can't handle the climate and, even more importantly, the extremes of day and night, usually wind up returning to the Lower 48.

Alaska's Native Peoples

Part of the fascination of visiting Alaska is its unique population which includes more than 120,000 Native Alaskans. The Native peoples can be divided into five main groupings, two of which – the Inuit in the interior and the Tlingit along the coast – are more important in terms of numbers and the likelihood of your exposure to them.

The **Aleut** and **Alutiiq** live almost exclusively in the remote and usually barren islands of the Aleutian chain. The **Athabascan** are part of a much more numerous tribe that still resides in large areas of northern and western Canada. The Alaskan Athabascan can be found mostly along the border with the Yukon and British Columbia. The **Inupiaq** and **St. Lawrence Yupik** form a third group, while the **Yup'k** and

Cu'pik combine to form a fourth. These groups are all part of the larger Inuit culture. Americans still often refer to the Inuit as Eskimos but that isn't what they call themselves. In fact, many Inuit consider Eskimo to be a derogatory term (it means eater of raw fish) and it should be avoided. The Inuit are one of the most widely dispersed cultural groups in the world. Their greatest numbers reside along the coast of Greenland, across northern Canada and in the Arctic regions of Alaska. Their economy has always been based on fishing and hunting. The Inuit have a complex social structure that is largely dictated by the harsh conditions of where they live. *Igloo* is an Inuit term that means house. In the summer months the Inuit igloo is either a walrus or sealskin tent. In the winter it is generally built of stone around a frame of driftwood or whalebone and is covered with moss or sod. Rare is the snow and ice igloo that is so often associated with this arctic-dwelling people. The Inuit are highly skilled craftspeople and their work is much sought after by visitors.

But the native groups you are most likely to encounter on your Alaska cruise include the **Eyak, Tlingit, Haida** and **Tsimshian**. The Eyak are a small tribe. The much larger Tlingit (KLINK-it) and Haida (HY-dah) groups are closely related and are the best known of the tribes. The Haida originated on the Queen Charlotte Islands and are renowned as skilled carvers of totem poles and highly decorated canoes. These three groups occupy virtually all of the Alaskan panhandle and have historically relied on fishing to sustain their economies. The Tsimshian (SIMP-shee-ane) are fishers and hunters. They originally came from an area along the Skeena River in what is now British Columbia. Traditionally, the Tsimshian divided themselves into clans of about 30 to 40 people, all living together in the same large house. They are also excellent carvers.

What's Included in This Book

*T*he scope of this book's port and sightseeing coverage is dictated not so much by geography as it is by the various ship and land itineraries that are available to Alaskan cruise passengers. For Alaskan ports of call it includes primarily what was described in the *Geography* section under the Pacific Mountain Range because that encompasses Anchorage, the Inside Passage of the Alaskan panhandle as well as ports along the shore of the Gulf of Alaska and its neighboring peninsulas. Because land tours are a popular extension of the cruise experience, the area between Anchorage and Fairbanks, including Denali National Park, is also a part of this book. Largely excluded except for brief mentions are the vast stretches of Alaskan territory in the far north, the Aleutian chain in the south and the western coastal region by the Bering Sea; mainstream cruises simply don't go to those places.

Since every Alaskan cruise covers some territory outside of the Great Land, it makes perfect sense that these be addressed in this book. Thus, the Canadian portion of the Inside Passage is covered even though the port calls here are rather limited (but they are starting to grow in number due to the cruise lines' constant search for new places to take their repeat guests). Likewise, the beautiful city of Victoria is becoming an increasingly popular port of call. I have chosen to cover it here. Finally, ports of embarkation and disembarkation in the Pacific Northwest (such as Seattle and Vancouver) are all destinations in and of themselves. I offer limited coverage of the sights in these cities for those who pass through them as gateways.

Cruise Lines & Their Ships

*T*he majority of Alaska cruises share many common attributes and even common ports of call, but the available variety still may come as a big surprise to those who are new to cruising. The typical cruise can be classified in several ways, including by destination, duration, level of luxury and type of ship (that is, large cruise ship or smaller explorer-type vessel).

Types of Cruises

Destination

Within the Alaskan cruise market, destinations fall into one of two basic formats, although there are variations in each one. The first basic type is the "Inside Passage" cruise (round-trip from either Seattle or Vancouver) and the second is the "Gulf of Alaska" cruise. The latter also generally departs from either Seattle or Vancouver and ends up in one of the ports serving Anchorage, or vice-versa since these itineraries alternate northbound and southbound runs. Inside Passage cruises embark and disembark in the same place, one of the Pacific Northwest gateway cities. Although the names I've used to describe the two main cruise destination formulas are common in the cruise industry, you will find that some lines use other monikers for the same thing such as "Voyage of the Glaciers" or whatever. Check my evaluation of the various itineraries on page 79.

Duration

The greatest number of cruises are for eight days and seven nights, regardless of their destination. This is especially true of the mass-market lines. You will find some 10-day cruises – and a few that are even longer – but the extra length is usually determined by the departure point (such as San Francisco, which is farther away) rather than the route followed in Alaska. While shorter cruises of three to five nights can be found in many cruise markets, this is not the case when it comes to Alaska. The exception is some short cruise tours which will be discussed later.

Level of Luxury

The wide range of cruise lines has an equally big range in the level of luxury and cost options, although the variety isn't as notable in mass-market lines. Many specialty "luxury yacht" lines also sail to Alaska from time to time.

Type of Ship

This comes down to whether it is a traditional cruise line or the "explorer" lines. Even the smallest of the major line cruise ships dwarfs the biggest of the "explorer" vessels and there is a big difference in the two types of cruise experience. While I'll explain more about the small ships later, the emphasis in this book will be on the traditional cruise ships because they're the ones that carry well over 90% of Alaskan cruise visitors.

Cruise Lines

The primary traditional big-ship cruise lines operating in Alaska are Carnival, Celebrity, Holland America, Norwegian, Princess and Royal Caribbean. You can see that this list includes the biggest cruise lines in the industry sailing from US ports and covers almost all of the ones that most American travelers are familiar with. Below are complete details on the lines and their ships, along with information on several other operators.

Ship-by-Ship & Line-by-Line Evaluations

Reading the Statistics

Statistical information for the cruise lines and individual ships is mostly self-explanatory. However, a few items are worthy of some clarification.

The number of ships shown under the *Fleet* heading is the total vessels in service or scheduled to have been placed in service as of the beginning of the 2005 Alaskan sailing season. This includes all ships of that line and isn't limited to the number serving Alaska. The figure for *under construction* includes projects currently in the shipyards and firm order commitments.

Sometimes, a year of refurbishment will be shown after the year that the ship entered service. This will be done only if the refurbishment was major and if the original service entry date was 1998 or prior. In addition, you will find useful definitions of some of the other terms in the ship listings in the sidebar "A Nautical Primer" at the end of this chapter.

The *Passengers* header indicates the number of passengers the ship will carry based on double occupancy of all staterooms.

You might well see other numbers given in various sources of information on any particular ship. Because of additional persons in any number of rooms, a ship that is fully booked may well be carrying far more people than the double occupancy figure. However, I use the double-occupancy basis because it is the most commonly accepted and understood method and is frequently used in the cruise industry.

The *Passenger/Crew Ratio* is determined by the number of passengers divided by the number of crew members, expressed as a ratio, such as 2.4:1. In theory, the lower the number, the better the service. This is logical since you can assume that if there are three passengers to be taken care of by each crew member, that would not be as good if that same crew member only had to serve two passengers. While the luxury lines are the only ones that have ratios of less than 2:1, I have yet to find any reliable correlation to minor variances in the ratio. I have been on ships with a 2.6:1 ratio where the service was better than on a ship with a 2.2:1 ratio. Again, it is a general indication of service rather than a hard and fast rule.

Stateroom Size: You'll soon see that cabins are a lot smaller than most hotel rooms, or even inexpensive motel rooms for that matter. This is important to keep in mind if you have never sailed before. The measurements are in square feet and the range shows the smallest to the largest type of accommodation, including suite sizes. Measurements are for the room only – that is, they do not include the balcony space (if applicable), but I don't think too many readers are planning to sleep out on the balcony!

The *Space Ratio* is a measure of how "roomy" the ship is. It is calculated by dividing the Gross Registered Tonnage by the number of passengers. The higher the number, the more space you have per passenger, at least in theory. Many cruise experts consider this figure as gospel and, while I agree that this ratio does provide some indication of available space, there is no way to mathematically account for the "feel" the ship has.

The design of the ship (including passenger flow) is a more important indicator of how much space you have. Extremely low space ratios, however, should be a warning to expect a crowded-feeling ship.

One fact that I've deliberately omitted for each ship or line is the nationality of the crew (that is, non-officers). Although in the past it was the norm for each line to draw its crew from mainly one national or ethnic group, this is no longer the standard practice. It is not uncommon for crew members who directly serve passengers to encompass 40 or more different nationalities. In effect, every ship is a United Nations and that adds a lot of flavor to your experience. A few lines still emphasize one or two nationalities. Holland America crews, for instance, are dominated by Indonesian or Filipino men and women.

Mass-Market Lines

The term "mass market" isn't meant to be derogatory in any sense. It simply means that these cruise lines appeal to the broadest section of the traveling public because they offer choice and luxury at an affordable price. They also have the most ships servicing Alaska. The largest lines are innovative in terms of onboard activities and services and are also known for constantly introducing new vessels, including the largest that can be found operating in any part of the world.

In this book, each major line will be profiled, followed by a ship-by-ship description of their vessels. Only those ships serving Alaska will be described. Some things apply to all ships of a given cruise line. For example, cuisine and entertainment policy won't vary much from one ship to another on the same line. Thus, general information that is provided in the cruise line profile won't be repeated in the individual ship descriptions unless it significantly differs in some way.

CARNIVAL CRUISE LINES

Contact: ☎ (800) 227-6482; www.carnival.com
Officers: Bridge officers are Italian, but others may be international
Registry: The Bahamas for most, with a few registered in Panama
Fleet: 21 ships; 1 under construction

The world's largest cruise line has played a major role in making affordable cruising available to the public. While Princess' "Love Boats" caught the imagination of the public on television back in the 1960s, it was the then just-established Carnival line that introduced more new ships and more ideas that appealed to the less-than-millionaires crowd ready to take a cruise. Carnival offers excellent value and a casual, mostly informal experience on their self-proclaimed "fun ships." The entire Carnival fleet features a striking all-white exterior, except for the mostly red-and-blue Carnival logo, trim and distinctive funnel, which is shaped more like the tail of a jet airplane rather than a ship's smokestack. This may not seem very important when you read it, but it definitely adds a graceful flair to the entire fleet. One of the most notable features of Carnival's vessels are the large main showrooms that put an emphasis on rather lavish Vegas-style entertainment. Glitz is in evidence in more than just the production shows. The interior décor emphasizes eye-popping features and tries to dazzle you with the "wow" factor. This is especially true in Carnival's famous large atriums and the public areas surrounding them. Those who prefer a more refined appearance may need sunglasses! Activities are geared toward the fun side of cruise travel, as opposed to cultural enrichment. In fact, entertainment is so important at Carnival that towards the end of dinner in the main dining room your wait staff will put on a brief song and dance act that differs each night of the cruise. It's definitely a lot of fun as many passengers get involved.

Speaking of dinner, Carnival vessels offer a wide variety of dining choices and their newest ships even have an elegant supper club. Although Carnival doesn't break much culinary ground, they always provide excellent meals that are color-fully presented by a friendly wait staff. You won't, however, get white-glove treatment. The buffets are excellent and feature many stations, including a New York-style deli on the larger and newer vessels. A 24-hour pizzeria and ice-cream bar are other popular features with ever-hungry cruise passengers. Midnight buffets are big at Carnival, but their once-per-cruise Midnight Gala Buffet is an experience to remember. Concentrating on sweets, it's such a visual spectacle that guests are invited to view it an hour earlier just for picture-taking! Carnival's handling of the Captain's cocktail reception is also something special as practically an entire deck becomes a walk-through feast of hors d'oeuvres and colorful exotic drinks. Children's activities are generally extensive and the bigger the ship the more they have. In general, Carnival provides a cruising experience that is equally good for couples and families with children.

Carnival is one of the great innovators in the world of cruising and was a pioneer in the mega-ship category for contemporary cruising. They also offer a great deal of flexibility.

Given Carnival's size it seems odd that they haven't yet made a decision to expand their presence in Alaska, which has been stuck at just one vessel since they first debuted in this market about five years ago.

⚓ CARNIVAL SPIRIT

Entered Service: 2001	Gross Tonnage: 88,500
Length: 963 feet	Beam: 106 feet
Passengers: 2,124	Passenger Decks: 12
Crew Size: 930	Passenger/Crew Ratio: 2.3:1
Stateroom Size: 160-388 sq ft	Space Ratio: 41.7

The *Spirit*-class vessels are no longer Carnival's largest, but I still give them the nod as the most beautiful ships in what is a fabulous fleet. (The larger *Conquest*-class is not represented in Carnival's Alaskan itineraries.) The first ship in its class, the

Spirit features some of the most spectacular décor of any ship on the high seas. Although somewhat less ornate and opulent then the succeeding *Spirit*-class ships, glitz is still the term that applies to this vessel. And nowhere is this more visible than in the eight-deck high atrium with its fabulous murals. If the ship has an overall theme, it is Art Deco at its wildest. However, the main showroom is a three-deck affair with the look and feel of an elegant opera house, even though it's done up in an exquisite Egyptian style. One feature of this class of ship is the unusually large lounge/showroom that is placed immediately beneath the main showroom. On the *Spirit*, it's called the Versailles Lounge and it is beautiful as well as being a comfortable venue for watching the varied forms of entertainment that take place there. There are many other lounges and entertainment facilities of varying sizes. One of the most eye-catching decorative features is the unusual fountain which spans two decks.

The main, two-level dining room is simply gorgeous. However, because of its size, some people might feel that the noise level is too high. Alternative dining takes the form of (besides the buffet) the extra-fee Nouveau Supper Club. Located high atop the ship and connected to the Lido deck by a glass staircase suspended above the atrium (those prone to vertigo might wish to take the elevator or inside stairs to get there), it is an artistic masterpiece. The angled, rose-colored glass ceiling over the club lends a special atmosphere during the day. The glass dome, by the way, appears to be part of the funnel from the outside. If you go up to the very top of the ship on the outside you can look down into the club!

A two-level disco, wedding chapel and a gently curving "shopping street" are other important public areas. Although the promenade doesn't wrap around the entire outside of the ship (it skips the bow end), it is wrap-around if you go inside and walk through the exotically decorated "jungle" walkway. This beautiful spot isn't used by a lot of people and, therefore, provides a nice place where you can get away from it all to have a drink or just relax and contemplate the world. The *Spirit* has plenty of recreational facilities, including its two large main pools, water slide, gymnasium and full-service spa.

Accommodations are also excellent as even the smallest rooms are fairly spacious by cruise ship standards. The décor is pleasant and the functionality is just fine. If you've been on other Carnival ships, you'll notice the familiar style. The major difference is that these rooms are larger than those on older Carnival vessels. Except for a few somewhat smaller cabins, the interior rooms are generally the same size as outside rooms minus the balcony. This makes them an especially good value. The majority of outside rooms do have private balconies.

CELEBRITY CRUISES

☎ (800) 437-3111; www.celebritycruises.com
Officers: Greek
Registry: Liberia, except for *Mercury*, which is registered in Panama
Fleet: 9 ships

Celebrity's ships, like most other cruise line fleets, have certain distinguishing exterior characteristics that make them easily recognizable. Their vessels feature a mostly white upper superstructure with large broad bands of dark blue across the bottom section of the hull and additional blue trim on the superstructure. Some also have a more colorful trim in places. But every ship features their hallmark funnel marked with a huge white "X." (The "X" is the Greek letter *chi*, a holdover from the days when Celebrity was known as Chandris, a Greek cruise line.) The overall effect may not be as beautiful as the more common all-white exterior, but there is no denying that Celebrity vessels are both beautiful and sleek. Although light-color exteriors seem to have become more popular on the cruise ships of today, dark exterior colors are actually more traditional. Regardless, Celebrity is consistently rated as one of the best cruise lines in the world by experienced travelers, including the most experienced cruisers. This shouldn't come as a surprise when you consider that Celebrity ships usually carry between 300 and 600 fewer passengers than similarly sized ships. The cruise experience is refined. There are sommeliers to help you choose the right wine (and glass), cooking workshops, interesting lectures and educational programs relating to the places you're visiting. Beautiful works of art, from the masters to modern, grace all Celebrity vessels.

Excellent cuisine is another Celebrity hallmark, and the sophistication of food preparation, presentation and service is higher than on most mass-market lines. Dining flexibility is not as great as on some lines because many of their ships aren't as large, but this varies quite a bit from one Celebrity ship to another. Their larger ships offer plenty of choices, while the smaller ones do not. The Cova Café Milano is a wonderful feature of all their vessels. Here you can select from a wide variety of specialty coffees while treating yourself to a delectable European pastry. All Celebrity ships have the usual array of amenities and facilities of a large cruise ship. Their AquaSpa by Elemis is a Celebrity feature that warrants special attention, with spa facilities that may well be the best available anywhere on the sea. In addition to the usual exercise equipment and beauty treatments, the area has sauna, steam, aromatherapy and other goodies for those who appreciate the being pampered. Gymnasium patrons can even avail themselves of a certified personal trainer.

Celebrity does cater to adults and has incorporated additional facilities for children in order to extend the appeal of the line beyond just couples. Children's facilities are sometimes divided into four age groups (during peak sailing periods), but most of the time all children are grouped together regardless of age. Celebrity also offers "adults only" (minimum age of 21) cruises to most of its destinations, including Alaska. There are limited sailing dates for these cruises.

⚓ Infinity/Summit

Entered Service: 2000/2001	Gross Tonnage: 91,000
Length: 965 feet	Beam: 106 feet
Passengers: 1,950	Passenger Decks: 11
Crew Size: 1,000	Passenger/Crew Ratio: 1.9:1
Stateroom Size: 170-1,432 sq ft	Space Ratio: 46.7

Along with its sister ships of the fabulous *Millennium* class, these are the largest vessels in the Celebrity fleet and they show that a mega-sized ship and top-notch quality of service don't have to be conflicting concepts. While Celebrity has always been known for its fine and elegant facilities, it takes a ship of this size to offer the full range of activities that today's cruise traveler has come to expect. The two vessels are exactly the same in layout and facilities, although the décor varies considerably. Some public facilities even have the same names but, here to, each ship goes with its own set of names to complement the interior design of the room. The three-level Grand Foyer is gorgeous in an understated way. More drama awaits guests as they ascend up to 10 decks above the sea in one of the outside glass elevators. Some of the glass elevators overlook the ship's interior.

Despite the ship's large size, the main dining room is not so overwhelming as to be distracting and it is simply beautiful. The sister vessels have a wide range of shopping options, bars and lounges, plus fabulous recreational facilities. The Constellation Lounge (*Infinity*) or Rendezvous Lounge (*Summit*) at the bow end near the top of the ship make wonderful multi-purpose venues for entertainment, dancing or lectures to just taking in the view. The *Summit* will be using this lounge beginning in 2005 for a very special Cirque du Soleil event (see the sidebar on page 27 for details). When it comes to big shows, this class of ship provides more extravagance as the large stage in its beautiful three-level theater is Broadway quality.

The Right Cruise For You

When it comes to accommodations, it's hard to beat these ships. Even the smallest inside stateroom provides passengers with use of Egyptian cotton bathrobes, mini-bar, safe and a host of other amenities in attractive surroundings that are surprisingly spacious. Of course, as you rise through the many stateroom categories those amenities and features keep on growing with the size of the room. Most outside rooms feature balconies. Hey, if you like balconies then how about the Penthouse Suite – in addition to its more than 1,400 feet of inside space, the balcony is almost 1,100 square feet. That's bigger than many homes!

⚓ Mercury

Entered Service: 1997	Gross Tonnage: 77,713
Length: 866 feet	Beam: 106 feet
Passengers: 1,870	Passenger Decks: 10
Crew Size: 909	Passenger/Crew Ratio: 2.1:1
Stateroom Size: 171-1,514 sq ft	Space Ratio: 41.6

From the beautiful two-level Manhattan Restaurant and its adjoining foyer and champagne bar to the showroom with its European-style opera house balcony boxes, the interior décor is delightful. The four-deck Grand Foyer is visually appealing with its understated elegance. Especially noteworthy is the Navigator Club, a multi-purpose facility with wrap-around windows and seating at different levels that makes it an ideal indoor venue for those who like to spend time gazing at the sea or the passing scenery. The colorful and cheerful décor maintains a mostly informal look despite retaining a feel of luxury and elegance.

The buffet is called the Palm Springs Café and is especially nice. Besides having a great selection of excellent food (much better than most buffet food), the eight bay-type windows provide a degree of privacy and views that are not usually part of buffet dining experiences onboard ships. Even though *Mercury* isn't nearly as large as many of the ships now being put into service in Alaska, it has just about all of the features and facilities of its bigger competition. It even boasts the latest in onboard recreation – a golf course simulator. The shopping arcade is surprisingly large and varied.

The exceptionally spacious and well furnished staterooms are among the most comfortable of any ship. Little amenities are numerous, even in the lower-priced categories, and include things like private mini-bar, hair dryer, personal safe and interactive television. Choosing a room on *Mercury* can be somewhat easier than on many other ships because the number of room categories isn't as great. The lowest-priced suite category (Sky Suites) are mostly near the top deck of the ship and are great for people who like to stay high up. There are even some inside rooms on this level. This is an option that is less available on many of the newest ships where the top two or three decks are often devoted exclusively to public facilities. The service onboard *Mercury* is consistent with the high standards that have been established on all Celebrity ships.

CIRQUE DU SOLEIL AT SEA

The famous Montreal-based entertainment giant has shows all around the world, including four in Las Vegas! So, where does the successful avant-garde circus go next? Well, it seems that the sea is the answer. Cirque de Soleil is currently performing on two Celebrity ships, including *Summit* in Alaska, and it is generally agreed that the show will be expanded to other ships, at least those in the *Millennium* class. Cirque du Soleil at sea started in December, 2004. For those who are familiar with Cirque's shows, don't expect your "typical" Cirque du Soleil show because this isn't a fixed and static performance. Taking place in the "Bar at the Edge of the Earth," a specially redecorated lounge on the ships' top deck, the special characters of Cirque (including some created just for Celebrity Cruises) interact nightly with passengers in a masquerade ball. Sounds like fun. The festivities take place between 11 pm and 2 am, but the costumed Cirque characters also roam the ship throughout the day creating all sorts of fun, including some for kids who won't be attending the nightclub-style festivities in the bar.

HOLLAND AMERICA LINE

☎ (800) 426-0327; www.hollandamerica.com
Officers: Dutch
Registry: Netherlands, except for one ship registered in the Bahamas
Fleet: 12 ships; 1 under construction

This line has always been the largest or one of the largest players in Alaska and its presence continues to grow with its seven ships and wide assortment of cruise tours. With almost 140 years of sailing experience, it's little wonder that traditions are very important at Holland America. Although they've adapted to the modern world of cruising, HAL is still, in many ways, an old-fashioned and traditional cruise line that appeals to a large segment of the cruising public seeking that kind of experience. It starts with the basic exterior design and features such as their traditional midnight-blue hull, as well as the color trim on the white superstructure. Public areas (including those ships with atriums) on most of the fleet tend toward a classy styling that features understated elegance rather than a deliberate attempt to "wow" you. The result is a fine setting for a sophisticated cruise experience. Works of art, including paintings and sculpture, are a big part of HAL ships, and sometimes these vessels seem like floating art galleries. The art work is mainly themed to Dutch nautical traditions. All ships have a wrap-around promenade deck with rich teak woods; you can walk around the entire ship without going inside. This is another way that all Holland America vessels keep older cruising traditions alive. Not that the new world of cruising hasn't had an effect on HAL ship design and décor. Their new and fabulous *Vista* class vessels have some of the splashiness and eye-catching glitz that is so popular elsewhere. However, even these ships do it in Holland American style.

Holland America has a well-deserved reputation for fine food and outstanding personalized service. Their recent introduction of the *Signature of Excellence* program is a re-commitment to fine service. With a host of onboard activities, they do a good job of combining both fun and culturally enriching activities. Informative lectures and discussions on the ports of call are one of HAL's strong points in this regard, although educational aspects on this line run the gamut of topics from finance to cultural enrichment. Also in this vein, HAL is one of the most active lines when it comes to "theme" cruises. The themes can be on just about anything but might, for example, concentrate on a particular type of music during the course of a cruise.

Accommodations are quite varied, especially when it comes to size. This is largely a factor of the ship's age; HAL's older vessels have a number of room categories with very low square footage. Many amenities are a feature of HAL staterooms and this selling point is beefed up further as you look at the upgraded suite categories which include such things as personal concierge service and an invitation to the *Rijstaffel* (literal translation is "rice table"), a traditional and extravagant Dutch-Indonesian buffet lunch hosted by the Captain. Unfortunately, it is no longer HAL's practice to have the *Rijstaffel* as a feature for all guests.

The Right Cruise For You

NOTE: *A few final notes about Holland America. Tipping is not included in the basic cruise fare. Social hosts, that is, dancing or dining partners for unescorted female guests, are available. This is something that used to be a common practice in the cruise industry. HAL is the only mainstream cruise line that still offers it.*

⚓ Amsterdam

Entered Service: 2000	Gross Tonnage: 61,000
Length: 780 feet	Beam: 106 feet
Passengers: 1,380	Passenger Decks: 10
Crew Size: 600	Passenger/Crew Ratio: 2.3:1
Stateroom Size: 182-1,126 sq ft	Space Ratio: 44.2

The current version of *Amsterdam* is the latest in a long series of ships carrying this name. In fact, the name goes back all the way in the long history of the line and it seems that HAL's passengers like the idea of having a ship with this name. They also like the more traditional design and feel of this ship. As a result of this history and tradition, and despite the fact that Holland America has newer and larger vessels, *Amsterdam* still has the distinction of being considered the fleet's flagship.

The ship has two funnels that are placed side-by-side almost at the stern of the ship, giving it a unique profile. There is also a lot of space at the bow before the steeply sloped superstructure begins to rise from the deck. Overall, the graceful design is mostly that of a traditional vessel, although there are certainly some elements of more modern ship design visible on the exterior. There is a most attractive three-level atrium that serves as the focal point of the ship. The layout of the two primary public decks is a bit confusing. However, you will get used to it after a short time at sea. One positive feature of the design is the use of gently curving public passages that helps to avoid the tunnel vision effect you can get on some big ships.

Gold is a popular color and is most prominent in the gorgeous main dining room, a rather extravagant affair compared to the generally understated elegance of the rest of the ship. The two-level main restaurant has lots of brass and showy "palm" trees all counterbalanced by the soothing strains of a strolling string quartet. Alternative dining is available in the form of a fine Italian restaurant in addition to the ever-present "Lido" deck buffet. There are several swimming pools, one of which can be covered during inclement weather. Be sure to take note of the wonderful bear sculptures beside the main swimming pool.

The staterooms are large and nicely equipped. Most have good-sized windows, although the floor-to-ceiling windows and balconies are saved for the suite categories. Speaking of suites, the Amsterdam has a large number of rooms designated as mini-suites. Although they do have a somewhat separated sitting and sleeping area, they would be more properly described as oversized staterooms. The décor is attractive but, as would be expected, somewhat understated. Beige and light browns are featured colors. All of the accommodations on this ship have full bathtubs, a nice feature (now found on just about the entire HAL fleet) that will appeal to many people.

⚓ Oosterdam

Entered Service: 2003	Gross Tonnage: 85,000
Length: 951 feet	Beam: 106 feet
Passengers: 1,848	Passenger Decks: 11
Crew Size: 842	Passenger/Crew Ratio: 2.2:1
Stateroom Size: 154-1,343 sq ft	Space Ratio: 46.0

Not that HAL would ever say so, but the debut of this and other *Vista*-class vessels in the fleet is, in my opinion, a response to the introduction of ever-more extravagant ships by other lines. The *Oosterdam* (pronounced OH-STER-DAHM) is the second of Holland America's four magnificent new *Vista* ships. It represents a dramatic departure from the line's "typi-

The Right Cruise For You

cal" vessel. Not only is it significantly larger than most other ships in the fleet, but it has a dazzling, colorful and often extravagant style. In fact, the change was so great that they toned down the décor on the two following ships in this class because some of their tradition-oriented guests found the *Oosterdam* a bit too much! I can understand their surprise, but I have to say that I like the lively appearance and feel of this ship. Moreover, despite the unusual degree of glitz, the décor doesn't detract from the fine service and overall classy experience that a Holland America cruise always offers.

Perhaps it is just as important to emphasize how this ship follows the traditions of HAL. That begins with the full wraparound promenade deck, the three-level atrium and the Crow's Nest Lounge, above which is an open observation area. The *Oosterdam* features extensive use of glass and curved, flowing lines to create a dramatic and airy atmosphere. This is most evident in the two-level main dining room and the magnificent tri-level main showroom called the Vista Lounge. It has an alternative theater and more dining options than can be found on other Holland America ships. The recreational facilities are larger and more extensive than on any other class of ship in the fleet. Among the options are a golf simulator and tennis and basketball courts. Spa facilities are among the largest and most sophisticated at sea. There are separate facilities for small children and teens, respectively called the Kid Zone and Wave Runner. While these will be welcome news for parents, one still cannot say that HAL represents the best choice for family-style sailing.

When it comes to accommodations, the *Oosterdam* raises the bar a few notches compared to this line's more traditional ships. This begins with the higher percentage of outside rooms that have private balconies. Spaciousness is generally the order of the day, with most rooms being larger than cruise industry norms.

NOTE: *Be careful when booking inside rooms. HAL's brochure shows 185 square feet, but this refers to large inside rooms. Those that are standard measure in at 154 square feet, which isn't bad but is a far cry from what you are led to believe.*

While the décor isn't that different from other ships of the HAL fleet, there is a generally more cheerful color scheme that gives the rooms an airier look. The *Oosterdam* offers bathtubs in all but the lowest-priced stateroom categories.

⚓ Ryndam/Statendam/Veendam

Entered Service: 1994/1993/1996 [all refurbished 1998-1999]
Gross Tonnage: 55,451

Length: 720 feet	Beam: 101 feet
Passengers: 1,258	Passenger Decks: 10
Crew Size: 602	Passenger/Crew Ratio: 2.1:1
Stateroom Size: 156-1,126 sq ft	Space Ratio: 44.0

These are identical vessels as to their deck-plans, and are almost identical triplets regarding the interior details. All are experienced Alaskan cruisers as each ship has been going to the Great Land since it was placed into service. They are now among the smaller ships in the Alaskan market and can make it into some tight places that the mega-ships have to skip. Referred to by HAL as "S-class" vessels, they all definitely fit the more typical description of what most people expect from this line. As ships of the finest cruise line in the world with a well deserved reputation for excellence in all categories, these vessels are not deficient in any important way. In fact, old-time cruisers who don't especially care for some of the trends on today's bigger ships might well prefer them. And that's just fine if they fit your style. However, if you're looking for a mega-ship, these won't fit your plans. They offer a distinguished and refined cruising experience in keeping with the older traditions of this line.

The sterns reflect the traditional raked design with terraced levels affording lots of outdoor space and great views. The Lido buffet is unusually large given the overall size of the ship and passenger count. The interior is beautifully designed and exudes the luxury that is associated with Holland America. Public areas make generous use of teak wood, many works of art and beautiful fresh flowers. Interior architectural highlights include a multi-story atrium, and both the main dining room and showroom span two decks. There's also a cinema, a Holland American fleet-wide standard, where free popcorn is offered. As always, the Crow's Nest Lounge is a great place to watch the passing scenery. These were among the first ships to have a retractable glass dome over one pool, so any unexpected bad weather won't spoil your time in the water.

All of the staterooms feature easy-on-the-eyes pastel tones and comfortable, tasteful furnishings. While most ships require significant upgrading to go from shower to bathtub, the S-class offers tubs in all categories except for inside staterooms. Almost all rooms (including the majority of inside cabins) are at least 182 square feet, making them exceptionally spacious. However, if you take the two lowest-priced inside categories then you will wind up with the smallest rooms on the ship, ones that might well be just a tad too small for most people's tastes.

⚓ Volendam/Zaandam

Entered Service: 1999/2000	Gross Tonnage: 63,000
Length: 780 feet	Beam: 106 feet
Passengers: 1,440	Passenger Decks: 10
Crew Size: 561	Passenger/Crew Ratio: 2.6:1
Stateroom Size: 113-1,125 sq ft	Space Ratio: 43.8

Somewhat newer and a bit larger than the preceding triplets, these very attractive sister ships are much more similar in size, layout and facilities to HAL's more famous *Amsterdam* and *Rotterdam*. Both are mostly traditionally designed vessels with a deliberately older-looking appearance, although the public areas show the influence of more recent trends in ship design. The attractive three-deck atrium serves as a focal point for many public facilities and that's a plus because some areas of these ships are not as easy to navigate as they could be. However, you'll quickly get used to the peculiarities of the layout. The main two-level dining room is an elaborate and luxurious facility. Dining options are not as varied on a ship of this size, but there is an alternative restaurant in addition to the buffet. What can be said with confidence is that just about everything on theses vessels has the rich feel that makes Holland America so popular with a large segment of the cruising population.

> NOTE: *It should also be noted that Holland America is one of an increasingly small number of cruise lines that has a naturalist/Alaskan expert on board. These two ships are no exception to this practice. They, along with the others, also have a Native Artists-in-Residence Program so you can observe skilled crafts people as they sculpt, paint or create other works of art.*

The tastefully designed staterooms and suites feature shades of beige and taupe and are generously sized, even in many of the lower-priced categories. However, there is one potential problem that you should be careful to avoid. While the overwhelming majority of staterooms on these ships are comparable in size to HAL's usual larger standards (beginning at around 180 square feet), the lowest priced cabin is so small and cramped that it could spoil your cruise if room space is important to you. Fortunately, there are only a few rooms in this category.

The Right Cruise For You

A VIEW FROM THE CROW'S NEST

One of the pleasures of cruising has always been to enjoy the view from a special interior spot where you could sit and gaze out on the water or the passing scenery without getting blown away by the wind. Fortunately, Holland America has retained one of the most enduring institutions in the cruise industry and that is the "Crow's Nest" – their observation lounge. The name comes from an even older nautical tradition: a lookout high up on the ship's tallest mast. But on HAL you don't have to climb a rope or ladder to get there. An elevator will whisk you to a beautiful lounge located on the top or next-to-top deck that provides unobstructed views on three sides. The Crow's Nest also has a small dance floor, so there is often entertainment. It is a common venue for lectures and other shipboard events. If you sail on Holland America, be sure to spend some time at the top. It is ideally suited to the scenic splendors of cruising Alaska.

NORWEGIAN CRUISE LINE

☎ (800) 327-7030; www.ncl.com
Officers: Norwegian
Registry: The Bahamas or Panama
Fleet: 12 ships; 2 under construction

The beautiful ships of NCL mostly feature an all-white exterior except for the graceful dark blue trademark funnel that is placed far toward the stern. A few of their newest and biggest ships have introduced a flashy and unique design on the fore section of the hull – colorfully painted "ribbons" or other decorative touches that lend a festive atmosphere. The response from the public seems to be positive and I wouldn't be surprised if this becomes standard throughout their fleet. In general, the ships of NCL have a nice combination of both traditional and modern styling that is pleasing to the eye. Norwegian has a reputation for efficient and friendly service that is not particularly fancy or intruding. Likewise, their food hasn't earned special honors but it would have to take a very fussy eater to find anything significant to complain about. Norwegian is justly popular with both young couples and families as much for their casual and fun approach to cruising as for their relatively low prices. If I have one complaint about NCL (and this even applies to their newest and best ships) it is that many staterooms are smaller than those on most contemporary ships. It is not uncommon for many classes of cabins to be only 135 square feet or so. Thus, when booking a cruise on NCL make sure you upgrade enough to get a somewhat larger room, unless the size really doesn't matter to you. When it comes to other facilities, Norwegian's vessels have everything that big ships can offer, including extensive children's programs (divided into three age groups), top-notch entertainment that varies from Broadway to Las Vegas-style and full-service spas.

The degree of flexibility offered by NCL also attracts many passengers. A trend that began in earnest perhaps five or six years ago and continues unabated today is to offer a greater freedom of choice when it comes to where and when you dine, how you dress and other things. NCL has been a pioneer in this field with their *Freestyle* cruising. Although other lines have followed suit, Norwegian's *Freestyle* offers passengers the greatest degree of flexibility. Depending on the ship, there can be up to 10 restaurants representing a wide variety of cuisines and styles. There is a fee for some of the specialty restaurants. Dining times and seating arrangements are completely flexible (open seating from about 5:30 pm to as late as 10 pm). This applies even in the more traditional main dining room, if you can call it that anymore. Regardless of where you eat you can dress as you wish (within reason – beachwear, for example, is taboo in dining establishments) and even in the most formal

The Right Cruise For You

restaurant you can go casual. Of course, you can dress up as much as you want and many people still do. Formal nights are designated in various restaurants but that just means it's dress-up time for those who want to do so. Norwegian also points to *Freestyle* when it comes to activities, but this is stretching it a bit since every cruise line allows you complete freedom of choice in this area. NCL has flexible disembarkation procedures that allow you to spend more time onboard, but be warned that this feature might cost you some extra money.

Norwegian has heavily promoted its "Homeland" cruising program and cruises to Alaska are a big part of this. In terms of the number of ships sailing to Alaska, this line is now the third-biggest among the Alaska players. Norwegian has also decided to be the first to embark on a program of renovating and building vessels mostly in the United States. This includes having a staff that is mostly American. As a result, by the time you read this they will have at least three ships that are U.S.-flagged, something that hasn't been seen in this country for a long, long time. Although none is currently scheduled to be in Alaska in 2005, I believe it's a strong possibility that one could show up there in the next couple of years, so this needs to be addressed. Because of legal and financial considerations, these ships will operate under the label of NCL America. Although the line hopes to eventually make the experience on NCL America just like that of other Norwegian ships, early reports from passengers do indicate that there is a difference that hasn't pleased a lot of people. Guests have reported that the level of service by American crew members, although still good, has been noticeably less than what past cruisers have come to expect. Since it is still early in the game, NCL America has to be given a bit of time to play catch up. Also, see the information about gratuities in the *Practical Information* chapter for some other differences.

⚓ Norwegian Dream

Entered Service: 1992 [refurb 1998]	Gross Tonnage: 50,760
Length: 754 feet	Beam: 94 feet
Passengers: 1,750	Passenger Decks: 10
Crew Size: 700	Passenger/Crew Ratio: 2.5:1
Stateroom Size: 136-350 sq ft	Space Ratio: 29.0

This attractive world traveler is a relatively small ship by today's standards but it comes with a good mix of the feel and features of a bigger ship. During its major refurbishment in 1998, the vessel was stretched and more rooms were added. That is why the beam is so narrow compared to most other ships of this length. Unfortunately, in adding all of the features on a ship of this size it created a situation where you may feel a bit crowded. Note that the space ratio is considerably lower than most ships of the major lines, including other ships in the NCL fleet.

The ship's layout is fairly simple. The top-most decks contain a good variety of recreational facilities, ranging from basketball courts to a fitness center and massage facility. It doesn't have a lot of big public lobby areas and goes for a more subdued form of elegance rather than dazzle. There are six restaurants to choose from, a large number considering the size of the ship and a big plus to those who like variety. The two main restaurants are the Four Seasons and the Terraces. The former is roughly oval in shape and extends out over the sides of the ship, providing excellent views and a feeling of spaciousness at dinnertime. Even nicer is the Terraces room, with its four gently sloping levels that give the restaurant its name. It overlooks the stern.

The two-level main show lounge is quite nice, although productions have to be somewhat less extravagant than those on bigger ships with larger showrooms. There are numerous other bars and lounges, all comfortable and attractive. The Observatory Lounge at the bow end of the Sports Deck is a

The Right Cruise For You

good place for socializing and viewing that great Alaskan scenery you'll be passing by. The wrap-around Promenade Deck is very traditional and contains the ship's main lobby and entrance area.

The staterooms are colorfully attractive and generally quite comfortable; however, several of the lower categories are very small and I can't recommend them. You have to go up to the middle price categories if you don't want to feel cramped. Only the best suites have balconies. *Norwegian Dream* provides a decent cruise experience at affordable prices and is well-suited to families and those seeking value. Those who demand higher levels of luxury and space will probably want to look elsewhere.

⚓ Norwegian Jewel

Entered Service: 2005	Gross Tonnage: 92,000
Length: 965 feet	Beam: 105 feet
Passengers: 2,376	Passenger Decks: 11
Crew Size: 1,100	Passenger/Crew Ratio: 2.2:1
Stateroom Size: 142-5,320 sq ft	Space Ratio: 38.7

The newest jewel in the NCL fleet, this ship will not make its Alaska debut until the 2006 season. *Norwegian Jewel* is very similar to *Norwegian Star* because it's built on the same platform, but it has enough differences so that passengers who have been on the *Star* (or *Norwegian Dawn*) will feel as if they are on a completely different vessel. For one thing, it holds a few more passengers.

The most important element of NCL's *Freestyle* program is the variety of places to dine that are available on your schedule. In line with that, *Norwegian Jewel* will have 10 restaurants, including some that have become very popular on several Norwegian ships. These include Le Bistro, Blue Lagoon and Cagney's Steak House. New to the dining scene with *Norwegian Jewel* is the Tsar's Palace. This will be one of two "main" restaurants and it may well be the most elaborate at sea.

Based on the palaces of St. Petersburg, it boasts white and gold ceilings, green marbled pillars and 24-carat gold-plated chandeliers. A unique touch are the balustrades around the room that will remind diners of Fabergé eggs. The second main dining room is Azura, featuring pop art with back-lit glass that glows and sets the mood for intimate dining. How chic! Other specialty restaurants are Mama's Italian Kitchen, a trattoria-style eatery complete with a long wooden table running through the center of the room; Tango's, a brightly decorated restaurant that goes well with the decidedly hot and spicy Latin menu, including a selection of tapas; and Chin Chin, an Asian restaurant. Something new is also in store for bar patrons. Three bars will be placed together, creating a sort of "Bar Central" (the term is NCL's, not mine), with each one somewhat physically separated and having a different theme. There's Shakers Martini and Cocktail Bar; Magnum's Champagne and Wine Bar (an Art Deco design that evokes the atmosphere of both 1920s Paris and the former grande-dame of cruising, the *Normandie*); and the contemporary Maltings Beer and Whiskey Pub. Not to be outdone by this trio, the Sky High Bar, based on the beer garden on the other two ships of this class, will be decorated to resemble a hot air balloon. A cabaret lounge called Fyzz will feature three private Karaoke rooms. I'm glad they're private – who wants to hear some of those Karaoke-types sing anyway?

Although *Norwegian Jewel* will feature similar staterooms and other accommodations, including the huge Garden Villa suites (see the *Norwegian Star* description below for this and other general stateroom information), it will have a completely new class of rooms called courtyard villas. These will share a common private courtyard, swimming pool, Jacuzzi, sun deck and small gym. These suites come with more than the usual amenities associated with cruise ships and their location at the top of the ship will provide spectacular vistas.

The Right Cruise For You

⚓ Norwegian Spirit

Entered Service: 1998 [refurb 2004] Gross Tonnage: 77,000
Length: 880 feet   Beam: 106 feet
Passengers: 1,966   Passenger Decks: 10
Crew Size: 965   Passenger/Crew Ratio: 2.0:1
Stateroom Size: 151-638 sq ft   Space Ratio: 39.2

Formerly the *Superstar Leo* operated by Star Cruises (the Asian company that owns NCL), the ship was transferred to Norwegian because the need for larger ships is far greater in the North American market than in the still-developing Asian market. This is good news for Alaska-bound passengers because this is a fine ship under any name. Although there was substantial "refitting" to bring it more in line with the *Freestyle* requirements of Norwegian, the ship is quite a bit different than the other ships in the fleet, something that might add spice for people who've already cruised NCL and like it but, at the same time, want a change of pace.

With an exterior repainting, the ship fits in with the image of the NCL fleet. However, the interior architecture, and even the décor, is more dazzling than is usually found on Norwegian's vessels. This begins with a very dramatic and glitzy six-deck atrium complete with three glass elevators for great interior views. Two "boulevards" provide convenient access to the shopping promenade and many other public facilities. The large Moulin Rouge theater has an appropriate name given its fiery red look. No less sedate is the Galaxy of the Stars, a lounge on the top deck. It's a popular entertainment venue in the evening and serves as an excellent observatory for viewing Alaska's scenery during the daytime. There are lots of other bars, including the Bier Garten, an NCL feature on several new ships that seems to be extremely popular with guests. Recreational facilities are extensive. The beautiful main Tivoli pool area has four hot tubs, each capped by a cylindrical cone-shaped covering that is rather unusual for a ship. The fine spa even has an exercise pool with artificial currents that you can swim against. The strength of the "tide" is adjustable. Children's facilities are also excellent and the kid's pool has its own hot tub. There's an elegant wrap-around promenade and several decks of outdoor space that give a spacious feel.

The *Spirit* has eight restaurants, including a French bistro, trattoria, steak house and buffet. Shogun's is a three-in-one restaurant with areas for teppanyaki, a sushi bar and an Asian fusion restaurant. There are two main dining rooms. If you like opulence, however, go for the beautiful Windows Restaurant, so-called because of its two-story windows that will remind you of the great room in a mansion.

The cabins on this ship are uniformly good when it comes to size. Even the smallest are considerably more roomy than is the case on many other NCL ships, including some of their newest. Unfortunately, the décor could be a little more colorful – the walls are too pale. There are lots of balcony rooms and an unusually high number of inside cabins. This ship also has a very large number of connecting staterooms, which is good if your kids are going to have their own room.

⚓ Norwegian Star

Entered Service: 2001	Gross Tonnage: 91,000
Length: 965 feet	Beam: 105 feet
Passengers: 2,240	Passenger Decks: 11
Crew Size: 1,100	Passenger/Crew Ratio: 2.0:1
Stateroom Size: 142-5,350 sq ft	Space Ratio: 40.6

This was the first ship in the growing NCL fleet that was truly designed around the concept of a *Freestyle* cruising program. As such, it offers an extraordinary array of dining options. In fact, there are no fewer than 10 different dining choices, including Soho (fusion cuisine); Ginza (Asian); Aqua (contemporary); and Le Bistro (French and Mediterranean). There are many other more casual options, and you'll even find a beer garden! If you want to opt for a more traditional-style "main" dining room, then the beautiful Versailles room fits the bill.

The Right Cruise For You

Speaking of décor, there are a variety of styles in the dining venues commensurate with the variety of cuisines, but thoughtful attention to detail is a hallmark throughout. Both the food and the service are just fine. NCL has been improving their staff ratios in recent years and the result is a level of service that is considerably better than what would have been expected from a budget-oriented line just a few years ago.

The ship's other public facilities are no less varied or beautiful, beginning with a host of bars and lounges of all sizes, from intimate places to the large Spinnaker Lounge high up on Deck 12 and affording great views from three sides. The tri-level Stardust Theater handles production shows which are some of the most elaborate at sea. A nightclub and cinema are among the other entertainment options. The tapas bar is an unusual feature and provides a more grown-up alternative to burgers and hot dogs when the urge for a snack arises. There are extensive recreational facilities, including a large spa with accompanying full-service fitness center. You'll find plenty of deck space for lying in the sun, although the ship could use some more swimming pools to match its size. The *Norwegian Star* offers a full children's program separated by age group.

Turning now to the accommodations, *Norwegian Star* is generally above the level you'll find on most ships of this line. Even the smallest of the outside rooms are a nice size with or without a balcony. The décor is colorful and attractive and the design is functional although the furniture on this and other new Norwegian vessels looks a bit chintzy compared to the competition. However, the most significant criticism I have about this class of ship concerns inside accommodations which, at only 142 square feet, are quite small for today's biggest ships. At the other end of the scale, most suites are in the 300- to 800-square-foot range, but the two huge 5,350-square-foot Garden Villas bring a new dimension in accommodations at sea that is surprising considering that NCL isn't usually considered for that kind of luxury. The villas, which are the biggest suites at sea, have five rooms plus a private garden with hot tub and come with their own butler and concierge service. The roughly $12,000 per-week tab isn't likely to appeal to most travelers but, if you have a few couples sharing it, the cost per person does come down quite a bit.

A minor makeover in 2004 altered some of the interior décor. Perhaps the most notable change is outside where the hull now features large and colorful flowing "ribbons" painted on the otherwise snow-white ship. NCL began this with some of their ships in Hawaii and the reaction from the public seems to be mostly favorable.

⚓ Norwegian Sun

Entered Service: 2001
Length: 848 feet
Passengers: 1,936
Crew Size: 950
Stateroom Size: 121-459 sq ft

Gross Tonnage: 78,309
Beam: 118 feet
Passenger Decks: 10
Passenger/Crew Ratio: 2.0:1
Space Ratio: 40.4

The *Norwegian Sun* is typical of many ships of this line with similar statistics. For a short time it was the biggest ship in the fleet, but it has been surpassed by a number of other vessels in the past three years, especially with the introduction of the Dawn-class. The ship has a rather broad beam for its length, but it still has graceful lines. The *Sun* was, along with the *Norwegian Sky*, among the first NCL line ships to have been specially configured for *Freestyle* cruising, although this has been carried even further with later ships. Thus, for example, you'll have a total of nine different restaurants to choose from. It has a rounded three-deck atrium and a two-level showroom at the stern, a somewhat unusual location for modern ships (not that it makes any difference if you watch a show at the front or rear of the vessel). A dozen bars and lounges assure that you'll have plenty of places to whet your whistle as well as be entertained. Like all of the newer Norwegian ships, these facilities

The Right Cruise For You

are often quite eye-catching, with a number of different themes.

The *Sun* has a wide assortment of recreational facilities and a darn good program for children. Until recently it might have been fair to say that Norwegian didn't pay quite as much attention to spa facilities and their ships' spas often didn't compare favorably with most of the other major lines. This is no longer the case and, once again, beginning with this class of ship, the spas have been upgraded and are first class. The ship has lots of outdoor deck space and, although this may not be as significant as on a Caribbean cruise where you spend lots of time outside, it is nice to know that you'll have plenty of room to spread out when everyone comes out on deck to see the glaciers or a passing whale!

Accommodations are very attractive, comfortably furnished and highly functional in design and space utilization. However, once again, there is a drawback when it comes to staterooms in the lower-priced categories. Too large a percentage of the rooms (all inside and a great many outside) are small. It's not just the very smallest ones at 121 square feet. Several other categories fall below my acceptable level of 150 square feet. So if you want a nice-sized room you're forced to upgrade considerably – and likely to a price level that might be higher than you wanted to pay. On the other hand, ocean-view staterooms on the two highest decks have private balconies and are much more generously sized. For anything below that class, I recommend you ask for the exact cabin size from the reservation agent before you make a booking.

PRINCESS CRUISES
☎ (800) 774-6237; www.princess.com
Officers: British or Italian
Registry: Britain or Bermuda
Fleet: 12 ships; 2 under construction

Princess, of *Love Boat* fame, can be said to have started the current popularity of cruising as a result of the television series that featured a Princess vessel. While the original *Love Boat* is no longer in service, the tradition continues with newer and better vessels. When the mega-ship *Grand Princess* was introduced in 1998 it began a revolution in cruise ship building that opened up a whole new world to the cruising public. It was called "Grand Class" and meant not only that you were on a ship of grand proportions, but that you had far more on-board options than were previously available to cruisers. The public response was so positive that Princess extended the concept of Grand Class in one form or another to the entire fleet; ships that were too small to accommodate the changes were phased out. "Grand Class" as a style of cruising has been renamed by the Madison Avenue ad executives and now goes under the moniker of *Personal Choice* cruising, obviously meant to compete with Norwegian's *Freestyle*. One thing it encompasses is Princess' so-called "anytime dining," which means you can choose between specialty restaurants without fixed seating arrangements and traditional fixed dining in the main restaurant. The buffet becomes a late-night bistro so you can have a light or even a full meal at two in the morning if you so desire. This feature has replaced the traditional midnight buffet on Princess vessels. The newer and bigger the ship, the more *Personal Choice* options there are.

The modern and rapidly growing Princess fleet (three fabulous new ships were introduced in the short span of four months in 2004) features all-white exteriors with generally graceful lines and gentle curves. The cuisine on Princess is excellent, falling somewhere between Carnival and Celebrity in sophistication. The same can be said to apply to the nature of the service throughout the ship. Entertainment is among the most lavish and spectacular to be found at sea and boasts shows in Broadway and Vegas styles. Princess' vessels have become increasingly popular with families as activities and programs for children (three or four groups depending on the ship) are extensive. Other features are the Asian-style Lotus Spa, varied recreational opportunities including a putting green, and extensive personal enrichment programs. The latter are known as the *Scholarship@Sea* program and it is safe to say that Princess has developed this more than any other cruise line. Also on the cultural side is the art gallery that is part of every ship in the fleet. This is in addition to works of art that are displayed throughout their ships. A dedicated concierge staff is available to all guests and provides a convenient way of making reservations for dinner and other *Personal Choice* services.

Stateroom facilities on Princess are uniformly excellent, with very few cabins that I would consider sub-par and these are limited to the very lowest categories on the small number of older vessels in the fleet. When it comes to accommodations, Princess boasts balconies, balconies and more balconies. They were among the first to promote this as a basic feature of ship design and all of their ships have a majority of rooms with balconies. This is all very nice, no doubt, but do keep in mind that such rooms cost more. Don't fall into the trap of cruise line advertising (certainly not limited to Princess), which implies that you can't have a wonderful trip unless you've got a balcony!

Princess currently is sending seven ships to Alaska for the summer, the same number as Holland America. And, like HAL, it shares the lead for the variety of its cruise tours.

⚓ *Coral Princess/Island Princess*

Entered Service: 2002/2003	Gross Tonnage: 88,000
Length: 965 feet	Beam: 106 feet
Passengers: 1,970	Passenger Decks: 11
Crew Size: 900	Passenger/Crew Ratio: 2.2:1
Stateroom Size: 156-470 sq ft	Space Ratio: 44.7

The *Coral Princess* and *Island Princess* are identical sisters that form a new class of Princess vessels designed to have the amenities and facilities of the largest ships in the fleet but carrying considerably fewer passengers. The result is a fabulous ship that has everything you could want but doesn't scare away those who are turned off by the thought of sharing their cruise with 2,500 to 3,000 other people! Except for the missing nightclub on the upper aft-section, the *Coral* and *Island Princesses'* exterior profiles are similar to the so-called *Gem*-class vessels, including the "jet engines" (see the *Diamond/Sapphire* descriptions below).

There are two main dining rooms, stacked one on top of the other but not connected. Unlike many ships with this kind of arrangement, the second room is not put in some hard-to-find place. In fact, the layout of these ships is superb. In addition to the bistro, alternative dining options include the now almost standard Sabatini's trattoria and the new Bayou Café, featuring New Orleans-style cuisine and live jazz entertainment. These cruise lines are always coming up with something new – another of the delights of cruising.

Somewhat unusual is the arrangement of the ship's Lido deck – the Horizon Court (buffet for breakfast and lunch but a bistro at all other times; never closes) is at the bow, rather than amidships. This gives passengers views on three sides while dining. Other public areas of note include a retro-style martini bar, a cigar bar, wedding chapel and Princess' popular Explorer Lounge. The art collection is wonderful on both ships and the atmosphere is one of elegance.

The stern section has the fabulous Lotus Spa and accompanying fitness center. These facilities are very extensive on all of the newer and bigger Princess ships, but these particular ships are even larger, practically making this a "spa" ship. There are plenty of other recreational facilities, including a nine-hole mini-golf range and a golf simulator.

The Right Cruise For You

Accommodations are first-rate and feature plenty of space, comfort and lovely décor in all categories, with top-notch luxury in the uppermost categories. Furnishings feature the light pastel shades that are common to most Princess vessels. In fact, these rooms are hard to distinguish from those on almost all Princess ships built since the late 1990s. That's only a negative if you must have a room that looks different each time you cruise. I prefer to look at it as more of a guarantee that you're going to have a beautiful room that won't disappoint.

⚓ Dawn Princess/Sun Princess

Entered Service: 1997/1995	Gross Tonnage: 77,000
Length: 856 feet	Beam: 106 feet
Passengers: 1,950	Passenger Decks: 10
Crew Size: 900	Passenger/Crew Ratio: 2.2:1
Stateroom Size: 135-695 sq ft	Space Ratio: 39.5

When the *Sun Princess*, the older of these two sister ships, hit the waves in 1995 a lot of people thought it would be the ultimate in cruising for a long time to come. How wrong they were. While both of these vessels are still beautiful and should please just about everyone, they already seem somewhat dated compared to the newer Princess fleet as a whole (including the four other ships that the line is currently sending to Alaska). There's little doubt that this was the ship that set the stage for all of Princess' Grand-class vessels and the whole concept of "Grand" cruising that has evolved into their *Personal Choice* program.

The beautiful exteriors are among the first to feature the more modern style, with the superstructure moved forward, toward the bow. However, the design retains a degree of traditional grace by having this section gently raked, or terraced. On the other end, the stern is less raked, with little terracing effect.

The main interior feature is the lovely Atrium Court, spanning four decks and featuring graceful curving staircases, lots of rich woods offset by brass, towering palm trees and glass elevators, all topped by a colorful Tiffany stained-glass ceiling. Numerous shops surround one level of the atrium. The one-deck main theater is not particularly impressive in itself, but from a technical standpoint it's a good facility that is capable of hosting Princess' most extravagant shows. At the opposite end of the ship is the almost-as-large Vista Lounge. (Names of public facilities sometimes vary from one ship to the other.) This multi-purpose entertainment venue is eye-catching and a great place to watch informal shows or to go dancing. There's also a rather large casino with a spiral staircase in the middle that connects it with the deck below, where you'll find the ship's lovely wrap-around promenade.

When it comes time to eat you'll find that the *Dawn* and *Sun Princess* have two main dining rooms, something often seen in the Princess fleet. They are exactly on top of one another and are of the same size and layout but with different decoration. The two rooms are not directly connected by a staircase inside; each is a single deck high and is more to the liking of those who prefer smaller dining rooms. The flip side is that this makes them somewhat less visually impressive. Other dining options include the forward-facing buffet/bistro and a patisserie where you can purchase mouth-watering cakes and pastries to go with your specialty coffee.

These ships have an exceptional amount of open deck space so you should never feel crowded when trying to find a good spot to view the scenery. Maybe you'll even get a chance to soak up some sun. There aren't that many pools, but there are lots of hot tubs, something that has added appeal in cool Alaska! These were the first ships to feature "Princess Links," a mini-golf facility. When it comes to children's facilities, the sisters don't come close to what's available on the newer and larger vessels in the fleet. However, the child care staff is good, so don't let the facilities stop you from taking children on either of these ships. Likewise, while the spa and fitness facilities are

The Right Cruise For You

more than adequate, they are a notch or two below what Princess guests have come to expect on their newest ships.

All staterooms boast beautiful décor and warm color schemes that are typically Princess. They fall somewhat short compared to the rest of the fleet in their size; all interior rooms are less than 150 square feet and even the lower-priced outside categories can be between 135 and 155 square feet. If having a lot of space is important to you and you don't want to upgrade to much more expensive accommodations, be sure to verify how big the room is at the time you book and don't hesitate to ask for a larger room. Some may be available at little difference in price.

⚓ Diamond Princess/Sapphire Princess

Entered Service: 2004/2004	Gross Tonnage: 113,000
Length: 952 feet	Beam: 123 feet
Passengers: 2,670	Passenger Decks: 13
Crew Size: 1,133	Passenger/Crew Ratio: 2.3:1
Stateroom Size: 168-1,329 sq ft	Space Ratio: 42.3

These ships are a newer and slightly altered version of Princess' unbelievable *Grand*-class ships. Their introduction into service on Alaskan routes definitely raises the bar an additional notch when it comes to mega-sized luxury vessels in this market. With ship competition being extremely fierce, it's likely that these type ships will result in other lines improving still further the quality of their fleet assigned to Alaskan runs. Although these are *Grand*-class ships from a shipbuilder's point of view, they have been tweaked quite a bit and Princess refers to them as their *Gem* class. Indeed, they are beautiful gems that have just enough differences from the original class of ships to make them a distinct entity. These two ships are virtually identical.

The exteriors of *Diamond* and *Sapphire Princess* present an impressive and beautiful all-white profile. If you have ever traveled on one of the original *Grand*-class vessels you are familiar with the rather bulky-looking stern section resulting from the Skywalkers nightclub being perched atop the highest part of the aft. On *Gem*-class ships, the club is located slightly forward of that point, resulting in a much more pleasant appearance. In fact, despite the ship's immense size, it is the epitome of grace. (Do go into Skywalkers during the day for a wonderful view of the ship looking forward. An opposite view is available when you're in port from the open deck above the bridge.) An unusual exterior feature are the "jet engines" perched above the decorative grillwork that surrounds the funnels. Well, many people are convinced that they're jet engines. In reality, they are just decorative features that have become something of a conversation piece in the Princess fleet.

Dining on *Gem*-class ships is a wonderful experience. Passengers choose from traditional or alternative dining options. The "traditional" means you have fixed seating in the so-called main dining room. I refer to it that way because this attractive restaurant is rather small and intimate compared to what you would see on most ships of this size. That's because a very large number of guests opt for the alternative dining program. Each evening you can select from one of four specialty restaurants – Oriental, Italian, Southwestern or a steak house. They feature the full main dining room menu plus a number of specialty items. It is best to make reservations so you don't have a long wait. If you choose the traditional dining it is possible to sample the specialty restaurants on a space-available basis. In addition to these wonderful dinner choices, there is Sabatini's, a popular upscale Italian trattoria available at additional charge. The fine service is a seemingly endless parade of well-prepared favorites along with unusual items. The buffet option is available for dinner, in addition to breakfast and lunch. After hours, the buffet turns into a late-night bistro where you can choose from a variety of delectable treats. There is table service.

Public areas are spacious and appealing, beginning with the three-level atrium. It isn't the biggest at sea, but certainly one of the most beautiful with its abundance of white marble and exquisite detailing. Those seeking recreation will find plenty of activities, including tennis and basketball courts, mini-golf at Princess Links and cyber-golf simulators where you can select from dozens of famous courses throughout the world. The Lotus Spa and its adjacent aerobics room and gymnasium is one of the largest and most beautiful facilities on the water. There are plenty of pools and hot tubs, including a tidal pool in the spa and the fabulous Conservatory with its retractable roof. It features beautiful tile work featuring colorful fish designs. The balcony surrounding the Calypso Reef pool hosts many activities and events. The variety of entertainment is equally astounding. Among the larger lounges are the wildly Egyptian-themed Explorers Lounge (a popular feature on many new Princess ships) and the multi-purpose Club Fusion. The more traditional Wheelhouse Bar is another great place, but Skywalkers late-night disco (14 decks above the sea) is the undisputed hot spot. There are also several smaller and more intimate places to have a drink or chat. The main theater is rather plain and disappointing visually, but you still get those elaborate Broadway-style shows for which Princess is known. There is an extensive children's program with three separate facilities catering to separate age groups.

Staterooms occupy five consecutive decks that have no public facilities. A large percentage have a balcony. There are also a large number of mini-suites that provide an opportunity to upgrade to a more luxurious level without getting into stratospheric prices. But you may not care to upgrade much at all since even the smallest rooms on these *Princesses* are a nice size and feature easy-on-the-eyes pastel shades with rich wood trim and beautiful fabrics.

⚓ *Regal Princess*

Entered Service: 1991	Gross Tonnage: 70,000
Length: 804 feet	Beam: 106 feet
Passengers: 1,590	Passenger Decks: 12
Crew Size: 696	Passenger/Crew Ratio: 2.3:1
Stateroom Size: 190-587 sq ft	Space Ratio: 44.0

The *Regal Princess* is considerably smaller than any other Princess vessel currently serving Alaska. That's positive for people who don't wish to have a mega-ship experience and *Regal* has always had a good reputation and following among its past guests. The ship was designed by the noted Italian architect Renzo Piano and it met with immediate controversy. The architect envisioned a ship based on the graceful silhouette of a dolphin and the rounded corners and high arching top near the bow do, indeed, evoke some comparison to the shape of a dolphin. While I don't see anything wrong with this style, especially the large enclosed forward section that it creates on the Sun Deck, a number of ship industry critics have had bad things to say about the appearance. And it is a fact that neither Princess nor any other cruise lines asked Mr. Piano to design another ship!

The design issue isn't of such great importance to the average cruise passenger, since most of the time you'll be *on* the ship and not looking at it. Regardless of its shape, this Princess has a spacious and generally well planned interior design with most of the public facilities placed on the beautiful Promenade Deck. *Regal Princess* offers a grill as an alternative dining option, but the choices are considerably fewer than on any other Princess ship sailing to Alaska. The numerous recreational facilities include a pool with a swim-up bar like those in a Caribbean or Las Vegas resort. The extensive use of rich teak wood and lots of shiny brass give the ship an elegant feel, which is further enhanced by an almost museum-like art collection.

The Right Cruise For You

Every stateroom is spacious. The smallest rooms and average room size are well above industry norms and you don't have to worry about feeling cramped, regardless of the category of accommodations you choose. In addition to the big size, both the room layout and design are first rate. Décor is similar to what you'll see throughout the Princess fleet. As one of Princess' oldest ships, *Regal* has a lower percentage of staterooms with balconies, but you can certainly go out on deck when the urge to view the scenery comes on you.

ROYAL CARIBBEAN INTERNATIONAL

☎ (800) 327-6700; www.royalcaribbean.com
Officers: Primarily Scandinavian or Italian with some international for non-bridge positions.
Registry: The Bahamas or Norway
Fleet: 19 ships; 1 under construction

Royal Caribbean has the second-largest fleet, trailing Carnival by only a small margin. That gives you an idea of how successful they are and what a good product they deliver at affordable prices. Although Royal Caribbean has a good number of ships serving Alaska in one way or another, the selection is not as great as it could be considering what Royal Caribbean has in its inventory. The *Radiance*-class ships are just dandy and are among the stars of the cruising world. Unfortunately, the almost unbelievable *Voyager*-class ships aren't likely to be in the Alaskan market because they're too big to get through the Panama Canal and Royal Caribbean isn't likely to send them around Cape Horn at South America's tip. But, competition being what it is, you never know. (Do read *Now That's a Big Ship!*, page 61, for some fun and interesting information on *Voyager*-class ships.)

The almost all-white exteriors of Royal Caribbean's vessels are an appealing part of this line's impressive fleet. The easily recognizable Royal Caribbean funnel with its dark blue crowned anchor symbol is generally placed fairly far back on the vessel. All of their newer ships (those built since 1995) are definitely in the mega-liner category. Royal Caribbean has been an innovator in ship design and it is reflected both in ship size and varied facilities, as well as in the brilliance of their architecture. Among their innovations were new recreational ideas, such as a rock climbing wall. This feature first appeared on their giant new ships and proved so popular that it has been extended to almost the entire fleet. This line also realized that a ship's eye-appeal is a genuine part of the cruise experience for many passengers. Thus, they were among the first to incorporate an atrium. They call it the "Centrum" and it is always something spectacular. Royal Caribbean ships also feature the Viking Crown Lounge high atop the vessel. Similar to Holland America's Crow's Nest, this makes for a great place to socialize while enjoying the passing view.

Royal Caribbean offers excellent food and friendly service. They are on much the same level as Carnival in terms of formality and quality. While the majority of Royal Caribbean ships feature numerous alternative dining options, many do impose an additional fee. The entertainment and onboard activities are extremely varied and cater toward those seeking a fun time over the more culturally oriented programs found on more sophisticated luxury lines. This line also can boast one of the most extensive children's programs at sea. Called "Adventure Ocean," it features five different age groups. For parents who want a romantic evening by themselves now and then, the children's activities include dining separately with their friends at least one evening per cruise. They also have a kids' menu in the main dining room.

With three ships sailing to Alaska, Royal Caribbean is one of the medium players in the market.

The Right Cruise For You

⚓ Radiance of the Seas/Serenade of the Seas

Entered Service: 2000/2003	Gross Tonnage: 90,000
Length: 962 feet	Beam: 106 feet
Passengers: 2,501	Passenger Decks: 12
Crew Size: 859	Passenger/Crew Ratio: 2.9:1
Stateroom Size: 166-584 sq ft	Space Ratio: 36.0

In the Royal Caribbean fleet, the *Radiance*-class vessels are second in size only to *Voyager*-class vessel (and none of those is used in Alaska). Second-biggest, yes; but definitely not second class because these are gorgeous ships with a host of wonderful features and facilities. Encompassing all the good things people have come to expect from Royal Caribbean, this class of ship features a visual brilliance that is a joy to behold. The ships are very large by any standard but, given their dimensions, are far more spacious than most. For example, although they are nearly 10% longer and a deck higher than the next biggest RCI class, they actually carry about 10% fewer passengers. This comes as welcome news to a segment of the cruising public that feels Royal Caribbean packs too many people onto many of their ships. An open, spacious feeling and a generous amount of glass are the hallmarks of these vessels.

Radiance and *Serenade* are identical, except for the names of most public facilities and the décor that goes with them. For such big ships they display a graceful profile, with a gently sloping superstructure at the bow and an imaginatively designed funnel nearer the stern. The three uppermost decks are almost entirely devoted to recreational facilities and, in addition to the usual fare, you'll find a high-tech golf simulator, a separate swimming pool for the teen crowd and even the aforementioned rock climbing wall. There's a multi-level fitness center and one of the best-equipped spas at sea.

As is the case with the entire fleet, the Viking Crown is a gorgeous facility and, like all of the newer ships in the fleet, it goes beyond those on older ships in both size and luxury. The spectacular central atrium has glass-enclosed elevators and extends almost the entire height of the ship. This visually stunning area provides convenient access to most of the ships' public areas as well as the staterooms. Equally beautiful is the Solarium, which sports exotic themes and statuary. A large game room even has pool tables (self-leveling, of course, to compensate for the ship's motion). A wide variety of facilities and programs are available for children of all age groups.

The three-level theater hosts lavish production shows, while numerous smaller and more intimate venues will keep you entertained throughout the day and night. The two-tiered main dining room has a gorgeous grand staircase, a waterfall, exquisite color schemes and graceful tall columns to go with a huge central chandelier. As is the case with most rooms of this size, the noise level can sometimes be a bit high, although it's not as severe as in some other ships. There are two alternative restaurants (one at additional charge) in addition to the buffet option.

All of the staterooms are a good size, even those in the lowest price category. Most rooms below the suite level are very attractive and decorated with modern furniture and cheerful colors and fabrics. Interior rooms are a little more on the Spartan side, but they are still comfortable and highly functional. Bathtubs don't come into the picture unless you're at the suite level. However, the showers are oversized. The majority of outside cabins have private balconies and those that don't have large round windows. This is meant to produce the traditional feel of a porthole, but on a bigger scale.

⚓ Vision of the Seas

Entered Service: 1998	Gross Tonnage: 78,491
Length: 915 feet	Beam: 106 feet
Passengers: 2,435	Passenger Decks: 10
Crew Size: 775	Passenger/Crew Ratio: 3.1:1
Stateroom Size: 149-1,059 sq ft	Space Ratio: 32.2

The Right Cruise For You

Vision of the Seas is the third sister in its class and it brought with it a new standard of size and luxury to the world of cruising. Regarding that, it's almost unimaginable what has followed in little more than a half-dozen years since this ship made its debut! It's clear that the popularity of many features on this and similar ships was translated into the *Radiance*-class, which followed *Vision*. Perhaps because of its impressive size, *Vision* avoids a cramped feeling despite having a space ratio that is definitely lower than most of the competition. Another reason for this is due, at least in part, to the extensive use of glass throughout the ship. Entire walls are made of glass and it almost always seems that you're actually out on the open seas while on board. Views from Royal Caribbean's trademark Viking Crown Lounge are among the best on any ship and the more quiet observatory located directly beneath it. Many other public areas also provide great viewing and this even extends to the large and well-equipped gym. The latter is on the sports- and view-oriented Compass Deck, which features a large retractable canopy. *Vision* has an excellent art collection and you'll encounter paintings in just about every nook and cranny of the ship. The extensive public areas are designed to dazzle you from top to bottom and from bow to stern, but especially impressive is the stunning décor of the two-tiered Masquerade Theater. This first-rate facility has top-notch shows. Other entertainment options are offered in the Some Enchanted Evening Lounge at the ship's stern. The ship boasts many facilities that are almost mandatory in today's cruise vessels, including an excellent spa/fitness center and separate programs and areas for teens and younger children. This was one of the first ships to do that.

Although you can't go wrong with the experience in the highly decorative two-level Aquarius Dining Room or the Windjammer Café buffet, *Vision of the Seas* did come out before the trend that offered a wider choice in alternative dining. Consequently, there isn't much else available. Some of the older ships in the Royal Caribbean fleet are being done over to expand dining choices. This ship isn't quite ready for a major retrofit but, if it does get one, additional restaurants are sure to be among the top items on the agenda for change.

In general, good-sized staterooms are a hallmark of this class of ship. The most common type of cabin has 153 square feet, which barely exceeds what I consider to be a minimum requirement for comfort. Moreover, it is nicely decorated and well equipped. Colorful curtains add an informal touch of home and are also used to separate the sleeping area from the living area. The majority of outside rooms have private balconies. I suggest avoiding the small number of staterooms that measure less than 150 square feet.

NOW THAT'S A BIG SHIP!

When Cunard's *Queen Mary II* made its maiden voyage in early 2004 it created a stir in the cruise world (and beyond), the likes of which I've never seen. Certainly a big part of this was due to the fact that it was highly touted as the world's largest cruise ship, and so it was in terms of length (1,132 feet), height and gross registered tonnage (150,000). Yet, it isn't that much bigger than Royal Caribbean's Voyager-class vessels that were first introduced in 1999 and now number five sisters, with the final ship in the class having been delivered in 2004. In fact, each of these 1,020-foot, 138,000-GRT ships holds more passengers (3,114) than the *Queen Mary II* (2,620), and in terms of passenger capacity, they are now the largest ships in the world. Perhaps it is America's love affair with British-style royalty that made the difference in media attention.

So let's take a look at how the Voyager-class vessels compare. The ships have a main shopping promenade that extends for most of the vessel's

The Right Cruise For You

length with shops and eateries on both sides. It looks like a shopping mall. Above this promenade are the cruise industry's only "outside" inside rooms. How's that? Well, they're interior rooms but they have windows that overlook the promenade. These ships are the only ones afloat that have an ice-skating rink. And, they're so big that they have two Centrums, one toward the bow and one toward the stern. Now that's a big ship! But, bigger is on the way. Although the ship name (and even the "official" class name) haven't been decided on, Royal Caribbean is working on a larger version of the *Voyager*-class that, for the time being, is called *Ultra-Voyager*!

Other Cruise Lines

These lines have fewer ships and fewer Alaska itineraries than those covered above. In fact, they generally don't send a ship to Alaska for the entire summer season, but rather offer a limited number of sailings; often, the itineraries will differ from one sailing to another. But perhaps an even more important distinction for the average traveler is that all the lines in this section are more luxury-oriented than the mass-market lines. They feature smaller ships with a more intimate and personalized service experience. Of course, all of these factors contribute to their being considerably more expensive than any of the mass-market lines, often as much as three times the price or greater. I am not trying to discourage people who have the financial means or a strong desire to travel in this style from doing so. However, because most readers are not likely to be willing or able to afford this type of experience, I haven't included detailed ship-by-ship descriptions.

CRYSTAL CRUISES

☎ (800) 446-6620; www.crystalcruises.com

Crystal is one of the most honored of all cruise lines and those looking for luxury simply can't go wrong by traveling with them. What makes Crystal different from the other lines with prices going into the stratosphere is their ships. While the other high-budget lines such as Radisson, Silversea and Seabourn are almost exclusively small-ship operators (under 500 passengers and sometimes considerably less), Crystal's ships have a capacity for about 1,000 passengers. As such, their ships do have the amenities that the large vessels of the mass-market lines feature, such as a big showroom and even an alternative dining option. This is attractive to many people and gives Crystal a niche in the cruise market. It sort of gives its passengers the best of both worlds. That's if you can handle the fare. Crystal's cruises, including those to Alaska, tend to be longer than a week and visit places that major lines do not. These attributes can be another plus for many travelers. On the other hand, because Crystal has a fleet of only three ships and they move them all over the world, the number of Alaska sailings is rather limited. The beautiful *Crystal Harmony* is currently serving Alaska.

RADISSON SEVEN SEAS CRUISES

☎ (866) 314-3212; www.rssc.com

This upscale line is considered one of the best in the world if you are a member of the *Conde Nast*-set. Their fleet of about a half-dozen ships are all quite small and personalized service is the name of the game. All of their accommodations are suites, so you'll have plenty of room to spread out. The beautiful *Seven Seas Mariner* is the ship that RSSC now has deployed on its Alaskan runs.

ALTERNATE CRUISE LINES

In addition to these two luxury lines, there are some other options, depending on when you're going.

Silversea, ☎ (800) 722-9955; www.silversea.com, seem to have an unofficial policy of alternating years when it comes to Alaska. They last cruised to Alaska in 2004. Silversea has small and luxurious vessels that to most observers are even more upscale than Radisson Seven Seas.

Currently, Seabourn (in the same class as Silversea) and the famous Cunard line are not going to Alaska. And what about the Disney Cruise Line? Well, their two ships were exclusive to the Caribbean until recently. They're running a test with a Mexican Riviera itinerary in 2005 and rumors abound that they're going to soon be placing an order for two more ships. So, in a few years, who knows? Mickey Mouse ears on the funnel may be a part of Alaskan cruising!

WHO'S WHO IN THE CRUISE INDUSTRY

There are literally dozens of cruise lines throughout the world, many of which are completely unknown to the American traveler because they don't cater to this market. But, even if you limit yourself to the North American cruise market, there are more than a dozen major lines. At least in name. Consolidation, so common in every industry, is also a trend in the cruising business. There are relatively few cruise companies if you consolidate brands by their corporate banner. Here's the lineup:

Carnival: This industry behemoth owns Alaska-cruising Holland America and Princess, as well as world-famous Cunard, Costa Cruises, Windstar and Seabourn – in addition to the Carnival line itself.

Royal Caribbean: Royal Caribbean is, by itself, the second-largest cruise line after Carnival. That goes for the group as well, because RCI also owns Celebrity Cruises.

Most of the remaining lines are independent. However, Norwegian Cruise Line is owned by a large Asian cruise company called *Star Cruises*, which also owns the smaller Orient Lines. As far as the two giants are concerned, it is the practice of Carnival and Royal Caribbean to let each line operate independently, thereby allowing for more variation in cruise style. Despite the consolidation, there has yet to be any significant upward trend in prices, although this could happen once the current ship-building boom comes to a close. On the positive side, the cruise lines will give you credit for traveling on a sister line. Thus, for instance, you can get past-guest treatment and prices on a Carnival Cruise if you sailed in Europe on Costa or Cunard. Of course, there are lots of details in the fine print when you try to do this, so take the promise with a grain of sea-salt.

Small Ship Lines

One cannot compare the small ship lines with the large mass-market cruise lines. They are not in the same category, which means you're comparing apples and oranges. The small lines detailed below carry between 35 and 150 passengers on each of their ships. They have limited public facilities, but good food and fine service are traits they share with the big lines. However, people who travel on the small ships are doing so not for the cruise experience, but because the small vessels provide an in-depth sightseeing experience by getting into places that large ships simply cannot reach. For the most part

The Right Cruise For You

they cover a smaller geographic area because they aren't as fast as big cruise ships. Itineraries vary greatly, but the majority are a week long; two-week cruises can also be readily found. The cost of small ship cruising is considerably higher than on the big lines because they do not have the economies of scale in their favor. On average you can expect to pay at least 75% more for a week-long cruise on these lines. Leaders among the Alaskan small-ship cruising field are listed below.

AMERICAN WEST STEAMBOAT COMPANY

☎ (800) 434-1232; www.alaskacruisetour.com

CLIPPER CRUISES

☎ (800) 325-0010; www.clippercruise.com

CRUISE WEST

☎ (888) 851-8133; www.cruisewest.com

GLACIER BAY TOURS & CRUISES

☎ (800) 451-5952; www.glacierbaytours.com

LINDBLAD EXPEDITIONS

☎ (800) 397-3348; www.expeditions.com

THE RIGHT CRUISE FOR YOU

If you are considering a small-ship cruise, then you should ask yourself the following questions:

▸ Do you have a spirit of adventure?

▸ Have I been to Alaska before on a bigger cruise ship?

▸ Is the experience of a cruise definitely secondary in importance to seeing more of Alaska?

▸ Can you afford the additional cost?

If you answered "Yes" to all four questions then you're a candidate for small-ship cruising. Explore this option further.

ALASKA MARINE HIGHWAY SYSTEM (AMHS)

6858 Glacier Highway
Juneau AK 99801-8909
☎ (800) 642-0066; www.ferryalaska.com, www.alaska.gov/ferry

The AMHS provides an informal way of getting around southeastern Alaska. The biggest difference between the company's ferries and traditional cruising vessels is that they do not provide a luxury experience. Staterooms are available (you can also occupy just desk space), but this is transportation only. Because ferry schedules aren't designed for day-by-day touring, they don't always leave at convenient times. You may find yourself having to spend more time in a given town than you planned because there's no ferry leaving when you want one. Overall, seeing Alaska by ferry requires a lot of time and quite a bit of patience. You also have to be willing to travel with the free spirits who make use of the ferries for sightseeing purposes. Many travelers on the AMHS are Alaskans who use the ferry service as a lifeline to reach other remote communities.

There are three basic routes. The most important one for visitors is the Inside Passage/Southeast route from Bellingham, Washington (about 85 miles north of Seattle via I-5 to Exit 250) to Skagway, with about a dozen intermediate stops in towns large and small. The other routes are the Cross Gulf (Southcentral) route in the Gulf of Alaska and serving Anchorage, Valdez, Cordova, Seward, Homer and Kodiak, among other places; and the Southwest route serving the Aleutian island chain from Kodiak. You can transfer between the Southcentral and Southwest lines at Kodiak. A relatively new service connects the Southcentral route with the more important Southeast route. However, while this can allow visitors using the AMHS to cover the same territory as the cruise lines (with an even greater choice in the number of ports of call), the connecting service has a rather limited schedule that requires a lot of time.

The Alaska state ferry fleet is comprised of 11 vessels all named according to state law for Alaskan glaciers. Quite a few of the ships are small and older vessels, but some are quite large, such as the 418-foot, 625-passenger *Columbia*, the 500-passenger *Malaspina* and *Matanuka*, and the 748-passenger *Kennecott*, the biggest ship in the fleet, introduced in 1998. The most significant change in fleet history occurred in 2004 with the introduction of the high-speed *Fairweather*, a 259-passenger catamaran-style ferry that has a cruising speed of almost 40 mph. A sister vessel, the *Chenega*, joined the fleet in 2005.

Fares for passengers range from $50 to $400, depending on the length of trip and whether or not you take deck space or a cabin. Smaller vessels on shorter runs do not have overnight accommodations. There are additional charges if you are taking a car onboard the ferry.

Ferry terminals aren't usually the same ones used for cruise ships and are normally located out of the main town.

FERRY TERMINAL LOCATIONS	
All distances are from downtown via the main road	
INSIDE PASSAGE/SOUTHEAST ROUTE	
Ketchikan	2.5 miles north
Juneau	14 miles north
Petersburg	0.9 miles south
Sitka	7.1 miles north
Skagway	3 blocks south
Wrangell	2 blocks north

FERRY TERMINAL LOCATIONS	
All distances are from downtown via the main road	
GULF OF ALASKA/SOUTH CENTRAL ROUTE	
Anchorage	605 W. 4th Avenue
Cordova	4 blocks north of downtown on main road
Homer	4558 Homer Spit Road
Kodiak	100 Marine Way
Seward	At the Alaska Railroad dock
Valdez	West end of city dock

The AMHS has very limited service in towns along the Canadian portion of the Inside Passage. If you want to explore this region in more depth, the province of British Columbia operates an extensive and reliable ferry system that has high quality ship facilities. Contact BC Ferries at ☎ (250) 386-3431 or on their website at www.bcferries.com.

Both the small ships and the ferry systems are what I would term alternative choices to cruising the mainstream lines. Although there are lots of people who select one of these options (especially those who already have some experience traveling in Alaska), the rest of the general information on cruising that follows will be limited to the large-ship cruise lines.

Setting Priorities

Selecting Your Dream Cruise

With so many Alaska cruising options – different cruise lines, different ships and even different itineraries – it can be somewhat of a difficult (although fun) task for you to select the right cruise for *you*. So, how does one go about that? Begin by defining "best" on a personal level since what is best for one person will not be the best for another. People have different priorities when vacationing and cruising is no exception. Let's take a look at some of the major factors that determine which cruise is going to be your dream cruise come true.

The Cruise Line

As you have just read in the section on the cruise lines and ships, each line has a distinctive style or personality reflected throughout its fleet. Do you want a sophisticated luxury experience or a more fun-oriented cruise? Do you like refined elegance or is glitz more your style? Is this a romantic getaway for two or a family affair? Formal or informal? More or fewer dining choices? These and many other questions can help narrow down which cruise lines are in the running for your dollars. To a large degree, your available budget will also help determine what line or lines to consider. *Crystal* is, for example, a whole bunch more expensive than *Carnival*. You have to judge how much certain features of a cruise line (and the ship) are worth to you.

The Ship

Many ship features are determined by the line that owns them. However, even in one specific cruise line, there can be a great variation in the age, size and facilities of its various ships. The newer and larger ships are likely to have the most diverse facilities, dining choices and activities. But larger does not always mean better; a lot of experienced travelers prefer a somewhat smaller vessel. It is often the case among the major lines that there is a big difference in the size of their largest ship compared to their smallest. Even limiting the list just to ships with Alaskan itineraries, as I did in the preceding section, will reveal many ship types. The earliest editions of this book tended to favor "smaller" cruise ships for Alaska because they could sail into some of the Inside Passage's tighter spaces. These days, however, even the smallest of the major cruise line ships in Alaska are too big to reach those off-the-beaten-path spots. But again, a first- or second-time Alaskan cruise means plenty to see from even the biggest ship. And don't get too caught up in the hype you might read from the small-ship cruise lines about all the places that they can get to that the big ships can't. While it is true that they have unique access to *some* areas, the maneuverability of today's biggest vessels is remarkable. In fact, restrictions are just as likely to be due to water depth as to tight places. With bow and stern thrusters, a giant cruise ship can even move sideways!

The Stateroom

Not only is the stateroom the single biggest determining factor in the cost of your cruise, it might well determine how happy you are with the ship and your cruise overall. The two major components of the price-determinant are whether the room is *inside* or *outside*, and the location of the room (how high up, how far fore or aft).

Inside rooms, obviously, have no window. However, on many ships (especially the newer ones) the size of an inside room is not much different from an outside room without a balcony. So, unless you think you'll feel claustrophobic in an inside room or you just have to have that view or balcony, you can save a lot of money by going for an inside cabin. Outside rooms have a greater variety. They can be with or without balcony, regular window or floor-to-ceiling window, and so on. You will pay the extra price for such extra amenities. The cruise lines make it seem as if you just have to have a balcony in order to enjoy your cruise. Nonsense! How much time are you going to spend on the balcony? One other item of caution. Some outside rooms are priced lower because the view is obstructed, or partially obstructed, by lifeboats. In my opinion, they are not worth the savings. If you're going to get an obstructed view, you might as well save some money and get an inside cabin. Prices generally are higher in a specific cabin category if the room is towards the middle of the ship or if it is on a higher deck. The reason for this is that the farther up you are from the water or the farther away from the front and back, the more comfortable the ride. But the difference is slight; cruise ships have great stabilizing systems that limit the effect of the ocean's movements. On the other hand, cabins on the lowest deck or two sometimes have an isolated feel to them, especially on older ships where there may be only a few cabins of this type. I recommend these only if you must conserve every penny.

Another very important consideration in selecting a cabin is the size. Excepting some of the most upgraded suites, which cost *mucho* bucks, ship cabins are considerably smaller than rooms at a land-based resort hotel. While many cruise line brochures don't give you a good picture of how big the cabin is (they'll tell you if you call and ask), you can count on a typical modern ship stateroom being anywhere between 150 and 185 square feet. This does not include the size of a balcony (if the room has one). Some ships, especially the older ones, may have a number of cabins that are even smaller, while at the other end of the scale, a few can go up to around 200 square feet or slightly larger. Just to give you something to compare this to, motel rooms typically start at around 250 square feet and luxury hotel rooms today are generally built in the 400- to 550-square-foot range. Ship cabins are well designed from a functionality standpoint, but they don't offer a lot of walking room. If you are going to be traveling with your children, try to select a ship with bigger cabins. I usually downgrade any vessel where the size of the standard cabins is under 150 square feet; 165 square feet and up is what I consider a decent size. Over 180 square feet is better for more than two people. Be aware that cabin sizes can vary by more than a few square feet even within a single category depending on its location. Do not hesitate to ask the cruise line or your travel agent for the exact size of the cabin they plan to assign to you. Ask for a larger cabin if it seems too small to meet your needs.

The Ports of Call

In many instances people going on a cruise select a destination and then try to find the best ship for them. The factors mentioned earlier would be the keys to influencing their decision. Often, the ship's itinerary is almost an afterthought. This is more true in places like the Caribbean where a beach is a beach and one marketplace begins to look a lot like another after a few port calls. The same can be said about some other places where the primary purpose of the trip is the cruise experience itself, rather than the destination. While I largely disagree with that view for any cruise destination, there is little doubt that it exists among some people. Regardless of what the situation may be in other places, it is most certainly not the case in Alaska. If you decide to cruise in Alaska, it is just as likely that the reason for your cruise is to see the wonderful sights of America's Last Frontier. While the atmosphere, luxuries and activities onboard will, no doubt, immensely add to your enjoyment, the fact is that many people will consider those aspects of an Alaskan cruise to be of secondary importance. Therefore, when choosing an Alaskan cruise it becomes very important to also select the ship based on its itinerary. Keep in mind that a good Alaskan itinerary is actually more than the ports of call. The number of key scenic areas visited plays an almost equally important role. More will be said about this later when I discuss how to evaluate Alaskan itineraries.

CRUISE LINES & THE ENVIRONMENT

In the late 1990s cruise lines were not very environmentally friendly. Several major companies (we won't point fingers here because the guilt was pretty well spread around) received public relations black-eyes when it became publicly known that the cruise ships were illegally dumping waste into pristine Alaskan waters... waters that they always featured in their advertising. The cruise lines constantly spoke in green terms, but their actions belied the image they were trying so hard to promote.

But the bad publicity had more effect on correcting the problem than the efforts of any government or environmental group, individually or collectively. Regulation of ships is largely through international organizations and oversight is often slippery. The cruise lines, for the most part, successfully resisted imposition of higher standards. However, in "voluntary" association, all of the lines have now undertaken serious efforts to reduce dumping, legal or otherwise. The newer ships are being designed to be more fuel efficient and have better onboard waste treatment facilities, so what is dumped into the water isn't as wretched as it used to be. The practice now is to dump only waste that is suitable as food for fish. So, if you are an environmentally conscious person, you can be somewhat optimistic that the worst is over. And now the larger ships don't mean more pollution. In fact, with advanced technological systems, they will pollute far less than a smaller but older ship ever did.

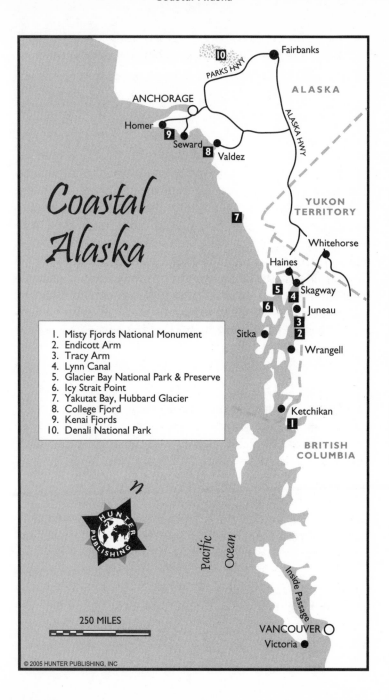

Coastal Alaska

1. Misty Fjords National Monument
2. Endicott Arm
3. Tracy Arm
4. Lynn Canal
5. Glacier Bay National Park & Preserve
6. Icy Strait Point
7. Yakutat Bay, Hubbard Glacier
8. College Fjord
9. Kenai Fjords
10. Denali National Park

The Right Cruise For You

© 2005 HUNTER PUBLISHING, INC

The Two Basic Itineraries

Previous editions of this book listed the actual itineraries for each ship and evaluated them on a case-by-case basis. But these days cruise lines change itineraries so often that it's impossible to keep the information timely in a book. I've even begun to see itinerary changes for a particular destination (including Alaska) before the expiration date of the cruise line's current brochure. Moreover, Alaskan itineraries tend to be much more similar in nature than those run in the Caribbean or the Mediterranean, where the number of ports is much greater and the combination of possible ports of call is almost endless. The greater similarities in Alaskan cruising do make things easier to discuss in general terms. Check the cruise lines' website for any possible late changes to itineraries and make sure that the itinerary is the one you wanted at the time you book.

There are two basic types of Alaskan cruise itineraries, the Inside Passage and the Gulf of Alaska. Note that different cruise lines often give their own names to these categories. For instance, Gulf of Alaska cruises are often referred to as the "Voyage of the Glaciers." Names aren't important. The composition of ports and scenic cruising is what counts.

Inside Passage Cruises

These cruises are round-trip journeys from either Seattle or Vancouver (but as far south as San Francisco in a few cases) and are almost always eight days and seven nights. Inside Passage trips thread through the waterways that stretch along Canada's British Columbia coast and Alaska from the border near Ketchikan to as far north as Skagway or Glacier Bay. The most important ports of call along the Inside Passage are Ketchikan, Juneau, Skagway and Sitka. While you can make your own determination as to which ones are of most interest to you by reading the *Ports of Call* chapter, a good Inside Passage cruise should include at least three of these ports. If it does all four then you've found a really good itinerary. Other Alaskan cruise ports are Haines, Petersburg and Wrangell, as well as Prince Rupert in British Columbia, but these are much less visited by the big ships and, although interesting, they are far less important than the big four, especially if this is your first time visiting Alaska. Icy Strait Point is a "new" port of call. This is a special situation that will be addressed in the detailed information on the ports of call. One last possibility exists when it comes to ports on Inside Passage trips. This is the wonderfully fascinating and beautiful city of Victoria, British Columbia. Although Victoria has much to see, a port call here will, by necessity, reduce the number of other ports that a ship can stop at by one. If you're cruising to see Alaska, then Victoria isn't a good substitute for any Alaskan town. However, once again, it does come down to what interests you most.

When it comes to scenic cruising, the Inside Passage has much to offer. Among the possible places are the Misty Fjords National Monument along the Behm Canal, Tracy Arm or Endicott Arm near Juneau, and the Lynn Canal on the way to Skagway. Two important areas of scenic cruising are Glacier Bay National Park and Yakutat Bay's Hubbard Glacier. These can be a part of Inside Passage or Gulf of Alaska itineraries – it varies from one cruise line to another. No cruise will take in all of the above sights. Misty Fjords is a somewhat rare stop, while almost every cruise will visit either Tracy or Endicott Arm. It is uncommon that a ship will do both, and it isn't necessary since these two are quite similar in appearance and fairly close to one another. Only cruises with a port of call at Skagway will pass through the beautiful Lynn Canal. Therefore, this is an important combination to look for in selecting a good Inside Passage itinerary. Glacier Bay National Park is, as you will read about later, one of the most extraordinary sights in all of Alaska. It used to be common for almost all Inside Pas-

The Right Cruise For You

sage trips to cruise here, but that is no longer the case. The government is very concerned about protecting the fragile environment of Glacier Bay. Thus, the number of ships that can visit there is restricted by law. And with so many ships cruising Alaska these days, a majority will not get to cruise Glacier Bay. A cruise to Alaska without Glacier Bay is missing something that is, indeed, very important. I consider it a major plus if you find an itinerary that you otherwise like and it includes Glacier Bay. On the other hand, an Inside Passage cruise with Hubbard Glacier is also a big plus and a reasonable substitute for Glacier Bay.

Gulf of Alaska Cruises

These itineraries are one-way trips from Seattle or Vancouver to Anchorage (northbound) or a reverse southbound routing. The ships begin or end their voyage not actually in Anchorage but in either of two nearby ports (Seward or Whittier) and passengers are taken by bus or train to or from Anchorage itself. Although Gulf of Alaska trips are also usually one week in length, a large number of cruise passengers extend these trips into the Alaskan interior either via a cruise tour or on their own. In order to allow time for additional sights in the Gulf of Alaska, these cruises will typically visit only three ports along the Inside Passage. However, those ports will almost always be from the list of four major ports I mention above, namely Ketchikan, Juneau, Skagway and Sitka. Additional ports of call along the Gulf of Alaska are either non-existent or limited, with Valdez being the only one that might be called on and that seems to be becoming increasingly rare for the big ships. However, the lack of extra ports is more than compensated for by the additional scenic cruising in store. This will often include Glacier Bay National Park, Yakutat Bay and Hubbard Glacier (these can be Inside Passage destinations as well), Prince William Sound, and magnificent College Fjord. There are many other sights that can be seen while cruising the Gulf of Alaska route, but two of the above three should be considered as basic requirements in selecting a good itinerary.

Itinerary Evaluation

Regardless of the cruise line, you'll find there is a pronounced similarity in ship itineraries for each of those categories. Yet, there are enough differences to merit careful examination before you make your choice. Some of the most important factors to take into consideration will be addressed shortly, but the first question that you need to ask before selecting a specific itinerary is "Which is the better trip: the Inside Passage or the Gulf of Alaska?" On the surface, the Gulf of Alaska comes out on top in my opinion. It does all, or nearly all, of the major Inside Passage ports of call that an "Inside Passage only" cruise does, plus it has the advantage of much more scenic cruising, whether it be Glacier Bay, Yakutat Bay or Prince William Sound and College Fjord. It can do this, of course, because the time an Inside Passage cruise would spend backtracking to Seattle or Vancouver is devoted to exploring new territory. However, one does have to consider the fact that connections to or from Anchorage aren't as convenient as from Seattle, and they also cost more. (The cruise itself is also somewhat higher priced than an Inside Passage itinerary.) So a lot depends on your budget. And available time. If you have more than a week to spend, then the Gulf of Alaska itinerary makes sense because it gives you access to Alaska's majestic interior. All of these considerations are most important if you plan on only one trip to Alaska. If you think you'll be coming back, then it becomes almost a moot point. In such a case you could almost flip a coin as to which one to do first. However, I would pick an Inside Passage cruise that concentrates on less-visited ports because you can see more of the "regular" ports on your Gulf of Alaska journey.

The Right Cruise For You

OTHER CONSIDERATIONS

Now we can get back to those other points you should be considering:

▶ *Does the itinerary visit the ports and cruise the scenic areas that you are most interested in?* While no cruise is likely to include every port that you want to visit (since you are not designing a custom itinerary), if it stops at the majority of what you consider to be the most desirable ports, then that is a good first step.

▶ *How much time is allotted in each port? Is it enough for you to see most of the things that are important to you?* The answer to the last question should be easy enough because the port descriptions that follow later in this book will give you a good idea of what can be done in one day. Of course, if you are going to be taking organized shore excursions, you will know in advance exactly what you will be seeing.

▶ *Even if the number of hours allowed is sufficient, be sure to check what time of day your ship is in port.* Some ships may spend a significant number of hours in a port, but arrive late in the day, leaving little time for sightseeing before attractions close. This is all right if the types of activities you are most interested in aren't restricted to certain hours. Just be sure that you factor this into your evaluation.

▶ *Compare the amount of time at sea versus that spent in port.* Depending on the itinerary, a one-week cruise may have anywhere from one to four days at sea and stop at as few as two ports or as many as four or five. Typically, week-long cruises spend two full days at sea. The relative importance of this will depend upon the primary purpose of your cruise. Many days at sea are fine if you are most interested in the cruise experience. But if you want a port-intensive vacation you will not be well served by an itinerary that spends three or more days at sea. However, days at sea are often filled with wonderful sights so they aren't necessarily a big negative even if you consider a port-intensive itinerary the best option. If you want your sea days to be kept to a minimum, don't book a cruise that leaves from San Francisco.

Other activities such as shopping and recreation are generally less important than sightseeing on a cruise to Alaska. However, the last few years has seen a large increase in the number of "active" shore excursions that require some degree of fitness and adventure. If any of these kinds of activities are going to be a major deciding factor for you, then look for itineraries that include those ports where these activities are best. Again, the port descriptions will help you with this aspect of itinerary selection. So, grab yourself a stack of brochures from the cruise lines and start carefully looking at their itineraries!

Options in Port

Unless you have sailed all the way to Alaska only for the undeniable pleasures of the cruise experience, the ports you visit will certainly be one of the most important aspects of your trip. Selecting the itinerary is only the first step in planning your land activities. Now it is time to decide how you are going to see what you have traveled so far to reach. (Read the section *Recreation in Port*, on page 131, to learn more about the type of activities that will be available to you.)

There are two basic choices: either you use the cruise line's shore excursion program of guided or escorted tours, or you head out on your own. As with everything else, there are advantages and disadvantages to each approach depending on

The Right Cruise For You

your interests, planning capabilities and spirit of adventure to go it alone. Of course, you may have every reason to take an organized shore excursion in one port and to go on your own in the next port. Some places are more suited to individual exploration than others.

Organized Shore Excursions

A long list of shore excursion options will be provided to you in advance for each port that your ship will be calling on. When it comes to sightseeing, I don't usually recommend a shore excursion, except in those places where it may be better to go on a tour because of local conditions. Alaska isn't a foreign country (nor is Canada, for practical purposes) so most of the reasons that people might opt for a shore excursion in Europe or Mexico (language, food, customs, etc.) don't apply here. The same is true when it comes to driving regulations, safety from crime and a host of other considerations. However, Alaska's unique geographic situation does create special needs. The lack of roads in most places requires some unusual methods of transportation to get to sights. In such cases, shore excursions are the way to go. These considerations aside, shore excursions are very popular with the cruising public. It comes down to convenience. You will be picked up at the ship, taken to all of the places listed in the itinerary with a knowledgeable local guide to explain things, and then be transported back to the ship. You don't have to do any real planning, worry about getting lost, or getting back late and missing the ship's departure. On the other hand, shore excursions do have definite limitations. Group travel is slower than individual travel, so you might see less. This becomes even more pronounced if a lengthy lunch stop is made or if time is allowed for shopping and you don't want to do that. Also, and perhaps most important, the excursions may not even cover places that you want to see. Finally, shore excursions are no bargain. Two people using public transportation, renting a car, or even using some taxis can expect to pay less for a day of sightseeing than they would on a shore excursion, even if all of the activities are the same.

The list of available excursions in each port will be almost identical regardless of which cruise line you take. The only exceptions are some very long excursions that may be omitted for those ships spending a limited time in a given port. The reason for the sameness is that the cruise lines aren't operating the tours. All the lines make arrangements with local tour operators and these are usually the same for all the lines coming to a particular port. Although the cruise lines obviously get group rates and claim that they don't get anything out of the independently run excursions, I have some difficulty swallowing that. Doing the math shows they profit.

Shore excursions generally take one of two forms. The first is the sightseeing variety, which is usually a highlight tour of the port city, although more detailed visits to specific points of interest are also common. Many full-day excursions leave the port town and explore the surrounding countryside. These trips frequently allow at least some time for shopping, whether or not you're interested in doing so. The other type of excursion is recreation-related. These essentially provide transportation to a site to partake in whatever sport or adventure activity you choose and you can do so with the camaraderie of your fellow passengers. Some excursions allow times for both sightseeing and recreation. As indicated before, I generally prefer seeing the sights on my own where possible. However, for recreational and sporting activities the organized excursion is much more convenient. Often, it is the only practical way for day-trippers to partake in these activities. Whether on a sightseeing or recreational excursion, lunch may or may not be included, so do check the itinerary. Also make certain you know the duration of your excursion. You may be able to do a guided shore outing in the morning, for example, and explore the town on your own in the afternoon.

The Right Cruise For You

BOOKING SHORE EXCURSIONS

You can find out about available shore excursions for whatever cruise itinerary you've selected either on the cruise line's website or by waiting for the shore excursion brochure they'll probably send you prior to your departure. Many cruise lines, including Princess, Holland America, Royal Caribbean and Celebrity, have implemented a system where you can book shore excursions online prior to your cruise. In most cases you can do this as soon as you've paid for your trip. Surprisingly, giant Carnival has yet to offer this service. If booking online isn't an option, you'll have to wait until you're onboard to make reservations. Do so as soon as possible so that you won't be closed out of an excursion you really want to take. Bookings can be made either at the shore excursion desk or via the ship's interactive closed-circuit TV system. Tickets are generally delivered to your stateroom. All charges for shore excursions will be put on your onboard account.

On Your Own

Travel on your own in port is best done where most of the sights are close by or where transportation is readily available. This type of independent travel allows you to see exactly what you want to see, to spend more or less time in a given place depending on how much you are enjoying it, and also often allows you to have a better feel for how the locals live. In those cases where you have many hours in port, including lunch time, you have the option of returning to the ship to eat or trying some of the local popular eateries. Either of those options has a greater appeal to me than being herded as a group to a restaurant chosen by the tour operator (not that they'll take you to a bad place).

One possible disadvantage of going on your own is that if you get lost, or lose track of time, the ship isn't going to wait for you. It will, however, always wait for the rare late-returning excursion. Whenever you venture out on your own (except in those tiny ports where you'll always be within a few minutes' walk of the ship), take the telephone number of the ship's port agent. If you are going to be a little late or have any other problem, you can phone ahead and let them know. Do not, however, use this as a means of getting more time in port. It should be used only in a genuine emergency. The telephone numbers will be provided to you, usually in the daily program. If not, be sure to ask for them.

Cruise Tours

Cruise tours are package plans that combine land travel either before or after the cruise (sometimes both). They are available from nearly all cruise lines in just about every destination, but seem to be most popular of all in Alaska. This is due, at least in part, to the heavy promotion given to Alaska cruise tours by the major lines. The combinations of places to see via cruise tours are almost endless, but the most common ones journey from Anchorage via the scenic Alaska Railroad (often in special trains or rail cars for cruise passengers only) to Denali National Park and on to Fairbanks. These trips always stay at first-class hotels (two cruise lines own hotel chains in Alaska), although in some out-of-the-way places accommodations are not quite as luxurious. Again, you will be better equipped to select the best cruise tour for you after reading more about the destinations in the *Beyond the Cruise* chapter. More details on various cruise tours will be found in that chapter. Remember to compare the cost of the cruise tour package with the cost of doing it on your own. In general, cruise lines aren't offering any bargains. In fact, I would char-

The Right Cruise For You

acterize most of them as overpriced, especially when you compare it to the good value you get for the cruise itself. Typically, the additional cost over the base cruise fare for a five-night land package will be at least $1,000. Of course, the convenience will be worth a lot to some people. Not only does it eliminate the need for detailed planning of your land vacation, but it makes the cruise and land portion one easy and seamless experience.

Information Sources

There are many sources for general information on the cruise lines and on cruising itself. The glossy brochures are a necessary piece of literature before you make any final decision, but I cannot emphasize enough that these are marketing tools for the cruise lines. As a result, they're far from objective. The same, of course, can be said about the extensive websites that each and every cruise line has. There are also more general sites about cruise ships but, here too, many are run by travel agencies looking for business or feature only certain cruise lines. The **Cruise Lines International Association** (CLIA) is an industry organization composed of all the major cruise lines and many smaller ones. Their website, www.cruising.org, also paints the experience in a purely positive light, as you might expect. Despite this, it is a useful site because it contains a wealth of information, both statistical and otherwise. You can call CLIA at ☎ (212) 921-0066.

Useful Websites

In addition to CLIA, I recommend that web surfers check out the following sites before coming to any decision on their cruise:

▶ www.alaskacruise.com

▶ www.cruise2.com

▶ www.cruisecritic.com

▶ www.cruisemates.com

▶ www.cruiseopinion.com

▶ www.cruisereviews.com

▶ www.sealetter.com

The primary features of most of these sites are the unbiased reviews submitted by individual travelers like you. In fact, you can send in a review of any ship you've cruised on and it will be added to their database. Because these "reviewers" are not affiliated with the cruise industry, you can be assured that their opinion is objective. Of course, you have to read the reviews carefully. Some people can get ticked off at one little thing and then decide to knock everything else about their cruise experience. Cruise2.com is a little different in that it offers a wealth of statistical and other information about all cruise lines and ships, although it's often a little slow in getting new ship information posted. Sealetter.com, too, is a more comprehensive site and is one of the best sources of information.

THE ULTIMATE CRUISE FANATIC'S WEBSITE

For people who just can't learn enough and read enough about what is going on inside the world of cruising, there's **Cruise News Daily**, which can be accessed at www.cruisenewsdaily.com. It is written in newspaper fashion with timely reports on everything from new ships to itineraries that are being altered because of current weather conditions. Their staff has inside access to what is going on and you can often learn of things here well before the news becomes generally known. I look at it almost every day. That's the good part. The bad part is that what you get on their free

The Right Cruise For You

website is just a synopsis of the full articles. You can see the full article only if you subscribe to their service. Subscription rates begin at around $20 for a month, with discounted rates for longer subscriptions and new subscribers. You receive the full text via e-mail either on a daily or weekly basis – the option is yours. Newsletters are published on weekdays except holidays. The free site does offer access to some of their other features, including photos of ships under construction and a complete rundown on what ships are being built in the yards. It's a fascinating site, but only for the dedicated cruiser.

A Nautical Primer

*T*hose who live and work on the sea have always had a language of their own. This continues today, whether it applies to the navy, commercial shipping or the cruise industry. Although most cruise ship staff will speak in terms that landlubbers understand, nautical terms will be heard frequently during the course of your journey. Here's a quick rundown on some of the ones you'll be most likely to encounter.

▶ *Beam:* The width of the ship measured at its widest point (generally mid-ship).

▶ *Bow:* The front of the ship (*fore* indicates toward the bow or near the bow.)

▶ *Class:* A grouping of ships of the same type. Two or more ships in the same class can also be said to be *sister* ships. It is customary to name the class after the first ship built of a particular type. The only major line not following this practice is Holland America. They make up a name for each class of ship in their fleet. Ships in the same class have identical or nearly identical deck plans and facilities. However, the décor can be and usually is quite different. Sometimes ships of a particular class that were built several years after the original one can wind up having significant differences.

▶ *Gross Registered Tonnage (GRT):* This has nothing to do with the weight of the ship. Rather, it's a useful measure of just how big a ship is. The GRT, although listed in tons or tonnes, is the available internal space of the ship.

▶ *Knot:* A measure of speed at sea equal to about 1.15 miles per hour.

▶ *Master:* In its most common usage, the commander of a non-military vessel; that is, the captain of the ship. In it's most technical sense, a "master" is anyone who has the necessary skills, experience and certification to be a captain. Thus, on a large cruise vessel the first officer (commonly referred to as the Staff Captain) and sometimes even a Chief Engineer may hold a master's license. If John Jones is the commander of a ship named *MV Cruiseship* you would address him as "Captain Jones," but you could also refer to John Jones as being the "master" of the *MV Cruiseship*.

▶ *Nautical mile:* The equivalent of 1.15 land miles.

▶ *Port:* The direction to the left when you are facing the ship's bow; it is the opposite of starboard.

▶ *Starboard:* The direction to the right when you are facing the ship's bow.

▶ *Stern:* The rear of the ship (*aft* is towards the stern or near the stern.)

The Right Cruise For You

A Practical Guide

*W*hether you are a first-timer or an experienced sea voyager, this A to Z directory of practical information should help to answer many of your questions and make your cruise a more enjoyable experience.

Accommodations on Land

Certainly one of the best parts of cruising is that once you unpack your bags in your stateroom, there is no living out of a suitcase. The ship is your hotel. And, if you take a cruise tour before or after the sea-based part of your vacation, the cruise line will arrange for all of your hotels. Depending on the type of Alaska experience you choose to have, you might need hotels in your embarkation city, including Anchorage, or in other Alaska towns if you are traveling on your own. Cruise lines provide the highest level of accommodations for passengers taking cruise tours regardless of which line you sail. Princess and Holland America each operate their own hotel chains in Alaska, although individual travelers can also book these places if space is available. **Princess Lodges**, ☎ (800) 426-0500, www.princesslodges.com, has locations in Copper River, Denali, Kenai and Fairbanks. **Westmark Hotels**, ☎ (800) 544-0970, www.westmarkhotels.com, is in Anchorage, Denali, Fairbanks, Juneau, Sitka, Skagway and Tok. They also have several locations in the Yukon Territory.

Embarkation Cities: All of the ports of embarkation in the Pacific Northwest have a wide choice of hotel facilities in every price category. If you are planning on taking a pre- or post-cruise package in either Seattle, Vancouver or San Francisco, think twice as the cost of hotels in these places is often outrageously high. It would be better to do a little independent planning and sightseeing. Consult your travel agent or use the Internet to find a place suitable for your needs.

In Alaska: Finding hotel accommodations in Anchorage is a simple task, as in any other big city. One difference that you'll notice is that a typical "three star" hotel in Anchorage will cost between $150 and $250 per night during the summer season, somewhat higher than in most places. The same is true in Alaska's resort areas. Prices run about $50 less per night in most other parts of the state. Luxurious "four star" hotels are much harder to come by in Alaska than elsewhere, although there are a few. Bed and breakfasts are popular throughout the state. These have a wide range of prices. In addition to the already mentioned Princess Lodges and Westmark Hotels, several major hotel chains are well represented. The most numerous of these are Best Western, Choice, Holiday Inn, Super 8 and several Marriott corporation hotels. The chain properties are concentrated in Anchorage, and both Best Westerns and Super 8s can be found readily in other parts of the state.

Lodging is rather limited in the vicinity of Denali National Park and is always in great demand. Thus, if you are planning an interior journey on your own, make reservations at least six months in advance. Other than Princess and Westmark, most of the major chains are not well represented there. Many properties in the vicinity of the park are affiliated with one another so it may well be useful to begin your search by contacting **Denali Lodges**, ☎ (877) 336-2545, www.denalilodges.com. The similarly named but different **Denali Lodging**, ☎ (866) 683-8500, www.denalialaska.com, is another choice for searching multiple locations at one time, as is **Denali Park Resorts**, ☎ (800) 276-7234, www.denalinationalpark.com.

Climate & When to Go

Don't let the beautiful full-color pictures in the cruise brochures fool you. Sunny days are the exception rather than the rule, especially along the Inside Passage. Fortunately, prolonged hard rains are relatively rare in the summer months. Alaska's fickle weather shouldn't deter you. Activities (except for flightseeing) are seldom canceled due to the weather and, if you're suitably dressed, you can laugh at the weather. Alaskans, mindful of copious amounts of water from the sky, refer to rain as liquid sunshine. And there is a bonus to the often cloudy weather – the beauty of the glaciers is enhanced by it. Their ice-blue color is most intense under cloud cover, much more so than if the sun is shining brightly, when they appear white. You must also consider the unpredictable nature of Alaskan weather. Seeing clouds when you get up in the morning does not mean it won't be much nicer in a short time. When talking with visitors about the weather, Alaskans say, "If you don't like the current conditions, just wait five minutes!"

CLIMATE CHART

The following climate figures are based on National Weather Service records for the 30-year period ending in 2003 and show monthly average high and low temperatures (°F) and precipitation (inches).

	Ketchikan	Juneau	Skagway	Anchorage	Fairbanks
May	56/41/4.7	55/39/3.5	59/39/1.6	55/39/0.4	59/37/0.6
June	62/47/7.5	61/45/3.0	66/47/1.2	62/47/1.1	70/49/1.4
July	65/51/7.1	64/48/4.2	68/50/1.1	65/51/1.9	72/52/2.0
Aug	65/52/11.1	63/47/5.2	66/49/2.2	63/49/2.4	66/46/1.9
Sept	60/47/14.1	56/42/6.9	58/44/4.0	55/41/2.6	54/36/1.0

Practical Information

May through September is the time when cruise ships will be doing their Alaskan itineraries. Exact dates vary from one line to another and can start in early to mid-May and run all the way into mid-September. As you can see, temperatures are always on the cool side. Too cool for a lot of people in May and September. Although costs are lower during these months, you have to weigh the savings against the potential for discomfort due to low temperatures. If you want more comfortable temperatures, you'll simply have to pay a little more and travel between late June and late August. The only place where summer rainfall is excessive is in the Ketchikan area, where you should expect rain. It's a fact of life. In most Alaska locations the summer sees less rain than other times of year. The interior, as you can see, is actually quite dry during the summer, as are some parts of the southeast, such as around Skagway.

Dining

The dining aspect of a cruise is one of the most important and obvious pleasures of this form of travel. Even if you have never cruised before, I'm sure you've met someone returning from a cruise who can't stop boasting not only about how great the food was, but how much of it there was. If you're on a diet, there's no doubt that a cruise isn't the best place to be. But, heck – you only live once. Forget about your diet and enjoy! You can lose the pounds when you come back or maybe even try to shed a few pounds before the cruise in preparation. (Should a special diet be essential for health, religious or other reasons, this should be arranged at the time you book your cruise. Most cruise lines can accommodate a variety of dietary requirements.) You'll savor wonderfully prepared cuisine, often from renowned chefs, and try delicacies from all around the world. The cuisine of the area where you're cruising is frequently highlighted. Alaska, of course, doesn't have a particular cuisine of its own, but you can count on fresh salmon and other delicacies of the sea that are purchased locally and served in a variety of ways.

In the old days of cruising, shipboard dining was pretty straightforward. You had dinner every night in the main dining room, while breakfast and lunch were offered either in that same dining room or in the buffet. The latter was often somewhat limited in selection. And, of course, there was the midnight buffet. How things have changed. In addition to the main dining room, almost all of today's ships have at least one alternative restaurant. This can take the form of a bistro, café or other type of specialty restaurant. It is usually open only for dinner, although you will find that the choice for lunch has also expanded greatly. The aforementioned buffet has been spruced up, too, with more choices and options. Many buffets are supplemented by specialty areas that feature a particular type of cuisine. There may even be a deli. Most cruise lines also have a pizzeria (sometimes open 24 hours, and certainly always available for long periods throughout the day). Buffets are especially popular for breakfast on port days when you want to make a quick exit to get on shore. Likewise, if you return from shore for lunch, the buffet will take less of your activity time away. Be advised that you will not receive any credit for meals on the ship that you miss because you are in port. In general, the larger the ship the more alternative restaurants there will be, some offering a casual experience, while others can be the most formal of the ship's dining venues. It is becoming increasingly common for some new ships (such as Princess' Gem-class or the newer Norwegian Cruise Lines ships) not to even have a "main" dining room in the traditional sense. Rather, there is a selection of several different restaurants, all included in the basic cruise fare. Unfortunately, along with the increase in choice, it has become almost a universal practice among the cruise lines to charge a fee for at least one of their alternative restaurants. Should you choose this dining option, plan on paying anywhere from $10 to $30 extra per person. This may seem like a high amount for an "all-inclusive" vacation, but a dinner like the one you'll get in these alternative eateries would most likely cost about $100 per person in a fine land-based restaurant. On some lines there may be one or more nights when a particular alternative restaurant may not operate. Typically this will be on the night of the Captain's Dinner, when they want everyone in the main dining room. However, even this seems to be becoming a thing of the past. Choice every night is definitely the wave of the future. Make sure you familiarize yourself with alternative restaurant policies regarding reservations.

The main dining room is always a beautiful place where the cruise line shows off. These days it is extremely rare (outside of the luxury cruise lines) to offer a single-seating dinner, with everyone served at the same time. The general way of doing things is to have early and late seatings. The early seating commonly begins around 6 pm, although it can be adjusted slightly to fit in with port calls. Late seatings usually commence about 2½ hours after the early seating starts. Some people avoid the early seating for fear that it will be rushed, but I haven't found this to be a problem at all. You will be given a choice of which seating you want at the time you book your cruise and every effort will be made to accommodate your wishes. Don't be afraid to ask for a different seat if you don't like the table you have been given. It is often possible for the dining room staff to make adjustments. If you have a preference, such as sitting at a small table as opposed to a large one with many people, make this known at the time you book.

Dinner in the main room is always a multi-course affair and, although the portions in each course aren't overly large, nobody walks away hungry. In fact, the dining room staff will gladly accommodate requests for additional servings or even two different selections if you can't make up your mind what you want to eat! Don't be shy in asking. If you don't see anything on the menu that you like, make it known. There are usually a couple of items available that aren't listed.

While a few lines (usually the more exclusive and expensive ones) may offer complimentary wine or other alcoholic beverages a few times during the cruise, drinks (including soft drinks) are always at additional cost. Your cruise ship will have a good selection of wines and champagnes and your wine steward (or headwaiter if wine stewards are not utilized on the line you select) will be happy to assist you in making the right choice to accompany your dinner. The more upscale the line, the better the wine selection. Spirits of all types are available throughout the day at numerous bars and lounges and, of course, during evening entertainment performances.

Three meals a day doesn't seem to be enough for hungry cruise passengers. Two other popular cruise line events that you may encounter are the afternoon tea (around 4 pm) and the midnight buffet. The former is generally comprised of small sandwiches, pastries and fruits, in addition to a variety of coffees and teas. As is the case with meals, however, there is often a charge for other drinks. The midnight affair is usually heavy on sweets, often sinfully so. Even if a late-night cheesecake isn't for you, do at least look at one of these beautiful and bountiful displays. See if you can resist taking something. Lines offering midnight buffets usually have them every night of the trip, but on a week-long cruise there will usually be one night where this becomes an extra-special affair when the chefs show off not only their cooking artistry, but their flair for the showy and dramatic with exquisite food and ice carvings. At least a few lines are so proud of this feature that they invite passengers in prior to the buffet opening time just to take pictures! It's that impressive. But not every line offers the midnight buffet. Princess, for example, uses their buffet area as a late-night bistro with waiter service. But don't fret about not being able to see all the exquisite food carvings and other visual delights.

Practical Information

These will be much in evidence at other times throughout the cruise.

No matter which ship you are traveling on, there's no doubt that plenty of opportunities to eat will present themselves. Sweets, such as ice cream, are often served out on deck in the afternoon, sometimes even 24 hours a day. Charging for ice cream isn't common, but I'm aware of at least one line that does impose a fee for premium ice cream (but they also serve "regular" ice cream for free). And pizzas, hamburgers and hot dogs are other choices. Finally, if you decide that you don't want to go to the dining room or elsewhere to eat, room service is a standard feature on all ships. Hours of operation are always long and 24-hour service is available more often than not.

Disabled Travelers

There has been some controversy in recent years about just how far the cruise lines have to go in order to meet the needs of handicapped travelers. The public relations staff working for the cruise lines will be quick to point out amenities for the handicapped are provided "voluntarily" (since there are few handicapped access laws required of cruise ships), but the fact of the matter is that cruising, by its very nature, can present some difficulties for the disabled traveler.

These days all of the major cruise lines offer rooms that are suitable for handicapped guests. This is especially true on the larger, more modern vessels. That's the good news. The bad news is that no matter how well they are designed, ships do impose some limitations for the disabled traveler. Even though you can get from one deck to another by elevator, corridors are often narrow and negotiating some areas in a wheelchair can be difficult. Because physically challenged persons, to their credit, are traveling more these days, the number of people bringing motorized scooters onboard to help get around has increased. But this can present safety problems, and some lines are now imposing size and other restrictions on the use of scooters. If you require oxygen (you must bring your own), make it known to the cruise line in advance. In general, despite the helpful nature of ship personnel, cruise lines do require that disabled persons be accompanied by someone who can tend to their needs.

All in all, shipboard limitations aren't such a big problem. The greater potential problem is actually in port, when it's time to get on and off the ship. Almost all of the most important Alaskan ports allow ships to tie up at the dock, thereby eliminating the need to use tenders (small "shuttle boats"), which would definitely present a degree of difficulty for almost all physically challenged individuals. However, airport-style walkways where you directly enter a terminal are rare, except at the largest gateway ports. It is far more common to use a gangplank or stairway that, depending on the nature of the pier, often sit at fairly steep angles and could be next to impossible for those with more severe disabilities to navigate. As a safety precaution, the cruise lines and their captains reserve the option to prohibit physically handicapped passengers from disembarking at certain ports if they deem the individual would be at risk of injury.

If you have any questions concerning this subject, contact the cruise line directly and ask specific questions about facilities, including access at ports of call on the cruise you're interested in. Be prepared to explain your level of handicap as this will help cruise line staff to assess your personal situation. Places requiring use of tenders will be indicated in the chapter on visiting Alaskan ports of call. Questions regarding access for persons with disabilities while in Alaska should be directed to **Access Alaska**, ☎ (907) 248-4777, or **Challenge Alaska**, ☎ (907) 344-7399.

Practical Information

Dress

On Board

Attire during the daytime is highly casual and comfortable. How you dress after dinner depends on what you are going to be doing. If you're going to take in a show or dance the night away, the general practice is to remain dressed as you were for dinner. Otherwise, you can return to your cabin and change back into more casual attire. The dress codes for dinner don't vary that much from one line to another. In the past it was customary (including for me) to divide dinner dress into three categories – formal, informal and casual. The past few years have seen a blending of the last two and some lines now "officially" list only two categories in their brochures. Regardless, the distinction between informal and casual has become so blurred that for practical purpose there are now only two categories. Let's take a closer look at what each one means.

Formal attire technically means a tuxedo or dark suit for men and a gown for women. However, the key word here is "technically," because on all but the most formal ships there is a big range in what people actually wear on the so-called formal evenings. While a lot of men do where tuxedos, they aren't necessarily in the majority, especially on the less-expensive lines. The dark-suit crowd is always well represented. You will almost certainly see quite a few men in suits that are definitely not dark, along with some in sport jackets. So, it all comes down to how comfortable you will feel, even if most other men are more dressed up. If that doesn't bother you, then you needn't be concerned about how spiffy you look. If you want to wear a tuxedo but don't have one, the cheapest option is to rent one through the cruise line. Each cruise line works with a tuxedo rental place or they have their own onboard service and they will take care of everything and have your tuxedo waiting for you in your stateroom on arrival.

Now for the ladies. Gowns of varying style and elegance are predominant but, again, there are quite a few women who choose not to be so fancy. Cocktail dresses and fashionable pant suits are becoming more and more common on formal evenings. Although women may feel more obligated to dress to the level of the occasion than men do, the level of formality has been dropping. Gowns, as well as other attire for women, can sometimes be rented from the same places that provide men's tuxedos.

There are typically two formal nights per week of cruising. These are the Captain's dinner (often the second night of the cruise) and the farewell dinner, which is usually the next-to-last night. The Captain's dinner is where people dress the best. Keep in mind that there are only two formal nights; even if you intend to follow all the dress guidelines, it will not pay for most people to go out and buy a whole new fancy wardrobe.

Alternative restaurants are often a means of avoiding more formal dress. But do keep in mind that the alternative restaurants may not always be open on formal evenings and some of these specialty eateries have formal dress codes all of the time. On some ships you may be limited to the buffet if you want to avoid getting dressed up. Some lines have at least one alternative casual restaurant that's always open. And, of course, lines like Norwegian allow you to dress the way you want all the time.

Casual attire has two meanings, depending on the time of day. In the afternoon, anything goes, from cut-off jeans to polo shirts to tank tops and halters. However, in the evening, casual translates into what most people would call business casual and what the cruise lines often refer to as "smart casual" or "resort casual." Not quite anything goes. Specifically,

jeans, shorts, halter tops and any kind of beachwear are definite no-no's in the dining room. Sandals and sneakers are likewise looked down on, although you can get away with nice
walking shoes that are in good condition.

Now, cruising Alaska isn't the same as cruising in the Caribbean because of the obvious differences in the weather. While
beachwear is often appropriate for daytime in many cruising
destinations, you will be cold if you choose to dress that way
on an Alaskan cruise. If you plan to be out on deck, then dress
as you would for a chilly fall day in most parts of the United
States and even warmer on those days when the ship is going
to be sailing by glaciers. A warm jacket and even a pair of
gloves will come in handy for those times when you want to
be outside to get a better view of the scenery. But this doesn't
mean you have to leave the bathing suit and sandals at home.
That was the case in the old days of cruising when ships generally had only outdoor swimming pools that they didn't even
bother to fill up for trips to Alaska. Now just about every ship
has one pool that can be covered by a retractable dome and
the area can be heated. So, taking a dip in the pool while the
outside temperature is a balmy 50 degrees can be done!

In Port

How you dress when in port depends not only on the weather,
but also on your activities. Casual and comfortable is generally
the best way to dress. When in port (or when on deck viewing
scenery) the best advice is to be prepared for just about anything. Dress in layers so that you can quickly adapt to changing conditions. Warm woolens, a heavy sweater, hat and
gloves are all advisable, as is a fairly heavy outer jacket. A
lightweight waterproof jacket comes in handy for intermittent
showers.

Wise packing extends beyond what clothes you are going to
take on the cruise. So don't forget to pack the following:

▶ Sunscreen is advisable even in often cloudy Alaska if you're going to spend a lot of time outdoors.

▶ Insect repellent. Brands containing DEET are considered somewhat more effective, but DEET-less brands are safer, especially for children. Stinging and biting insects aren't a big problem on an Alaskan cruise, but if you're going into the interior those Alaskan mosquitoes have a well-deserved fierce reputation.

▶ Sunglasses

▶ Hat

▶ Gloves. This may sound silly for a summer vacation but you will be cold when standing out on deck by the glaciers, especially if you're trying to hold a camera.

▶ Collapsible umbrella

▶ Sweater and two ro three jackets of varying heaviness. Although ship personnel will provide blankets when the viewing conditions are chilly, they aren't as easy to use as a warm jacket if you're taking pictures.

▶ Binoculars

▶ Camera and/or camcorder, and plenty of extra film, tapes and battery packs. You will be able to purchase film and other needs in port (as well as onboard ship), but the prices are much higher than at home. Do price film developing on your ship as it is less expensive than you might think. All ships now have full digital service.

▶ Medications. Making sure that you have all of your medicines with you goes without saying. However, you should also bring along a copy of your prescription in case you lose your medication and need replacements. In addition, this will assist in the Customs process. Although it is rare to be challenged by Customs officials about medications, a prescription will help clear things up rapidly.

▶ Documents. You won't believe how many people forget about bringing the necessary documentation, including tickets! Make sure you have copies of your ID (especially the information page of your passport) and keep them in a safe place separate from the originals.

Driving / Rental Cars

As a general rule, driving a rental car provides the greatest degree of flexibility. But most Alaskan ports of call are rather small, with many points of interest relatively close by. Thus, a car isn't usually necessary. However, there are almost always some sights that are distant. While you can usually get to them by shore excursion, a car might be a better way for the independent-minded traveler. In many towns along the Inside Passage, the road system extends only a few miles in any direction from town. While this makes it hard to get lost, it also decreases the need to have your own vehicle. Places like Ketchikan and Sitka definitely fall into this category, and Juneau does but to a lesser extent. Skagway, on the other hand, is connected to a much longer system of roads and may warrant a car rental. If you're starting or ending your cruise in Anchorage, then a car provides a viable alternative to cruise tours as there is a good system of roads extending from south of Anchorage all the way to Fairbanks.

Rental agencies are limited in the smaller towns and cities along the Inside Passage. Here's a rundown on what's available from the major companies. Some of these locations are not major ports of call or part of an Anchorage to Fairbanks routing. Rather, they are on the Kenai Peninsula south of Anchorage, where the road network is good. You can also check the Internet for local companies that might offer better prices.

CAR RENTAL COMPANIES

Alamo, ☎ (800) 462-5266, www.alamo.com. Anchorage, Fairbanks and Juneau.

Avis, ☎ (800) 230-4898, www.avis.com. Anchorage, Fairbanks, Juneau, Kenai, Kodiak, Petersburg, Sitka, Skagway and Whittier.

Budget, ☎ (800) 527-0700, www.budget.com. Anchorage, Fairbanks, Juneau, Kenai, Ketchikan and Kodiak.

Hertz, ☎ (800) 654-3131, www.hertz.com. Anchorage, Fairbanks, Homer, Juneau, Kenai, Seward and Soldotna.

National, ☎ (800) 227-7368, www.nationalcar. com. Anchorage, Fairbanks and Juneau.

Electrical Appliances

All cruise ships serving Alaska have the same 110-volt system found in the United States and their outlets accept the two-pin plug (including those with a third grounding prong) found on US appliances. Some European lines have 220-volt electrical systems and use the two-round-pin plug that is found throughout most of Europe, but even these ships may have dual voltage systems. If you're traveling on a vessel that has only a 220-volt system, you will need a transformer and, probably, an adapter for the plug. Although they may have some of the latter on board, it is best to bring your own.

You should be aware that some electrical appliances (usually those that heat, such as irons and hair dryers) are not permitted onboard. These items are usually supplied in the staterooms or will be brought to your room upon request. If you are the type of traveler who always brings along a host of electronic goodies, other than electric shavers and the like, then it is always a wise idea to check in advance concerning the cruise line's regulations.

Formalities, Documents & Paperwork

Passports & Other ID

You will have to present proper identification to the cruise line personnel before you embark. It is your responsibility to make sure that everything is in order, not only for embarking and getting into each port, but for the return trip too. Your embarkation can be delayed or even denied if don't have the required documents to satisfy both the United States and Canadian officials. Although a current, valid passport is not required for American citizens traveling to Canada, this is always the best form of identification for immigration and just about any other purpose. If you don't already have a passport, it might be a good idea for you to apply for one. You should begin the procedure at least 90 days prior to your departure. If you do not have a passport, then bring either your original birth certificate (with raised seal) or a certified copy of it and a photo identification issued by a governmental agency (such as a driver's license). Non-US citizens should consult American (www.immigrationagency.org) and Canadian immigration (www.canadavisa.com) authorities as to what documentation is required.

Cruise Documents

Cruise documents are a fancy name for your tickets and other little bits and pieces of information that the cruise line will send to you (either directly or through your travel agent). They are sent, more often than not, anywhere from two weeks to a month prior to your scheduled sailing date. Some lines will, on your request, issue them earlier at an additional cost (and a high one at that). The only time you should make this request is if you will be traveling for a week or more prior to your cruise. There are hefty fees for reissuing documents if you lose them or require a change, so keeping track of them is important.

For reasons I can't fathom, cruise lines have been way behind the times when it comes to electronic ticketing and avoiding the hassle of sending documents. As of press time, only Royal Caribbean had implemented a form of e-ticketing and it is offered only on a limited basis. But all this is bound to change, and I'm sure that your travel agent will be aware of the latest ticketing options.

Luggage tags will be included in your document package. These may have specific information identifying you and your stateroom number or they may simply be color-coded to the deck you're on and you have to write in your name and room number. In either case, be sure they're affixed to your luggage before you turn the bags over to dock personnel. It's a good idea to remove any old airline tags before you put on the cruise tags.

All cruise lines require that you fill out a passenger information form of some kind. The form includes information needed by US immigration authorities prior to your embarkation. Every line now gives you the opportunity to complete these forms online at their website or by fax. You should complete this paperwork no later than the time you make final payment. If you are unable to avail yourself of either the online or fax methods, ask your travel agent or cruise line personnel what procedure should be followed. Completing these forms on the day of embarkation causes delays and possible boarding problems.

Customs

It is almost a sure thing that at least a small portion of your Alaskan cruise experience will be in Canada. As a result, the US Customs Service will want to see you on your return to the States. The procedures are generally fast and efficient, but it helps to be informed in advance about what you may or may not bring back into the country. Exemptions from Customs duties depend on how much time you spent in Canada. If it was over 48 hours, then each person has an exemption of US $800, but families can combine their exemption so that three people, for example, get US $2,400, regardless of who bought what. Exemptions include a limit of 100 cigars and 200 cigarettes and one liter of liquor. Visits of under 48 hours reduce the exemption amount to $200 per person, 10 cigars, 50 cigarettes and 150 ml of liquor. Exemptions cannot be combined on these shorter visits.

You should also be aware of restricted articles, generally those that have safety questions or were manufactured in certain countries, such as Cuba and Iran. If you are planning on doing a lot of shopping in Canada, get more information from the US Customs Service at 1300 Pennsylvania Avenue NW, Washington DC 20229; ☎ (202) 354-1000; www.customs.ustreas. gov.

Finally, you should be aware that the "duty free" shopping that may be advertised in some ports has absolutely nothing to do with American Customs duties. It simply refers to the fact that there is no local tax on the items. Such purchases, however, are subject to the foregoing regulations and limitations. True "duty free" shopping does apply to purchases made onboard your ship. So, you won't have to pay any fees on that $25,000 painting you buy!

Gambling

Other than the Disney Cruise Line (which doesn't go to Alaska), there isn't a cruise ship afloat without a casino. Casinos allow passengers to enjoy the games and the cruise line enjoys the profit! Depending on the ship, the onboard casino can range from a very small room to a large and elaborate affair that is more reminiscent of Las Vegas. Today's biggest ships largely reflect the latter. There are both slot machines and table games. Small denomination slot machines are easy to find, but minimums at the tables will probably be higher than you are used to from stateside gaming. The majority of casinos are operated for the cruise lines by a well-known gaming company ("Caesars Palace at Sea" is the name given to some ship-board casinos).

Regulations prohibit ship casinos from operating when the ship is docked in port. Once a vessel enters international waters, however, the casino comes alive, day or night.

Minors are not allowed to play, but the onboard minimum age is sometimes as low as 18, as compared to 21 in the United States.

Don't expect good odds on slot machines, which are tighter than any you would find in Las Vegas or Atlantic City. On the other hand, table game odds are more akin to their land-based brethren, so you would be well advised to stick to them if you're serious about winning.

Practical Information

Home-to-Ship Transportation

Flight Arrangements

It would be nice to take a short ride to the cruise ship terminal, leave your car and get onboard. But, despite the increase in availability of American ports of embarkation, the fact is that the majority of Alaska cruise passengers will have to fly to their gateway port. Every cruise line offers you the option of including round-trip air transportation with your cruise package. In fact, there are a few lines that price the cruise with an air-inclusive rate and you then have to subtract an "air credit" if you book your own transportation. However, this type of pricing is rare and I haven't even seen it at all in recent years in the Alaska market.

Using the cruise line's air program will certainly be your easiest option. Everything will be taken care of, including transfers between the airport and your ship at both ends of the cruise. If you make air arrangements independently, you will almost certainly have to make your way to the ship on your own. You should also keep in mind that if several guests are arriving via a cruise-sponsored air program and the plane is late, the ship's departure will be delayed in order to accommodate those passengers or they will make arrangements for you to "catch up" with the ship at their cost if sailing can't be held up any longer.

Don't expect that courtesy if you're traveling on your own. (The possibility of that kind of disaster can be avoided by planning to arrive in the embarkation port a day early.)

So far it sounds like a really good deal to go with the cruise line's air program. But there are some disadvantages that need to be considered. The air fares offered by the cruise lines range from average to very high. For domestic flights, I've never seen a cruise line that offers a fare lower than what you can get on your own. Comparison is the key; you'll probably find it relatively easy to get a lower fare for individual travel even after adding in the cost of transferring from the airport to the ship.

What makes your task more difficult in comparing prices is that the cruise lines don't usually give you detailed information – such as the airline, departure times and number of connections – until final documents are issued (usually two to four weeks before your departure). You'll probably want to book your flight long before that if you're going to be doing it on your own. Furthermore, cruise line-sponsored flights are sometimes inconvenient as to both routing and times. Carefully weigh the advantages and disadvantages of the cruise line's air program as they relate to you and don't let the travel agent or cruise line bully you into something that you would prefer not to do. These days all of the cruise lines offer "custom" air arrangements. That is, you can pick the flight and airline that you want to take. Unfortunately, the extra charge for doing so is usually exorbitant.

Making your own air arrangements for a cruise to Alaska is a relatively simple task since there are a good variety of airlines and flights serving the embarkation cities. The possible exception is if your ship departs from Vancouver, where the choice is more limited but still shouldn't present any unusual problem.

Practical Information

AIRLINES SERVING GATEWAY CITIES		
Among the major airlines serving Alaska and/or cruise gateway cities in the Pacific Northwest are:		
Air Canada	☎ (888) 247-2262	www.aircanada.ca
Alaska Airlines	☎ (800) 252-7522	www.alaskaair.com
America West	☎ (800) 235-9292	www.americawest.com
American	☎ (800) 433-7300	www.aa.com
Continental	☎ (800) 523-3273	www.continental.com
Delta	☎ (800) 241-4141	www.delta.com
Northwest	☎ (800) 447-4747	www.nwa.com
Southwest	☎ (800) 435-9792	www.southwest.com
United	☎ (800) 241-6522	www.united.com

Getting to Your Ship

It's easy if the cruise line will be providing the transfers (that is, you book through their air program). Otherwise, the best bet, if available, is to take one of the special buses that run between the airport and cruise port, or a taxi when such services aren't available. Taxis, unfortunately, can cost a considerable amount. Fortunately for Alaska cruisers, public transportation is available in all of the embarkation/disembarkation cities.

If you choose to take part in a pre-cruise tour of the gateway city, all transportation to the ship will be included. Independent travelers will once again have to make their own way, but can minimize inconvenience by choosing a hotel that is relatively close to the cruise ship terminal. Some hotels in these locations will provide complimentary shuttle service to the port. If you have been renting a car in the gateway city you should be able to return it close to the cruise ship terminal.

Many cruise lines offer passengers who make their own flight arrangements the option to add on ground transfers to and from the ship. The fee for this service is very high and it will almost always be less expensive to take a taxi. Inquire at the time of your booking as to availability and cost.

> NOTE: *Your first priority as an independent traveler is to make sure that you allow enough time to make the transfer without missing your cruise ship's departure time. I cannot emphasize enough that the best way and most relaxing way to do this is to plan to arrive in your embarkation city the day before your sailing date.*

The section on *Ports of Embarkation*, page 144, offers driving directions to the cruise ship terminal for those who plan to arrive by car. It also provides details on things like charges for parking and how much time to allow between the airport and the cruise ship port.

Health & Safety Concerns

No one likes to think about the possibility of becoming ill while on vacation. However, a little advance planning and precaution is necessary because such things do, unfortunately, occur. As a cruiser, your planning to ensure a healthy cruise can be divided into two separate issues: health on the ship and health on shore.

Onboard Health

Despite big-time press attention to outbreaks of minor viruses on cruise ships that occur from time to time (see below for more on this topic), cruising is a healthy way to travel. As with any place that serves food, there can be occasional instances of food poisoning, but this is very rare and, when it does happen, it's usually mild. A greater risk are the annoyances resulting from over-indulgence in food and alcohol. This doesn't mean that you shouldn't eat more than you normally would at home or even take an extra drink or two (you are, after all, on vacation), but don't overdo it. Know your limits.

THOSE NASTY LITTLE VIRUSES

Beginning in the fall of 2002 the news media decided it was time to create a frenzy about a series of outbreaks of the so-called "Norwalk" virus that occurred on cruise ships. A little research reveals that these outbreaks have always occurred from time to time and that the reports made much ado about nothing. The mild virus is akin to what we commonly call a "24-hour virus." So let's put this picture into some meaningful perspective.

The Centers for Disease Control require that cruise lines report any contagious illness that affects more than four percent of the total passenger and crew count. Figuring an average of about 3,000 people per cruise, that means that whenever there are 120 or more cases, they are reported. Then it becomes public information (meaning that the news media gets their hands on it). The number of ships with cases reaching this percentage are typically about 30 a year, out of several thousand departures. And the outbreak is, more often than not, limited to fewer than 200 people or about seven percent of everyone onboard.

The viruses almost always originate on land. They are most common in winter (both on land and on ships). Anytime people are in close quarters, the virus can spread. Although outbreaks like this don't make news in a school or an office environment, let it happen on a cruise ship and .... Well, you know the rest.

The best you can do to protect yourself from becoming sick is the same as you would do at home – wash your hands frequently. Aside from that, you can rely on the good scrubbings that cruise ship personnel give their vessel after an outbreak. I don't see the need to take any special precautions, but for those who are a bit skittish about these things the best place for information on sanitation conditions for a particular cruise ship is the Centers for Disease Control & Prevention. Their website, www.cdc.gov/travel/cruise.htm, has the latest sanitation inspection report and rating for each ship. You can also call them at ☎ (888) 232-6789.

In-Port Health

Since health standards in both Alaska and Pacific Canada are the same as in the United States, there aren't any unusual things that you have to be aware of. However, even domestic travel has its little health risks that can't be ignored. Sunburn, heat exhaustion and other similar problems aren't as likely to occur in the cool and often cloudy climate of Alaska, but the sun does come out and people who are fair-skinned should take the proper precautions to protect themselves from over-exposure. You won't encounter any poisonous animals in Alaska either but, as mentioned briefly earlier, the Alaskan interior is known for voracious mosquitoes that swarm heavily during the short summer season. Even more annoying than the mosquitoes are the itchy effects of being bitten by sand flies and the tiny no-see-ums. All of these pests aren't much of a problem along the coast (including the major port towns and cities), but they become increasingly prevalent as you head inland. If you plan to do a lot of outdoor activity in ports, especially in the interior, make sure you use insect repellent and cover up as much skin as possible. Insect repellent isn't as effective against sand flies and *no-see-ums* as it is against mosquitoes. The best way to protect yourself against them if you're going hiking is to wear long-sleeve shirts, long pants tucked into your socks and gloves.

Ship Security

While it is impossible to be totally safe from crime in any environment, there is little doubt that cruise ships are one of the safest places to be. Few things are as rare as a person being mugged onboard a cruise ship. That said, a few simple common-sense precautions are still advisable.

▶ Women traveling alone or with another female friend should be aware of the intentions of men. There are, no doubt, some men out there who figure that a woman on a cruise without a male companion is looking for some action. Behave as you would in your home city and you should not have any problems.

▶ When it comes to safeguarding your possessions, don't leave cash or other valuables on display in your room. Always use the in-room safe that most ships provide or check valuables with the purser's office for safekeeping. Also, always be sure that your room is locked on leaving.

What more people are concerned with today in the aftermath of September 11, 2001 is ship security from outside threats, namely terrorists. Most of the cruise lines were paying more attention to this than the airlines were, even before that eventful day, and they have devoted more attention to it as of late. It is universal practice to X-ray all baggage that is being checked-in for delivery to a cabin. You will also have to go through metal detectors like those at an airport as you enter the cruise ship terminal and each time you get onboard at any port call. Inspection of carry-on luggage may also be done. You will be required to show proper identification before being allowed to embark and, again, each time you return to the ship during the course of your cruise. The IDs issued to all passengers usually have your photograph encoded into them. All American cruise ports are monitored by Coast Guard vessels with crew looking for anything suspicious; it is common in larger ports for cruise ships to be escorted in and out of the water channel.

As far as safety from the potential perils of the sea is concerned, today's cruise ships are technical marvels. They have the most modern and sophisticated navigational and collision avoidance systems. Officers are highly trained and experienced and all crew members receive extensive training in emergency procedures. It is a very remote possibility that you would ever be faced with an emergency situation that would necessitate evacuation of the ship. However, all ships are required by law to conduct a lifeboat drill and all passengers are required to participate. Listen to the instructions carefully and familiarize yourself with safety procedures that are posted in your cabin. As you would in a hotel, study evacuation routes and be familiar with the nearest exit and an alternative exit. Make sure that your children fully understand this information.

Safety on Shore

The good news is that the cities and towns of Alaska's Inside Passage have low crime rates. But Anchorage is not any different from the typical American city of its size. No area is free from crime and tourists almost always make an inviting target for thieves. Therefore, you need to take reasonable precautions, just as you would when visiting any other destination.

▶ Do not carry more cash than you need.

▶ Don't wear expensive jewelry.

▶ Keep valuables out of sight (a money belt worn inside your clothing is always a good idea): make sure you have a good grip on your camera; avoid carrying handbags (if you do carry one, close it securely and keep it facing towards your body).

▶ Seedy neighborhoods won't be encountered in the small towns of the Inside Passage, but even there you shouldn't wander around after dark (an unlikely event given when ships are in port and the long period of daylight in Alaska during the summer). If staying in Anchorage, however, stick to the main tourist areas after dark. See the separate section below concerning onboard security.

Those going into the interior (and this includes hiking just about anywhere in Denali National Park) have to be on the alert for large animals, but especially bears. While bears don't make a habit of going after humans, they will attack if they feel threatened. Should you encounter a bear, do not run. Stand your ground for a moment, and then slowly back away. Hikers should pick up the brochure from park officials about dealing with bears. This is even more important if you're going to be camping. The brochure details methods for storing food, which is what usually attracts bears. A few simple precautions will likely do the trick as the risk of dangerous encounters with bears, moose, caribou and other large animals is small for people who follow the safety rules.

Money Matters

Costs

This section will explore all of your potential costs, except airfare, something the brochures sometimes gloss over. A few things are important to keep in mind before you scan the prices. Cruise fares are always quoted on a *per person* basis and this assumes double-occupancy in a stateroom. Persons traveling alone will have to pay what two people traveling together would pay, or close to it – outrageous by any standard. (Some of the luxury lines are less drastic in this regard.) On the other hand, a third person in a room – either child or adult – pays a much reduced rate. The costs below are indicative of the so-called *brochure* rates, equivalent to the rack rate in a hotel. However, before you fall out of your chair, remember that significant discounts off the brochure rates are almost always available. See further details in the *Discounts* section of this chapter.

The fares shown below are for a seven-night cruise, because that is what the majority of cruise lines offer in Alaska. Cruises of less than a week are often higher priced on a per-night basis. Conversely, cruises of more than a week are frequently less expensive on a per-night basis. Now, let's take a look at the average brochure prices for each of the major lines, rounded off to the nearest $50.

AVERAGE BROCHURE CABIN PRICES				
Cruise Line	Inside	Outside no balcony	Outside w/ balcony	Suite (min.)
Carnival	$1,750	$2,100	$2,300	$2,900
Holland America	$2,150	$2,600	$3,850	$3,600
Norwegian	$1,250	$1,550	$2,050	$2,700
Princess	$1,900	$2,200	$3,100	$3,200
Royal Caribbean	$1,750	$2,200	$2,700	$3,100

The prices reflect the "luxury" level of each line. If you were to rank them from most expensive to least expensive, they would reflect the luxury and level-of-service scale as generally agreed-upon by most cruise experts. (The even more upscale lines that were briefly mentioned earlier would always be much more expensive, with fares often two or even three times as much.)

Practical Information

Average prices are affected to a great extent by two important factors. The first is the fluctuation in prices between low and high seasons. The difference of a week can sometimes mean a large drop or rise in prices, especially around holiday periods. The second reason for a range in costs is that there are so many different classes of staterooms. There are almost always a very limited number of staterooms in the lowest price category. Suites have the greatest possible range in price because of the wide variation in size and luxury level. So, while the minimum suite prices shown don't vary from one line to another by as much as you might expect, the maximum suite prices can be as low as $5,000 or possibly a little less on some lines and go up to as much as $15,000.

There is one other factor that affects pricing – the itinerary. Gulf of Alaska cruises are somewhat higher priced than Inside Passage cruises. Thus, Norwegian (which is always at or near the bottom of the pricing list regardless of destination) is even cheaper because most of their Alaskan itineraries are on the Inside Passage. Although prices from one ship to another in the same line don't usually vary a great deal, Carnival's Alaska prices are made a bit higher because they have only one ship going to Alaska and it has a high percentage of Gulf of Alaska itineraries.

You should also be aware that, depending on which ships are serving Alaskan routes, not all cabin/suite categories may be available on every line. Which type of accommodation to choose is discussed further in the *Selecting the Right Stateroom For You* section. The cruise prices shown above also include port charges assessed on each passenger, which are often quite significant. They do not include various other taxes and fees imposed by different governments (compared to port charges, these are not significant, typically running from about $20-$50 per person for the entire cruise). While cruise now quote rates with port charges included, many discount travel agencies and websites give you a low-ball figure by excluding them. Always be sure what price you are dealing with before you pronounce a price as good or bad.

The only other mandatory (or almost mandatory) expense that you will incur is for tips. Although there is no law that states you must leave a gratuity, it is an accepted practice; rare, indeed, is the individual who will not tip. Each person can expect to spend about $100 for a week-long cruise. More guidelines on this topic will be given in the *Gratuities* section.

Other on-board expenses of an optional nature that you may incur are:

▶ Drinks and snacks: Both alcoholic beverages and soft drinks are (with rare exceptions) on a fee basis. Since the cruise staff will constantly be offering you drinks, this can become quite expensive. Most cruise lines offer pre-paid packages for children that include unlimited sodas. My suggestion is to head to the buffet when you get thirsty during the day. The majority of cruise lines offer free self-service fruit juices all day long. There's always plenty of free food to be found as well, but some lines may charge for things like premium ice cream, pastries and gourmet coffees at patisseries.

▶ Dining: While all of your onboard meals are included in the cruise fare, almost all of the larger new ships (and an increasing number of remodeled older and smaller ones) have one or more upscale restaurants for which an additional fee is usually imposed. More will be said about this in the next section on dining.

▶ Personal Expenditures: This includes a wide variety of items, including services at the spa or beauty salon, shopping, laundry service and so forth. The amount you spend on this category can run from practically nothing to hundreds of dollars. Prices are always available in advance, so when you receive the bill at the end of your cruise, the balance shouldn't come as a shock to you.

▶ Shore Excursions: The only other significant costs that you will encounter are for land-based activities, either on your own or as part of a guided excursion. Here, again, the cost will be highly variable, depending on the number and nature of the tours you take. In general, you should know the cost of available shore excursions prior to your cruise even if you wait to book them until you're on board. Many cruise websites list the cost of excursions. If not, you'll almost certainly be provided a descriptive price list along with your cruise documents. Those touring on their own will have to figure on the cost of a car rental, taxi or public transportation, admissions, and so forth. Lunch might also be an added cost. The practice of cruise lines offering a box lunch seems to have gone the way of the dinosaur, but you can still always ask about it. If you plan your day so that you are back at the ship for lunch, it can save a lot of money and maybe even time.

A TAXING ISSUE

There is no such thing as unlimited resources and that's especially true when it comes to government's ability to find money. Alaska has benefitted enormously from oil money, and the state was wise enough to establish a reserve fund from the proceeds which it has used to make annual payments to each and every Alaskan citizen. However, this has become something of a

Holy Grail issue as no one wants to give up their dividend or risk not having enough money in the fund by using it for general state expenditures. Thus, like most governments, the state of Alaska is hard-pressed to balance its current operating budget. Taxing tourists is always a popular way for state legislators to raise some cash and so there have been several attempts to impose a fee of between $50-100 per cruise passenger. The plan has been defeated on several occasions, including most recently in early 2004. However, it will probably resurface sometime in the future. Although it isn't likely that such an extra cost would discourage many people from taking an Alaskan cruise, you can thank the cruise industry for its not having been enacted to date. They vociferously oppose it and threaten (very quietly) to take their ships elsewhere. Of course, they wouldn't really do that, but it makes people a little skittish about passing a new tax that could kill the golden goose!

Discounts

Seeing is not believing when it comes to prices listed in the cruise brochures. Every line offers a price reduction for booking early. Some form of discounted pricing is always shown in the brochure as well. Most lines offer a straight cash discount, which may begin at around $400 for lower-priced staterooms and rise to well over $1,000 for more expensive accommodations. A smaller number of lines give a percentage off the regular fare, as much as 40% in some instances but typically more in the range of 10% to 20%. Additionally, your discount will vary within the same cruise line, depending on how far in advance you book. In general, the earlier you do it, the greater the discount. Refer to the individual cruise line brochures or

Practical Information

your travel agent for specific cruise line-sponsored discounts. If there's room available, you can also sometimes get aboard at a greatly reduced rate if you wait until the last minute. Cruise lines hate to sail with less than a full ship and they will offer ridiculously low prices to fill every room. However, I don't recommend this as a regular practice if your heart is set on a particular cruise. If sales are brisk (and cruise popularity means that they probably will be), a last-minute discount will never be offered and there's a good chance that you might not get on the ship of your choice at all if you wait too long.

Another way to cut costs is to book through a discount cruise travel agent who buys large blocks of staterooms at sharply reduced prices. Newspaper travel sections are filled with advertisements for such agents. To ensure that you are dealing with a reputable company, make sure they are a member of at least one of the following: CLIA (Cruise Lines International Association, www.cruising.org), NACOA (National Association of Cruise Oriented Agencies, www.nacoaonline.com), or ASTA (American Society of Travel Agents, www.astanet.com). There are other reputable travel organizations, but the preceding three are the standards. Consult your local phone directory to find the cruise-only travel agents in your area. Cruise Holidays is an example of a nationally franchised cruise-oriented agency that has offices in just about every large city.

Among the larger national cruise agencies are: **Cruises of Distinction**, ☎ (800) 434-5544; **Cruise.com**, ☎ (888) 333-3116, www.cruise.com; **CruisesOnly.com**, www.cruises-only.com, ☎ (800) 278-4737; **National Discount Cruise Co.**, www.nationaldiscountcruise.com, ☎ (800) 788-8108; and **White Travel Service**, ☎ (800) 547-4790.

An Alaskan-based travel service specializing in cruises of all types is the **Alaska Cruise Center**, ☎ (907) 874-3382, www.akcruises.com. As you review these sites, you might see mention of Seattle-based Cruise Advisors. On their website, www.alaska-cruises.org, you can request their list of Alaska cruise information that contains all of the sailings for the current year and has information on the ships and itineraries. Don't be misled by the "org" ending – this is not a non-profit website designed to give out objective information. It's a travel agency, plain and simple.

Package deals that include air sometimes work out to be less expensive than booking the air and cruise sections separately (see the upcoming section on *Flight Arrangements* for further details). But no pricing system is ever static in the travel world. Do some research. Price things separately and as part of a package deal to see which is the best price at the time. And don't hesitate to tell a travel agent or supplier of a good price you were quoted elsewhere. They may just come back and beat it.

Since all of the cruise lines are anxious to have your repeat business, it's standard practice for them to offer discounts to travelers who have sailed with them before. These discounts can sometimes be substantial. They usually start at 10% but sometimes can be much more, especially for those lines that increase the benefit the more times you cruise with them. You can take advantage of past cruising and request such discounts when you book on an affiliated line – that is, a different line than you've cruised in the past but which is owned by the same company. All of the industry works this way and the ultimate example is the "Vacation Interchange Privileges" offered by seven lines, all of which are part of Carnival Corporation. For past guests the news seems quite good. But here's the bad news. Popular cruise destinations, especially during peak travel periods, are often excluded from the list of departure dates that are eligible for discounts.

The essential point of all this is quite clear: with the variety of discounts available being so great, you should never have to pay the full fare!

Practical Information

Credit Cards & Currencies

Since shipboard life is "cashless," you don't have to worry about having a lot of money with you while you're at sea. Once in port, however, it's another matter, as your cruise line-issued card won't be recognized on land! Credit cards are accepted just as widely in Alaska as they are in other parts of the United States, so that should mitigate the need to bring a lot of cash on shore with you. ATMs are available in the larger ports. There are also ATMs on most ships, but be aware that they charge much higher fees than you're used to paying.

If your itinerary includes ports of calls in Canada or embarks from Canada, then you'll need some Canadian dollars (worth approximately US 75¢ at press time). Although tourist attractions and other businesses in Canadian cities near the United States (or along the tourist path of the Inside Passage) will often accept US dollars, they will do so either at face value or at a poor exchange rate and you'd be cheating yourself to use them. If you think you'll be spending a lot of cash while in Canada, get hold of some Canadian dollars in advance. Better yet, use credit cards or withdraw Canadian cash from an ATM in Canada. You get the best exchange rates using either of these methods.

Your Onboard Account

As for settling your onboard account at the end of the cruise, it is easiest to do so by credit card. Almost everyone will have given the cruise line credit card information at the time of booking; you can just leave that on the record and you won't need to do anything. If you do want to pay cash, you have the option of doing so. Those travelers who don't have or don't wish to provide credit card information to the cruise line will be asked to put down a cash deposit at the beginning of the voyage to cover onboard expenses. You will be notified if you get low on your available balance and, if the balance goes to zero, will be asked for an additional cash deposit.

Any amounts due to or from you will be settled at the end of the cruise.

Gratuities

Except for a few lines (mostly the top-dollar luxury lines), gratuities for ship personnel are not included in your fare. And, as is the case throughout the travel and leisure industry, tipping is a way of life. Most ship personnel that will be directly serving you (dining room staff, cabin attendants, etc.) earn a low salary and tips provide a substantial portion of their income. The question of how much to tip involves your evaluation of the service provided and your own personal preferences and beliefs regarding gratuities.

Cruise line management will always provide written guidelines as to what is an acceptable amount to tip. But it is important to remember that these are only guidelines and you – the customer – have the final say. Don't be intimidated into giving more than you think is warranted or is above what you can afford. On the other hand, exceptional service is always a good reason to consider tipping above the suggested amounts. Here are some commonly accepted guidelines:

▶ Dining Room Staff: $3-3.50 per person, per day for your waiter and about half of that for his or her assistant. Your dining room area head waiter (or captain) can also be given $1-2 per day, but in my opinion this can be reduced or omitted unless he does something special for you. Most cruise lines suggest tipping the restaurant manager/maitre d', but again, I don't see the need for that unless he also has performed some special service for you. If you frequently ask advice from the wine steward (where a separate individual handles this chore), then he should receive a tip of a dollar per day.

Practical Information

▶ Cabin Attendant: $3-3.50 per person, per day is acceptable. Some sources recommend a small amount for the chief housekeeper but, as above, I don't see the need for that unless he or she has handled a particular problem well for you.

▶ Other Staff: The other people you will likely consider tipping are bartenders, cocktail waiters and waitresses, as well as deck hands who help out with the lounge chairs. These individuals are tipped each time you use their services. However, all cruise lines have already included a mandatory gratuity (usually 15%) for those who serve you drinks, so you should not feel obligated to give anything additional. If you wish, you can give a buck to deck hands who offer assistance.

No tipping of dining room staff and cabin attendants takes place during the course of the cruise. All gratuities are given at the very end. Now we get to the tricky part: the procedure for handing over the tips. In the old days of cruising (even as recently as two or three years ago on many lines), it was common for gratuities to be given in cash. Marked envelopes for each staff member were left in your stateroom and you gave the envelope with the cash tips to the appropriate person on the last night of the cruise. This is now becoming an obsolete method and that's good because few people felt that comfortable with this procedure. The most common method in use today is for all gratuities to automatically be charged to your shipboard account in the amount recommended by the cruise line. If that is the amount you want to give, then you don't have to do anything at all. However, even though your account is charged automatically, you have complete freedom to raise or lower the amount to all personnel or to one or more specific people who have served you. Procedures to do so may vary slightly from one line to another, but you can make adjustments by going to the information desk (purser) and filling out a form that indicates how you want gratuities to be distributed. Do this on or before the last night of the cruise.

> NOTE: *In late 2004 Norwegian Cruise Line implemented a slightly different policy. They add a "service charge" of $10 per person, per day to your account, just as most lines do. However, you do NOT have the option of adjusting this either up or down. The reason for this is long and rather complicated. To make the story short, it has to do with their separation of operations into NCL and NCL America for their US-flagged ships. Due to differing maritime laws in the United States, it was necessary to have the tips handled in this way. To avoid a lot of confusion, NCL decided to use this method for the entire fleet. Those who want to show dissatisfaction by reducing the tips or eliminating them entirely cannot do so. But do make any concerns you have about unacceptable service known to ship personnel as soon as possible. Otherwise they can't do anything to try and correct it. Outstanding service can still be rewarded on NCL by giving an additional cash tip to deserving individuals.*

As mentioned before, there are relatively few lines that include gratuities in the cost of the cruise. And don't fall for the advertisements of "free" tips on some of these lines. It simply isn't true. The price of your trip has been raised to reflect this cost and the "deal" simply relieves you of the burden of having to do it on your own. If you're traveling with a line that does this, there's no need to tip more. Of course, if you feel that a particular crew member's service has been outstanding, show your appreciation by providing a small additional gratuity.

As this book went to press, the only mass-market cruise line that included tips was Holland America. (However, as policies always seem to be in a state of flux, it is a good idea to verify this at the time of your cruise.) Others that do so are in the luxury category such as Radisson Seven Seas.

Payments, Cancellations, Refunds

Although payment procedures for your cruise and the process of issuing cruise documents differ a little from one cruise line to another, there are so many similarities that a number of general guidelines can be safely stated.

Deposits

At the time you book your cruise, you will be required to make a deposit. This is usually around $250 per person for a week-long cruise, and sometimes more if you're traveling on one of the more expensive lines. In the past, a second payment was sometimes required after the initial deposit and before final payment, but this isn't the practice today and I am not aware of any major cruise line requiring this. The balance due must be paid anywhere between 60 and 90 days before your scheduled date of sailing. If you're doing a last-minute trip and book after the full payment deadline you will, of course, have to pay the full amount at the time of booking. Options are available to pay for your cruise on a loan basis. But as with any loan, this winds up costing a lot more in the end.

Cancellations & Refunds

All cruise lines have a schedule of refunds should you be unable to take the cruise. This varies according to cruise length, but typical penalty schedules go by the simple policy that if you cancel, you forfeit. The only exception might be if you make the line aware of your cancellation prior to full payment date; then, you lose nothing. But 30-60 days before sailing date, you lose the deposit; eight-29 days before sailing, you lose half the total fare; and a week or less before sailing, you will lose the entire fee.

If there is any possibility that you may have to cancel, or you just don't like to take chances, consider purchasing trip cancellation insurance. This can be done through the cruise line, but your travel agent or independent travel insurance companies can often give you the same or better coverage for less money.

Recreation in Port

Alaska doesn't offer beaches for swimming. Nor is it likely that you'll be snorkeling or scuba diving. Even things like golf, though available, isn't that popular with most Alaskan cruise visitors. Yet, there is much to do of a recreational nature and activity-filled cruise vacations are getting more popular with each passing season. Details on activities in each port and beyond the cruise will be given in specific chapters. Do keep in mind that in Alaska many activities blur the distinction between sightseeing and recreation. I will generally categorize as sightseeing those activities that don't require any special skills or physical capabilities. If they do, then refer to the *Sports & Recreation* section on each port. For now, here's a brief summary of the kinds of activities you'll easily find in Alaska.

On Land

Activities include wildlife watching, bicycling, rock and mountain climbing, and panning for gold. Dog-sledding is popular too, but available only on a very limited basis during the summer months. In fact, you won't actually be sledding (unless you fly onto a glacier) since there isn't any snow, but you can take a trip on a wheeled sled. And while all types of skiing and related activities are certainly available, they will not be found in the summer months.

Hiking is popular and takes many forms, including guided glacier tours.

Alaska is known for big-game hunting. For information on hunting season and other regulations, contact the Alaska Division of Fish and Game at PO Box 25526, Juneau, AK 99802-5526, ☎ (907) 465-4190.

On the Water

Wildlife touring by boat is just as popular as it is on land. Boating of all kinds is ubiquitous in Alaska. Choose your vessel – canoe, kayak, raft (either a peaceful float trip or some real whitewater) or just about any other kind of boat.

But fishing might well be the king of water activities here. Among the catches are cod, halibut, Dolly Varden char, red snapper and many species of salmon. Crabbing is also popular. If you are going to be on a cruise-ship sponsored fishing excursion, then you needn't worry much about fishing regulations since everything will be taken care of for you. Independent fisherman should contact the Alaska Division of Fish and Game (see above for address; their phone number for fishing information is ☎ 907-465-4180).

Shopping

Rare is the traveler that returns home to be greeted by friends and relatives with the question, "What did you buy?" That seems to be particularly true with cruisers, perhaps because of the popularity of shopping in the Caribbean – the biggest cruise market. While Alaska certainly isn't a shopping Mecca, there are plenty of opportunities for the enthusiastic shopper to find something interesting or useful that is unique to

Alaska. There are countless cheap souvenir places, but dedicated shoppers will be most interested in acquiring native arts and crafts items, including clothing and soapstone or whalebone carvings. Colorful knit sweaters are especially popular, as are warm outer jackets called *kuspuks*. Beads and baskets are also in demand. Specific suggestions as to where to shop for these and other items will be included under each port description.

Unlike some places in the Caribbean or Mexico, for example, Alaska's shops do not present much of a problem as far as phony goods or dubious quality is concerned. All genuine Native Alaskan-made articles have a label to that effect, so be sure to look for it before purchasing, especially if you're buying in a touristy souvenir shop. And you won't be confronted by street vendors here either.

People who have cruised several times will tell you that the cruise staff knows all the best places to get a good buy on the best quality merchandise. Furthermore, many cruise lines will guarantee an item if you purchase it at specific locations they've approved. All of this is true, to a limited extent. Cruise-recommended shops can all be relied on to give you authentic goods of high quality. But this doesn't always mean that the prices are the best. And those cruise line guarantees at specified stores sound a lot better than they really are. There are a host of limitations (which vary from one cruise line to another) and getting a refund or adjustment can sometimes be a frustrating process. Read the fine print concerning any guarantee and be sure you understand it before buying something because you assume the cruise line will back it up. One thing is certain: none of the guarantees covers a change of heart. Once the ship leaves port and you decide that you don't like what you bought after all, forget about returning it.

Practical Information

GOING ONCE ...

Going twice... Sold to the little lady in the front row with her hand over her mouth! Ah, the sounds of an auction. Auctions at sea, specifically art auctions, have become a standard practice that probably started when the cruise lines decided to make their vessels floating art galleries with wonderful works of art throughout. Although you can't buy the pieces you see hanging on the walls, you can bid on a wide variety of paintings that are often by well-known artists from all over the world. The auctions are conducted by professionals and the attraction is that you can buy yourself a nice piece of tax-free art to hang in your home or hold for investment purposes at prices that are said to be far lower than what you would pay in a land-based art gallery. The cruise line will even crate and ship your purchase to your home. So, should you buy? If you know anything about art and want to add to your personal collection, go ahead. However, if you are a complete novice, you might wind up overpaying for a piece you know nothing about. But beauty is in the eye of the beholder. If you see something you simply must have and you can afford to buy it, there's nothing wrong with doing so even if it might not be the best investment. You might want to attend one of these auctions just for the fun of it – check out the art and watch people bid or see the auctioneer begin to sweat when no one is bidding. An added bonus is that many art auctions at sea provide free champagne to those attending, whether or not you make a bid or ante up a penny of your hard-earned money!

Be sure to read the *Customs* section, above, to learn about tax payments on your purchases.

Staying in Touch

Almost everyone likes to be able to stay in touch with family or maybe even their place of work (for those unfortunate souls who can't separate themselves from their work). Being on a cruise doesn't prevent you from doing that. In the old days it was a complicated and very expensive procedure to contact someone. Today there are a number of ways that you can easily reach friends and family back home or that they can contact you. It's still rather expensive, but not as bad as in the past. (The expense isn't because of technology limitations, but because the cruise lines want to make some extra money on the deal.)

Telephone

Every stateroom on every ship of the major lines has its own direct-dial telephone that can be used to call anywhere in the world. Dialing procedures vary from ship to ship, but are simple and well documented in the information guide provided in your room. If you have any questions, just ask for assistance from the ship's operator. Prior to your sailing date (usually when you receive your documents) you will be given a toll-free telephone number that people in the United States can dial to reach your cruise line's overseas telephone operator. All they then have to do is inform the operator which ship you're on and then the call can be completed. Note that it is the recipient (you) who will be charged for incoming calls and the rate may not be any less than if you initiated the call. In general, rates for either in- or -outbound calls on the ship range from $7 to $10 per minute.

Practical Information

A less expensive alternative for calling home is to wait until you are in port. You're not in a foreign country when it comes to making phone calls (Canada is on the same system as the US) so finding a public telephone where you simply dial "1," followed by the area code and number, will put you in touch with places in the United States. Many nationwide calling cards are valid in Alaska. If you don't have one and plan to make calls from Alaskan ports, pick up a calling card in Alaska. As in the US, they're widely available.

Finally, since we're dealing here with Alaska and Canada, your cell phone might just work in some locations, depending on the distance from your cell company's nearest satellite link. If you are in a port of call (or even on the ship) you should consider taking your cell phone along and see if it works. It could be a money saver.

Internet/E-Mail

Computer lovers – and who isn't an addicted user these days? – will be glad to hear that every ship sailing to Alaska has PCs available for passenger use. The negative is that the fees, which vary from one line to another, are generally high and in some cases are exorbitant. Prices will be posted and you will find that the more you use the computer, the lower the per-minute rate. Various package plans are available and staff will be able to assist you in determining what best meets your needs and in resolving any problems that arise. If you opt to use the machines, you can do anything that you would do on your home computer, including surfing the Web and sending or receiving e-mail. Ship-board Internet facilities always used to be found in the ship's library; this is still the norm, but some vessels now have Internet cafés.

Time Zones

All of the embarkation ports in the Pacific Northwest as well as the entire Canadian province of British Columbia and the Yukon Territory are on Pacific time. Except for a few small islands at the western end of the Aleutian chain (which is an unlikely place to be for most visitors to Alaska), all of the state is on Alaska time, one hour earlier than Pacific time and four hours earlier than Eastern time. Alaska and parts of British Columbia participate in Daylight Savings Time.

Traveling with Children

Although children are much more commonly seen on cruises these days than in the past, this is still the type of vacation that appeals more to adults than to kids. But don't let that discourage you from bringing along your children. Most mass-market cruise lines actively encourage it, so as not to lose the business of couples that won't travel without the kids. Yet, there is a difference in the child-friendliness among the cruise lines, and that should be an important consideration in your planning. You know what your child's likes and dislikes are. Match those with what is available on the ship you're interested in to see if this will wind up being a positive experience for your child. In general, the more sophisticated the cruise line, the less child-oriented the ship. The fact that Disney doesn't sail to Alaska shouldn't be a reason to rule out taking a cruise with small children; several other lines do a great job in this regard. Carnival comes to mind first, but Royal Caribbean would be an equally good choice. Princess is much more child-friendly than in the past and has excellent facilities. While Celebrity and Holland America cater more to adults, even they have upgraded their facilities for various age groups.

However, to say that they're as good as the other lines in this regard would not be correct.

Alaska as a destination for youngsters might not be as good as warmer places such as the Caribbean or Mexico. We all know that swimming at the beach or snorkeling will be more likely to appeal to a child than taking in scenery. Regardless, it does seem that most children take quite well to cruising. They'll be able to partake in a wide variety of activities and special children's programs onboard most ships. It is common for cruise ships to have supervised activities all day long and into the evening so the parents can enjoy some fun times by themselves. Child care is usually grouped by age so that teens won't be bored by activities that are geared to younger children. In fact, teens can almost always opt to join in special social programs and dances for their age group and usually find these a good way to meet new friends. Any specific questions that you have about facilities and activities on a particular ship should be directed to your intended cruise line before you book.

So, It's Your First Time Cruising...

So I stretched the A to Z promise a bit, but I don't think I broke any laws! Getting more serious for a moment, newcomers to cruising will certainly have additional questions, but being a rookie cruiser is no cause for concern. You've probably got the impression by now that vacationing on a cruise ship is really like staying at a full-service resort that's on the move. Most things are done for you, including the handling of your baggage to and from your stateroom on embarkation and disembarkation. You'll find that cruises are well-organized and efficiently managed, especially given the extraordinary number of passengers carried on today's larger ships.

FAQs

If you have any questions or concerns, just ask a crew member – they're always happy to help. With that in mind, here are a few things that first-time cruises often ask about:

Documents: If you don't receive your cruise documents within a few days of the latest scheduled time for their arrival, then immediately contact your travel agent (if applicable) or the cruise line.

Seasickness: Motion sickness is not usually a problem for most people on cruises. In some parts of the world, ships have to pass through waters that are known to be rough, but this is definitely not the case in the almost always calm summer waters of Alaska's protected Inside Passage. The Gulf of Alaska is more open to the sea but, again, summer rarely has any significant storms. Furthermore, the contemporary cruise liner is stable enough to provide a comfortable ride even during unsettled weather and the captain will always select a route that avoids the roughest seas. However, if you have a history of motion sickness then an ounce of prevention can be very useful, since it is far easier to prevent this malady than to treat it. Non-prescription drugs such as Dramamine and Meclazine (stronger forms require a prescription) are highly effective if taken several hours before you set sail. If bad weather is anticipated, then you would be well advised to take something, but be sure to consult your physician about these drugs if you are taking any other medications.

If you become seasick, these drugs will provide some relief. How much seems to depend on the degree of illness and the individual. Symptoms can be minimized by focusing on the horizon, which helps you regain your balance. Some people say that placing an ice cube behind the ear can offer relief. The ship's doctor, in addition to having medications, will certainly have his or her own home remedies that will probably work as well or better.

Practical Information

Time Schedules: Although delays can occur for a variety of reasons, all cruise lines are known for their commitment to punctuality. The greatest possibility of delay is from your port of embarkation (because the ship might be waiting for late arrivals due to airline delays). At each port of call you will be provided with a time schedule that tells you when to be back onboard. Always be sure to comply with this schedule, as the ship will not wait long, if at all, for the tardy individual traveler.

Identification Card: Every cruise line today operates with a sophisticated system for keeping track of who is onboard and who is not. You will be issued a plastic credit card-like identification card that usually serves three purposes: as a room key, as your onboard charge card, and as a means of indicating your right to get back onboard at each port of call. Be sure you have it with you before disembarking – not a problem since you won't be able to get off the ship without it – along with your other identification documents.

Onboard Activities: From some of the ship descriptions given earlier you should already have gotten the idea that onboard activities are almost unlimited. Check the daily calendar to see what's happening when and to pencil out each day's events. First-time cruisers might especially enjoy a tour of the ship's main public areas that's given in order to familiarize passengers with locations and functions. An always popular tour is the galley (kitchen) tour, where you can walk through the amazingly large and spotless facilities. Another frequently offered tour is of the spa. Here, again, the idea is to familiarize you with what services are available and, of course, to promote use of these fee services. Often, if you take the spa tour you can get a discount on many of the services that are provided.

Safety: This is of utmost importance to the ship's crew. Pertinent safety instructions are posted in each stateroom and you should familiarize yourself with all of them. Every cruise will have a lifeboat drill soon after embarking (some might even have it before the ship leaves its gateway port). *You are required by law to attend.* You should be fully aware of emergency procedures, as should your children. The drill (you don't actually get into the lifeboats) is kind of fun and colorful for the first-time cruiser. Your behavior onboard is of prime importance when it comes to safety. Although it looks romantic in the movies, don't sit on the ship's railing or lean over. You never know when you will slip or the ship might suddenly roll because of the waves. It is also very important that your children be made to understand this. It is rare that people fall overboard, but it can and does happen, mainly because travelers had too much to drink and were feeling momentarily invincible! If you see someone fall overboard, try to toss a life preserver to them. After that, or in lieu of it if you are not near a preserver, notify the nearest crew member immediately. And as far as that romantic pose on the bow of the ship is concerned – forget that, too, if the ship is moving. They never tell you in the brochures that you'll practically be blown away trying to stand at the bow while underway. In fact, such areas of the ship are usually off-limits to passengers when the ship is moving for that very reason. Wait until you're in port to get that picture for your scrapbook!

Embarkation & Disembarkation Procedures: Checking-in for a cruise isn't all that different than what you go through at an airport and sometimes it can be frustrating due to long lines. However, the efficiency of the cruise lines is usually high and most of the time boarding goes quite smoothly. You'll be guided through each step of the process and it's simply a matter of following instructions. Disembarkation has never been a favorite part of cruising and not only because it means your trip is over. It, too, can sometimes be frustrating and involve long waits for Customs personnel or whatever. In fact, it is often a "hurry up and wait" proposition. Again, it's a matter of following instructions. Don't make up your own rules as to

Practical Information

what to do and when you want to do it. This will only delay you and others. Most cruise lines will hold a disembarkation briefing the day before the cruise ends. It is a good idea for at least one person in your party to attend, especially if you have never cruised before. The procedures will also be outlined in the daily program that is given to you. On the night before disembarkation, be sure to have your luggage packed and out in the hallway for collection by the time requested. And remember to keep hold of your overnight bag, along with clothing, toiletries and any other essentials; once your luggage has been collected there is no way that you will have access to it again until you're back on shore.

Although I've tried to anticipate all of the areas where you might have questions, it isn't always possible to cover everything. If there is something on your mind that hasn't been answered, the best course of action is to call or e-mail the cruise line and ask them. Your travel agent is also likely to know the answer.

Ports of Call
& Cruise Sightseeing

*O*kay. Now we get down to the business of touring. This chapter is divided into several sections. First will be a listing of general sources of information. This is followed by a section on the embarkation ports and several sightseeing sections, including onboard sightseeing. Last are the ports of call, broken down into major ports and less-visited ports.

Tourism Information

The following organizations are the best sources of general information for planning. Sources of specific localities, national parks, and so forth, will be found under the descriptions of those places.

Alaska Travel Industry Association, 2600 Cordova Street, Suite 201, Anchorage, AK 99503; ☎ (907) 929-2200; www.travelalaska.com

Interior road conditions, ☎ (907) 456-7623

Alaska Public Lands Information Center, 605 W. 4th Avenue, Suite 105, Anchorage, AK 99501; ☎ (907) 271-2737; www.nps.gov/aplic

Chugach National Forest: Forest Service Supervisor, 3301 C Street, Suite 300, Anchorage, AK 99503; ☎ (907) 271-2500; www.fs.fed.us/r10/-chugagh

Tongass National Forest: Forest Service Supervisor, 101 Egan Drive, Juneau, AK 99801; ☎ (907) 586-8751; www.fs.fed.us/r10/tongass

Ports of Embarkation

*A*s recently as a few years ago, just about every Alaskan itinerary embarked and/or disembarked in Vancouver, British Columbia, but Seattle now rivals it in terms of number of ships sailing to Alaska. While it is likely that Vancouver will continue to have a significant number of departures, the better air connections to Seattle and the expanded cruise ship terminal facilities will secure Seattle's place as the major port of embarkation to the Great Land. This chapter will provide important travel information, as well as details on travel from the airport and downtown areas to the cruise ship terminals. It is not a comprehensive review of what there is to see and do in these cities. Rather, just a few highlights will be noted for those who have a few hours or even a day to spend. If you have more time, it's a good idea to get a guidebook.

Seattle

Sailing out of Seattle is a breeze, complicated only a bit by the fact that the city now has two separate cruise ship terminals. The original terminal, called the **Bell Street Pier** (Pier 66), is in the heart of the downtown waterfront on Alaskan Way, making it the most convenient of the two terminals. It is used by Celebrity Cruises and Norwegian Cruise Line. The new and larger **Terminal 30** facility is on the southern edge of downtown about 2½ miles south of the Bell Street Pier at 2431 E. Marginal Way South. It is the embarkation point for Holland America and Princess cruises. **Seattle-Tacoma Interna-**

tional Airport (known by everyone as Sea-Tac) is roughly 15 miles from downtown.

Few cities have made it as easy to get to the cruise ship terminal as Seattle has done. A convenient Grey Line bus service (reservations not needed) runs every 20 minutes with stops at most major downtown hotels, some of which are very close to the Bell Street Pier. The cost is $9 each way. If you are flying in on the day of your cruise, Grey Line also operates a **Cruise Express** service, ☎ (800) 426-7532, to both terminals on sailing days. It runs every 30 minutes from 9:20 am until 3:25 pm. Going back to the airport, it leaves every 30 minutes from the terminals. The one-way fare is $12 and a round-trip costs only $20, much less expensive than the cruise lines' transfer services. Taxis will run you between $25 and $40 from the airport to either terminal or downtown, also not bad compared to many other port cities. If driving to your terminal, take I-5 to Exit 165 and follow Madison Street down the hill. This will bring you through the downtown area and all the way to Alaskan Way. A right turn on Alaskan will bring you to the Bell Street Pier. A left will lead you to Terminal 30. Parking is available at a cost of approximately $12 per day.

City Highlights

Long recognized as one of America's most livable cities, Seattle is also a nice place to visit. The Emerald City is tucked onto a narrow strip of land between Puget Sound and Lake Washington. Across the sound are the dramatic Olympic Mountains and many lush, green islands. The Cascade Range forms the eastern backdrop and includes (on clear days) majestic Mt. Rainier. Seattle is very hilly which, combined with its waterside location, reminds many visitors of San Francisco.

Many downtown attractions are close to the cruise ship terminals, especially the Bell Street Pier. City buses provide an inexpensive means of getting around (they're free on weekdays in the downtown core), along with the quaint waterfront trolley that stops right by the Bell Street Pier. Waterfront attractions are numerous, beginning with **Pier 59** and its amusements, which include the Omnidome Film Experience. Adjacent is the fine **Seattle Aquarium** and a few blocks north is the **Maritime Discovery Center**. The waterfront is, of course, the place to catch one of many **harbor tours** on Elliott Bay, a part of larger Puget Sound.

The fascinating **Pike Place Hill Climb** is the transition between the waterfront and the greater part of downtown. It consists of a series of stairs (elevators for the handicapped) and gives you a good idea of just how hilly Seattle is! At the top is the famous old **Pike Place Market**, where locals and visitors come to buy everything from fresh seafood to tacky souvenirs. Nearby in the heart of downtown is the fine **Seattle Art Museum**, worth walking around just to admire the many examples of beautiful modern high-rise architectural design. To the south of downtown is the **Pioneer Square Historic District**, which includes the Seattle portion of the Klondike Gold Rush National Historical Park. This makes a great educational connection if your cruise is going to be visiting Skagway in Alaska.

Perhaps the best "tourist" destination in Seattle is the **Seattle Center**, site of the 1962 World's Fair and today an outstanding urban cultural and entertainment venue. The famous **Space Needle** here is symbolic of Seattle to the entire world. An elevator ride to the top will, on clear days, reward you with a panorama of the city and the surrounding area that is second to none. Also at the Seattle Center are the **Pacific Science Center** and the **Experience Music Project**. The latter is housed in a most unusual structure designed by the eminent Frank Gehry and contains a high-tech history of American popular music. There is a children's museum. You can reach the center from downtown by a monorail. The short ride is another highlight of any Seattle visit, especially for kids. (Note that the monorail may be shut down sometime in the near future as it is to be incorporated into a longer monorail system due to be completed in about 2007.)

Farther from downtown but worthwhile if you're spending more time in the city are the **Lake Washington Ship Canal** and its **Hiram Chittendam Locks**. Other parts of the city have numerous museums, gardens, parks and an excellent zoo, among other attractions. A former Boeing facility is now home to the world-class **Museum of Flight**, a must for those interested in aviation.

> **Visitor Information**: Seattle-King County Convention & Visitors Bureau, 1 Convention Place (701 Pike Place), Suite 800, Seattle WA 98101; ☎ (206) 461-5840; www.seeseattle.org.

Vancouver

Since Seattle is now an important embarkation point, it is possible that Vancouver will become only a port of call. However, this is not presently the case. Therefore, it will be addressed only as a port of embarkation.

Vancouver International Airport is only about 10 miles from downtown. If you're driving, exit the airport on Sea Island Way, bearing left into Marine Drive and take this to Highway 99 northbound. (This is the same road you'd be on if driving in on from the United States via Seattle and I-5.) The highway will become Granville Street as it comes towards downtown. Cross the Granville Bridge, bear right onto Seymour Street and continue to W. Cordova where you make a left. In three blocks you'll be at **Canada Place**, the cruise ship terminal. (When returning to the airport, take Cordova to Howe Street and make a right – this will lead back into Granville.) As an alternative to driving, bus service runs throughout the day every 15 minutes from the airport to major downtown hotels, including the Pan Pacific, which is part of the Canada Place complex. There is on-site parking at a cost of CAN $12 per day. If you have any questions about Canada Place parking, ☎ (866) 856-8080. The fare for the airport-to-downtown bus is CAN $12 one-way, CAN $18 for a round-trip. A taxi will run CAN $25-$30 each way, plus tip. Based on the convenience and relatively low cost of transfers, there is little need to arrange transfers with the cruise line.

> NOTE: *If airline schedules make it easier for you to fly into Seattle and make your way to Vancouver by land, be aware that the cruise lines will usually offer you the option to purchase transfers between the two cities. This will run approximately US $45 per person each way.*

Canada Place is one of the finest terminal facilities in North America. Designed to resemble the profile of a sailing ship, it has hotels, restaurants and shops all in walking distance of the rest of downtown Vancouver.

City Highlights

Vancouver is one of the world's most beautiful cities, with a physical setting that equals or possibly even exceeds that of Seattle. (Of course, Seattle residents will dispute that.) On a fjord called the Burrard Inlet, Vancouver is edged to the north and east by perpetually snow-capped mountains. The down-town area sits on a small piece of land that juts into the inlet. It's a city of parks and beautiful flowers year-round, due to its mild and wet climate. It also has a wealth of things to see and do. If you stay downtown almost everything will be in walking distance, or you can take city buses and taxis to get around. A C-train (light rail) service is also available and you can get to attractions in North Vancouver by a combination of SeaBus ferries and buses. Taxis are plentiful but pricey.

Your activities can begin at Canada Place itself, which has an **IMAX Theater**. In the general area of downtown are Vancouver's historic and ethnic communities of Gastown, Robsonstrasse and Chinatown. In the opposite direction from downtown, but also close by, is one of the world's greatest city parks. **Stanley Park**, on its own small peninsula, has miles of scenic drives, pathways, a fine collection of totem poles, an aquarium, floral clock and outstanding views of the city skyline (including Canada Place), fjord and mountains.

Science World, just southeast of downtown, is a world-class facility that is especially good for school-age children. Not far from there is the outstanding **Queen Elizabeth Park & Bloedel Conservatory**, which contains one of the most colorful botanical gardens on the North American mainland. There are outstanding views from the park's hilltop setting. More fine botanical displays can be seen at the **Van Dusen Botanical Gardens**.

Some of the area's best attractions are in North Vancouver across the Burrard Inlet. **Capilano Canyon** and **Lynn Canyon** are natural gorges with lush vegetation and are spanned by swinging foot ridges that provide quite a thrill when you wobbly-walk across them. Capilano is significantly longer and, therefore, more of a thrill, but Lynn is in rockier and more interesting terrain. Not far from Capilano Canyon is the **Grouse Mountain Skytram**, a cable car that will take you to the top of the mountain for an extraordinary view of Vancouver that is spectacular by day and night.

> **Visitor Information:** Vancouver Tourist Info Center, 200 Burrard Street, Plaza Level, Vancouver, British Columbia V6C 3L6; ☎ (604) 683-2000; www.tourismvancouver.com.

Anchorage

Southbound "Gulf of Alaska" cruises begin in Anchorage. The city's actual port is no longer used by cruise ships because of the long time that is required to sail around the Kenai Peninsula and the silty conditions of the harbor. But so-called Anchorage-embarking cruises will actually board either in Whittier or Seward. The same applies to disembarking, Gulf of Alaska cruises arriving from Seattle, Vancouver or elsewhere.

Anchorage International Airport is only five miles from downtown. Unfortunately, it is some 50 miles from the port at Whittier and almost 130 miles from Seward. Although I have generally advised to avoid cruise line air packages because of their cost, cruises to or from "Anchorage" may be the exception because of the cost of getting to the city. If you make your own travel arrangements, most cruise lines will provide an Anchorage-Whittier bus transfer for between $55 and $65 per person (train transfers, if available, will set you back $90), while the bus tariff for Seward runs about $85. Wow! You can rent a car in Whittier (only through Avis) and drop it in Anchorage. However, they'll tack on an outrageous $125 one-way drop fee which brings the cost of a car rental to between $200-250 for one day. In addition, there's a $12 toll for the tunnel that gets you into or out of Whittier. (Only a family of four can still save something by driving, providing they rent the car for longer than a day.) Seward has a greater variety of car rental companies and most will allow you to drop the vehicle in Anchorage for a more reasonable rate. But shop around. The **Alaska Railroad** (☎ 907-265-2494; 800-544-0552 outside Anchorage; www.alaskarailroad.com) serves both Whittier and Seward. The latter is on the main line and makes a convenient place to begin your interior trip. Special trains meet cruise ships arriving in Whittier and run into Anchorage, where you can change for the main line service.

Cruise passengers taking a cruise tour of Alaska (either before or after the cruise) will not have to worry about transfers as they are included in the price of the package. For individual travelers who'll be spending time in Anchorage before making their way to the port and who won't be renting a car, there is both bus and taxi service from Anchorage airport to downtown at a reasonable cost. The one-way bus fare is only $6. There is also a station of the Alaska Railroad at the airport. If you're going immediately by train up to Denali or Fairbanks, this is very convenient.

Sightseeing and all other information on Anchorage is contained in the *Beyond the Cruise* chapter.

San Francisco

In the past, Alaska-bound cruises leaving from San Francisco were rather rare and, when they were available, were somewhat of a repositioning cruise. That is, the cruise lines were moving the ships from Mexico or the Caribbean to Alaska for the summer, or vice-versa at the end of the Alaska season. While this is still the case with a majority of cruise lines, there are now a couple of lines that have regularly scheduled Alaskan itineraries leaving from San Francisco. This is probably somewhat overdue in the minds of many in the cruise world considering that San Francisco, in addition to being a major population center, is a natural for cruising with its own attractions. However, be aware that because of the distance from Alaska, cruises originating or ending in 'Frisco will either be longer than a week or have fewer ports of call in Alaska itself.

The **San Francisco cruise ship terminal** is conveniently located near downtown along the famous Embarcadero at Pier 35, between the Fisherman's Wharf area and the foot of Market Street. Parking is available at the cruise ship terminal for a cost of about $15 per day. For those arriving at **San Fran-**

cisco International Airport without transfers arranged through the cruise line, a taxi ride to the ship will set you back between $35 and $40. If you are flying in on the same day as your cruise, you should book a flight scheduled to arrive in San Francisco at least five hours before sailing time.

City Highlights

Several days or even a week can easily be spent seeing the splendors of the City by the Bay. There are a number of great attractions located near to the cruise ship terminal, even within walking distance. **Fisherman's Wharf** and its related attractions (**The Cannery**, the **National Maritime Museum of San Francisco**, and several restored historic ships) are the closest points of interest. Also nearby is the ferry that goes to Alcatraz island. Downtown San Francisco (Union Square and Market Street) is a bit farther, but local buses will take you there if you choose not to walk. The same applies to the fantastic views from Telegraph Hill and its famous Coit Tower.

Other Cities

There are a relatively small number of cruises that head for Alaska from Los Angeles or San Diego. Because of the distance involved, these cruises are longer than most Alaska cruises and they sometimes visit fewer ports. Spending a great deal more time at sea than other itineraries, these cruises are best for people who come primarily for the cruise experience. If you're really interested in seeing Alaska, however, it is best to depart from one of the previously mentioned gateway cities. Since cruises from LA and San Diego represent such a small portion of the total Alaskan cruise inventory, I won't detail port information or attractions. The majority of these cruises are repositioning trips at the beginning or end of the Alaskan cruise season.

Onboard Sightseeing: The Major Attractions

*I*f you are used to cruising Mexico or the Caribbean, you are probably used to waiting to get into port and off the ship to begin sightseeing. Alaska is a completely different story. Much of the time you spend cruising during daylight hours will be in highly scenic areas, the most significant of which will be highlighted in this chapter. Although there are days along the Inside Passage where you'll always be in view of something worth seeing, most passengers aren't going to spend the entire cruise on deck or on their balcony. Consult the daily ship's calendar of activities to determine when your ship will be passing the best scenery or potential wildlife hotspots. Your card game or gym workout should wait for a time when nothing spectacular is happening outside. Don't be surprised, however, when dinner conversation is about some magnificent scenery and your neighbor says, "I didn't see it because I was at the beauty salon." It happens on every cruise!

A QUICK COURSE IN GLACIER GEOLOGY

It's helpful to know something about glaciers because you'll be seeing so much of them in Alaska. As an "A" student in high school earth science (okay, so it was more than 35 years ago), I feel somewhat qualified to give you this mini-course!

A glacier is defined as a large and usually moving mass of ice. It originates either in mountains or at high latitudes. When the rate of snowfall is greater than the rate of snow melt, a glacier forms. There are four basic types of glaciers. Two of these (icecap and continental glaciers) are found only in places like Greenland and Antarctica. The other two types, alpine and piedmont, are both found in Alaska. The alpine type is a single mountain glacier. Alaska's Hubbard is one of the largest alpine glaciers in the world. The piedmont glacier forms when several glaciers flow together and meet in a valley at the foot of a mountain range. Malaspina is an example of one of the many piedmont glaciers in Alaska. Tidewater glaciers are something you'll hear a lot about when cruising. These are simply a glacier of the alpine type (and, less commonly, the piedmont variety) that reach the sea.

Glacial movement is caused by the sheer weight of the ice. Glaciers that are growing are said to be "advancing," while those that are shrinking are "retreating." Retreating glaciers result when the melting rate exceeds the rate of new snowfall. Most glaciers move at a rate of less than three feet per day, but the world's fastest recorded glacier (which happened to be Columbia Glacier, located between Anchorage and Valdez), sped along for a time at the incredible rate of over a hundred feet a day. As glaciers move they carry with them rock and other natural debris that is deposited as the glacier moves. These deposits are called moraines. Alaska's many fjords are also byproducts of glaciers. They are glacier-created valleys that have been partially flooded by the open sea.

Calving is the term used when a chunk of ice breaks off of a glacier and falls into the water. It is so-called because, in effect, it is akin to the glacier giving "birth" to a new iceberg.

The Inside Passage

The Inside Passage is visualized by the inexperienced traveler as the waterway alongside the southern Alaskan panhandle. Actually, it is much more than that. It extends for approximately 950 miles from Seattle, Washington to Skagway, Alaska and serves as a busy year-round shipping lane. The passage is protected by a series of islands large and small. These islands afford two advantages for the traveler. First, rough seas associated with ocean travel are an extreme rarity here during the summer. Second, you never lose sight of land, which means there is always something to see. This is unlike an ocean voyage where the blue sea, although undeniably beautiful in its own right, can become rather tedious to look at after a few days.

If leaving from Seattle or Vancouver, your first full day onboard ship will be spent traversing the Canadian portion of the Inside Passage along the mountainous shoreline of British Columbia. It's a rocky shoreline covered with lush green vegetation that thrives in the Pacific Northwest's cool and wet climate. Settlements are scattered and become less frequent as you travel farther north. Particularly picturesque are the islands in the narrow inlets near the town of **Bella Bella** and along **Alert Bay**.

The coastal mountain peaks that form the border between the United States and Canada are generally around 6,500 feet high. These continue to rise and will eventually exceed 7,500 feet. Although you may have seen higher mountains, just remember that you are viewing these from sea level, which makes their height even more impressive. (For example, a 14,000-foot peak in the Rockies viewed from Colorado Springs is only about 8,000 feet higher than your vantage point.) By the time you reach these waters you will have probably spotted your first small glaciers and ice floes. The waterfalls, too numerous to count, will frequently cascade down the rocky slopes on both shores and are striking sights. Many have the appearance of thin silver threads, while others are torrents that gush into the cold greenish waters of the Inside Passage.

The next three sights below are all along or just off the main route of the Inside Passage. However, because of their exceptional beauty they are deserving of specific mention and description.

Misty Fjords

Located just past the Canadian border with Alaska, the remote Misty Fjords National Monument covers a vast tract of land bordered for more than 60 miles along both sides of the three-mile-wide **Behm Canal** (a natural waterway; the word canal in its name and in many other channels of the Inside Passage are misnomers). The narrowness of the passage enhances the many sea cliffs and sheer walls, which in some places rise more than 3,100 feet above the water. The sound and sight of rushing waterfalls is everywhere. One of the most spectacular and dramatic sights in the Misty Fjords is **New Eddystone Rock**, a nearly 240-foot-high rock pillar rising from the very middle of the Behm Canal.

The name Misty Fjords is appropriate to the most common weather condition here. While this can severely hamper a flightseeing visit (usually available as a shore excursion from the nearby port of call in Ketchikan), it presents only a minor setback for cruise ships. In fact, the mist that envelops the fjords is considered by many people to enhance the atmosphere and beauty of the natural surroundings. Unfortunately, the number of major line cruise ship itineraries visiting Misty Fjords is limited.

For more information on Misty Fjords, contact **Tongass National Forest**: Forest Service Supervisor, 101 Egan Drive, Juneau, AK 99801; ☎ (907) 586-8751; www.fs.fed.us/r10/tongass. The National Monument lies entirely inside the confines of the larger national forest.

Tracy & Endicott Arms

These inlets are among dozens of such waterways scattered along the Inside Passage. Tracy Arm and Endicott Arm both begin about 40 miles south of Juneau, where they form the two "arms" branching off of the Stephens Passage at Holkham Bay. Stephens is an important sub-branch of the Inside Passage that provides access to Juneau. It is at the end of the two arms that the first of Alaska's many magnificent glaciers will be found. In fact, icebergs from these glaciers (the Sawyer and Sumdum from Tracy Arm, and Dawes Glacier from Endicott Arm) will frequently be seen drifting along the Stephens Passage. Tracy Arm is approximately 20 miles long and only a couple of miles wide. Endicott Arm is longer. No major-line cruise ship will visit both arms, but that isn't a problem in that the scenery along each is quite similar. Tracy Arm is somewhat more easily navigated and is, therefore, more frequently visited. While Alaska has fjords even more spectacular than Tracy and Endicott, these are often the first significant ones seen by Alaska cruisers and tend to remain vivid in the mind for a long time to come.

Lynn Canal

Lynn Canal, the northernmost of the major navigable portions of the Inside Passage, is a natural waterway (another fjord to be more exact) and not a canal. It begins at the junction of waterways (Stephens Passage and Chatham Strait) leading south towards the other ports of the Inside Passage and the Icy Strait, which heads northwest towards Glacier Bay and beyond into the Gulf of Alaska. Lynn stretches for about 70 miles and measures up to 10 miles wide in some places, making it one of the Inside Passage's largest inlets. It's almost entirely surrounded by the thickly forested mountain slopes of the Tongass National Forest and nowhere on the Inside Passage are the mountains more beautiful than they are here. You're always in sight of the ice-capped mountain peaks, while hundreds of waterfalls of all sizes add to the gorgeous picture. Few glaciers of significance reach the water here, but they're never very far away.

Lynn Canal is a remote area with many smaller inlets that you can spot as you cruise along its icy waters. The two major communities on the Canal are Skagway and Haines; Skagway is at the northernmost end of the Canal. These towns are both on the mainland and are connected by road. However, although they are less than 20 miles apart by ship, you would have to drive for almost 300 miles to get from one to the other by car! That tells you something about the mountainous terrain that forms the northern barrier to these communities. No cruise line sails the Lynn Canal just for the simple pleasure of seeing it. It is used as a means of getting to Skagway. Therefore, the only cruises on which you will have the chance to see this splendid stretch of watery real estate is on those itineraries with a Skagway port of call.

While all of the above scenic cruising is part of an Inside Passage itinerary, the following may be part of a Gulf of Alaska itinerary. They are listed in the order that they will be reached if cruising northbound.

Glacier Bay National Park

Beginning at Cross Sound on the Gulf of Alaska and extending inland as far as the Canadian border, Glacier Bay is a unique national park. Covering more than 3¼ million acres, the park ranges from sea level along the almost 65-mile-long bay to the more than 15,000-foot summit of Mt. Fairweather on the international border. However, it is definitely the sights along the bay itself that will most captivate you. The park contains Alaska's and perhaps the world's greatest concentration of tidewater glaciers. As you cruise through the bay you will be able to see at least parts of almost all 16 glaciers, which are among the most rapidly retreating in all of Alaska. Glacier Bay, which varies in width from 2½ to 10 miles, was once all ice-covered. This retreating process could stop next year or it could go on for hundreds of years. The best scientists in the field cannot predict such a thing. You will encounter some glaciers that are advancing in other parts of the state.

As your ship enters Glacier Bay, a launch from the National Park Service will pull up alongside and a couple of rangers will come onboard to provide commentary, answer questions and distribute literature.

The bay is surrounded by the mighty Fairweather Range, which provides all of the snow that created the glaciers you'll see enveloping three sides of the horseshoe-shaped bay. These mountains also provide a magnificent backdrop to the glaciers, at least a dozen of which are currently calving icebergs into the bay. **Johns Hopkins Glacier** is the highlight of the group. Originating more than 11 miles back into the mountains, the glacier is 45 miles from the beginning of the bay. It is so active that ships are generally kept at a distance of two miles from its face to avoid getting in the way of newly created icebergs that fall from its 200-foot-high wall of ice. "White Thunder" is the term used to describe the tremendously loud noise made when the ice crashes into the sea.

> NOTE: *At certain times of the year, notably June, access to Johns Hopkins or other portions of the bay may be restricted so as not to interfere with the birth of seal pups.*

Among other glaciers that can be seen from the deck of your ship are Reid, Lamplugh, Grand and Brady, all originating from the massive Brady Icefield on the bay's western side. Because of the active nature of the glaciers, the waters that you'll be cruising are filled with thousands of icebergs, some already melted down to the size of a small rock, while others are still enormous. But even the smallest icebergs are larger than they appear because only one-sixth of the total surface of any iceberg stays above the water (hence the phrase, "That's just the tip of the iceberg"). You'll enjoy standing by the deck railing as your ship cuts through the thinner parts of the ice floes, often making a crunching sound not that different from the noise your car makes as it crushes ice beneath its wheels.

It isn't only the scenery that makes Glacier Bay so special. Few places can match this area for the opportunity to see Alaska's abundant bird population, seals, otters and whales. There are several types of birds that make the cliffs of ice in Glacier Bay their summer home and tens of thousands congregate here in large groups. As your ship approaches the glaciers, the noise from such a great number of birds can be deafening. Seeing these summer residents fluttering about, with even more resting in the rocky crevices and ledges, is quite a spectacle and would be worth the trip even if there were no glaciers! If you're lucky, you might catch a glimpse of the colorful Alaska puffin, although they are more likely to be seen in other, more remote portions of the state.

Hundreds of brown seals live in the waters of Glacier Bay and they love to lie around on icebergs, especially if it is sunny. From a distance, all you see are small dark spots on the floating icebergs. But someone with binoculars and sharp eyes will soon yell "They're seals!" and all will realize it a moment later. Often, seals will ignore the presence of the huge ship, but at other times they'll dive into the water. Sea otters are not as common as seals, but your Park Service hosts will probably point some out to you.

Everyone who goes to Alaska hopes to see some whales and you're most likely to spot them near the entrance of Glacier Bay. If your captain is especially kind (and they usually are), he'll stop the ship for a time if there are whales around. The two types of whales most common in these waters are the orca, or killer whale, and the humpback, with the latter being the most populous. Orcas average 20 to 25 feet and are easily recognizable by their six-foot-high dorsal fin. The larger humpbacks measure between 45 and 50 feet. These social animals are usually in large groups. While you might see just the tops of their huge bodies protruding above the water's surface, they often put on quite a show, rolling over on their sides or expelling water from their blow holes. The most spectacular sight of all is that of a whale breaching, when almost the entire body surges out of the water for a brief moment. Seconds later, only the graceful tail is visible above the surface.

As mentioned earlier, there are restrictions on the number of vessels allowed into Glacier Bay and this includes cruise ships. As a result, the majority of cruises bypass Glacier Bay. I have always felt that people who visit Alaska without seeing Glacier Bay have missed something very special.

Yakutat Bay & Hubbard Glacier

While these twin attractions don't quite measure up to the level of Glacier Bay, they do provide wonderful scenery and an acceptable alternative. As a matter of fact, Yakutat Bay and Hubbard Glacier, located 150 miles north of Glacier Bay, are seen on the overwhelming majority of Gulf of Alaska cruises. Beautiful Yakutat Bay forms a deep indentation in the coast of Alaska just north of the small town of the same name. This is where the panhandle of Southeastern Alaska ends and the Southcentral coastal area of the Gulf begins. The bay is sur-rounded by some of the biggest mountains of the entire Coastal Range, including 18,000-foot Mt. Elias. Many of the highest peaks in the area are in the rugged and largely inacces-sible Wrangell-St. Elias National Park. Aside from visits by the most adventurous wilderness hikers and explorers, your cruise ship provides the only other practical way to see at least a part of this huge park.

As you cruise around Yakutat Bay you'll see many glaciers, in-cluding the famous Malaspina Glacier at the western edge and the smaller Turner Glacier. However, the highlight of any trip into the bay is a close-up visit to the magnificent **Hubbard Glacier**, whose face is more than six miles across, of which about a three-mile segment is visible from your ship. It is ap-proximately 300 feet high and dwarfs even the largest of cruise ships. The river of ice that is Hubbard Glacier originates more than 90 miles away, making it one of the largest in North America. Over the last 20 years the glacier has seen periods of rapid advance and then retreat. A fjord was turned into a lake when the glacier closed up its access to the sea only to be re-opened when a chunk of wall came tumbling down. It is these actions of Mother Nature on a large scale that create the awe-inspiring atmosphere surrounding Hubbard. The glacier re-mains one of Alaska's most active and is often advancing. On your visit, you'll probably witness the calving process as large blocks of ice frequently crash into the bay. Often, you can hear the grinding and crunching sound of ice before it actually breaks off. Note the waves that form when a large piece of ice hits the water.

As you admire this natural wonder from the comfort of your ship at the face of the glacier (the term applied to the very front wall of ice), take notice of its many different features. You'll see deep fissures and cracks within the ice, some of which are so large they appear like a rocky mountain cave entrance. Another beautiful feature of this and other large glaciers is the fantastic array of shapes taken on by the ice at the very top of the glacier. They appear as pinnacles, arches and other forms similar to the unusual eroded land masses in America's southwest. The difference is that these being ice, they change shape and form much faster. Today's pinnacle might be a floating iceberg tomorrow.

Prince William Sound & College Fjord

Prince William Sound, like all of Southeastern Alaska, is a world of mountains, fjords, beautiful coastline and glaciers. It leads directly into the open sea, unlike the Inside Passage, and contains many islands and narrow inlets. The 15,000-square-mile sound is bordered by the high mountains of the Kenai Range to the west and the Chugach Range to the north and west. The magnificent coastal scenery alone would be enough to make a memorable visit to the brilliant blue waters of Prince William Sound, but the very best sights are the stunning glaciers and fjords in the sound's northern reaches.

Having passed mile after glorious mile of icebergs laden with sunning seals, your ship will approach the edge of the huge **Columbia Glacier** on a bay of the same name. If the weather isn't sunny, the seals will not be as plentiful but they'll probably still be around, so watch carefully. Columbia Glacier is another 300-foot-high wall of ice that stretches for almost three miles across its face. It's been receding rapidly in recent years, but it's still massive enough to make a lasting impression.

The true highlight of the sound region is when your ship cruises into **College Fjord**. This spectacular fjord contains no fewer than 26 separate glaciers, each named for an eastern college (mainly Ivy League) that supported an early exploratory expedition of this area. Harvard Glacier is the most famous of College Fjord's members and is also the one most cruise ships choose to stop at; it lies at the far end of the fjord. Harvard is about 340 feet high at the center and is over a mile wide. It is bordered by velvety green mountains on either side. Harvard is an excellent example of how rocks form those "dirty" lines in the glacier. The sides of Harvard are filled with debris and exhibit the features of a classic moraine. But the middle section is almost entirely clear and is a vivid blue. Among other major active glaciers in College Fjord are Yale and Wellesley. The huge Amherst Glacier stands as sentinel at the southern end of the fjord. While the last few years have seen mainly retreating glaciers, there are some along the fjord that are currently advancing. Of course, no glacier moves fast enough for you to see it do so, regardless of whether it's advancing or retreating. You'll just have to take the word of the experts or come back again in a few years to make your own comparison.

Male & Female Glaciers? Wow.

An interesting cultural history note concerning College Fjord... It seems that the people who gave the names to the various glaciers were very concerned with proper social etiquette. Since most of the schools for which the glaciers are named were not co-ed at the time, all of the glaciers named after women's colleges are on one side of the fjord while the men's are on the other side. However, don't take this matter of treating glaciers as if they're living things too far. There isn't any such thing as a male or female glacier!

The area abounds with wildlife and you'll most likely see one or more bird rookeries as you cruise by. College Fjord's beauty is renowned not only for the many glaciers, but for the majestic mountains that hem in the fjord and set it off from the rest of Prince William Sound. Take some time to gaze at the view. You'll see miles of mountains with a series of silver ribbons – the glaciers – dropping precipitously from them and finally reaching the icy waters of the fjord. It's not uncommon to see as many as six or seven major glaciers lining your route. The view is simply spectacular in any weather, with an eerie type of beauty on cloudy days becoming one of brilliant colors in the sunshine. Sometimes, thin bands of clouds hang across the upper or middle portions of the mountains and provide a vivid contrast to the lush green vegetation that clings to them, framed at both top and bottom by the beautiful blue of the sky and sea.

Ports of Call

The remainder of this chapter is devoted to providing you with a detailed description of each port that can be encountered on a cruise to Alaska, including those in Canada. Ports will be listed in alphabetic order and divided into two main sections: the major ports and the less-visited ports. There will not be as much information provided for the latter because there is often less to see and do in some of those places. Also, far fewer readers will have the opportunity to visit them.

For the major ports here's how the sightseeing information will be dealt with. The "tour" is a description of what you should be able to see during a full-day tour of the port. Keep in mind the following important facts when planning your day. First, the number of hours you have is *not* equal to the hours of the port call. For instance, a typical port call as shown in the cruise line brochure might be from 8 am until 6 pm. But you often won't be able to get off the ship until about an hour after the scheduled arrival. You must also be back on board from a half-hour to an hour before departure, depending on the ship. Thus, in this particular case your maximum available sightseeing time is from 9 am until 5 pm. It is a good rule of thumb to begin your calculation of available port time by subtracting two hours from the ship itinerary hours to determine how much time you have.

Second, the tours described here assume you are not planning other types of activities. If you are like most people, however, and do plan on spending at least some time shopping or participating in a recreational activity, then you will have to subtract that from the available sightseeing time. And, of course, most people will want to allocate time for lunch. Then again, with all of the eating you'll likely be doing on board, skipping lunch or just having a quick snack will be a good idea for those who intend to do some serious sightseeing.

The sightseeing tours in this book also generally assume that you'll have about eight hours available in port. To help your planning process a suggested amount of time will be given for some attractions, areas or segments of the tour as well as the travel time between attractions where appropriate. For most attractions the days and hours of operation will be shown. If not, then you don't have to worry because they're open all the time. Unlike in many other parts of the world, commercial attractions in most of Alaska's small towns are heavily dependent on cruise ship visitors. Therefore, they often arrange their hours to coincide with the time that ships are in port. Do take note, however, that the hours shown are for the *summer* season. While this pretty much coincides with the Alaskan cruise season, it can vary a little. Most attractions begin their summer season in the middle of May and run through the middle of September. There are a few cruises that may fall outside of these dates. If you take one of those be aware that hours of operation might be somewhat more restrictive. Since prices for attractions change so rapidly these days, only a price range indicator will be shown. If there is no indicator, then the attraction is free.

ADULT PRICE LEVELS	
$	Less than $5
$$	$5-9
$$$	$10-20
$$$$	More than $20

Although I will frequently mention many of the most popular shore excursions that are available in each port, I have not included specific pricing information. The cost of an excursion depends on the length of the trip, the types of activities, and whether or not it includes lunch. Rare, indeed, is the shore excursion that will cost less than $20 per adult. If it does, then it is probably only providing transportation to a place where you'll be on your own regarding everything, including admissions and costs of activities. Regular shore excursions that include these items generally run from about $25 to $100. In those instances where it involves unusual modes of transportation (including helicopters or flighseeing) it will inevitably be much higher. Some of these types of excursions can run $200-$400 per person. Admissions to museums and other attractions that are part of the shore excursion itinerary are, however, included in the price.

The itinerary for your shore excursion will also indicate if lunch is included in the cost.

The Major Ports

Icy Strait Point

Not visited with the same frequency as the other four ports in this section, Icy Strait Point is, nevertheless, an important development in Alaskan cruising. It's a newcomer to the Alaskan scene; the first cruise ship didn't make its maiden call on Icy Strait Point until 2004 and it is not a general port of call. Rather, it is the first of what might be termed the Alaskan equivalent of a Caribbean "private island" because it was developed specifically as a cruise ship destination. Currently, Icy Strait Point is called on only by Royal Caribbean and its sister line, Celebrity Cruises. Whether that will change in future years isn't known at this time. (Although Royal Caribbean and Celebrity have a complicated agreement with the private company that developed Icy Strait Point, it apparently doesn't guarantee that it will remain their exclusive domain.)

Icy Strait Point is in a magnificent setting about 22 miles from Glacier Bay National Park near the town of Hoonah. The plan is to keep the area's pristine condition by limiting visitation to a maximum of one cruise ship per day. Even at that, the number of people getting off a single ship will far exceed the resident population of Hoonah, which is about 860 people! The local populace, by the way, was thrilled at being the newest port of call because the move provides work for many of the Tlingits who make the area their home.

Arrival

Since Icy Strait Point was built for cruise ships, your vessel will conveniently dock and no tenders are required.

Tourism Information Office

There is no official tourism information office, but you should be able to get all the information you need either from your ship's excursion office or from staff at the museum in the cannery.

Getting Around

Everything that you can do on your own is within walking distance of the dock, so foot power is essential. Any excursions that you select will leave from very close to the ship. There are no car rentals available and no public transportation.

One-Day Sightseeing Tour

As a "port" for cruise ship passengers, all attractions will always be open while your ship is visiting. Because of the isolated and previously undeveloped nature of the Icy Strait area, the main attraction will be that you can have a "real" Alaskan adventure. The town itself features the **Hoonah Packing Company**, a salmon cannery from the 1930s that offers free tours of its facility. There is also a small museum with exhibits about the area. You can explore a bit on your own by taking a stroll through some of the specially developed nature trails or along the beaches (definitely not for swimming). The area is heavily wooded and surrounded by mountains so you'll always have pleasant views.

The amount you can do on your own is limited and shouldn't take more than a few hours unless you walk every trail. As a result, a shore excursion or two will be required to complete your day. The excursions from Hoonah vary from an hour to 3½ hours, so you may well be able to do two or even three if you plan carefully. The cruise line will tell you what excursions don't interfere with other excursions.

The nature of the excursions cover a range of options on land, on the sea, and even in the air. Land trips include a "bush country" bus tour into the surrounding forest to search for black bears and other big wildlife. Although the odds are quite good that you will see one of these beautiful creatures, it isn't guaranteed and no money will be refunded if you don't encounter any. Other trips on offer are a forest tour by a motorized tram and a salmon bake, in case you want a change of pace from the shipboard lunches. Two cultural programs are conducted by members of the native Tlingit tribe. The first is a colorful program of Tlingit dancers, while the second is an interpretive walk with Tlingit guides who tell of the tribe's role in area history.

The area around Icy Strait is known as a good place to see whales of all kinds, including gray, minke, humpback and orca. You might catch a glimpse of some from the shore or from your cruise ship as it arrives or departs Icy Strait Point, but the best chance of seeing them is in some of the smaller waterways that the cruise ships can't access. Therefore, a whale-watching cruise on a smaller boat is offered. In addition to whales, you'll see numerous other marine mammals and could well catch a quick look at some land animals, including bears.

Finally, flightseeing excursions to Glacier Bay are an option, although a very expensive one. There's no need to do this, of course, if your cruise calls on Glacier Bay itself. Hopefully, if you select this excursion it won't be ruined by poor visibility.

Shopping

This is not the place to go if you like to shop. The only available shopping is in the Hoonah Packing Company complex. It contains a few shops where you can purchase native crafts. Live artisans work on the premises.

Sports & Recreation

All activities will have to be booked via your cruise line's shore excursion office. The number one activity for most visitors will be fishing trips to catch salmon. Other activities include guided bike tours and, with the large number of nature trails, easy hiking is another alternative.

Juneau

With a population of almost 31,000, Juneau is Alaska's capital and the state's second- or third-largest city. (Fairbanks was officially second after the 2000 Census with about a hundred more people, but Juneau is growing faster and has probably surpassed it by now.) So far the city has withstood several attempts to move the capital closer to the population center of Anchorage. It has a quaint, small-town atmosphere far different from most American state capitals. Juneau derives its name from a 19th-century gold prospector named Joe Juneau. He and his partner, Richard Harris, discovered gold in 1880. Juneau was one of the most productive gold-producing areas of the state for a long time and it wasn't until 1944 that mining operations finally ceased. Today, the city thrives on state government and visitors. It is situated snugly in a picturesque setting at the base of two mountains that tower above the city's buildings on one side and the attractive Gastineau Channel on the other. The setting has been favorably compared to that of a Norwegian fjord. Not far from Juneau is the vast Juneau Icefield. Residents here are quick to point out that this icecap – the origin of almost 40 separate glaciers, including the famous Mendenhall Glacier – is larger than any found in the Alps and is, in fact, as big as all of Switzerland.

Arrival

The cruise ship pier is a few blocks south of downtown via Franklin Street. As will be the case in most major Alaskan ports, the pier can handle the largest cruise ships, but there is a slight possibility that tenders will be used if too many ships are in town at one time.

Tourism Information Office

The **Juneau Visitor Information Center**, 1 Sealaska Plaza, Suite 305, Juneau, AK 99801, ☎ (888) 581-2201, www.traveljuneau.com, is the place to contact for information. The above address is for information by mail. If you're in town already, look for the **Juneau Convention & Visitors Bureau** office in Centennial Hall at 101 Egan Drive. There are smaller information offices by the cruise ship docks.

Getting Around

The many sights of downtown Juneau are all in a reasonable walking distance of the pier. However, taxis and buses are available. If you plan to get out of town on your own rather than with a guided excursion, then renting a car is a better idea. Local car rental agencies will almost always be willing to pick you up at the dock. For walking tours, the most important streets to know are Franklin Street, which runs all the way through downtown, and the curving waterfront street known as Marine Way near where it branches off Franklin and then changes name to Egan Drive. Juneau Capital Transit operates a system of bus routes in and around the city; ☎ (907) 789-6801 for information.

One-Day Sightseeing Tour

There's a lot to see in this very interesting little city, which can support its claim as being the heart of the Inside Passage. Since most cruise ships spend a lot of time in Juneau, you shouldn't have any trouble seeing the sights. However, it will require a full day to see everything listed here. If you plan on doing a lot of shopping or recreational activities, something will have to give. Allow about a half-day for the downtown tour, while the rest of the day can be devoted to visiting Mendenhall Glacier and some other interesting attractions.

You can begin your walking tour within steps of the cruise ship terminal. Just south of the terminal via Franklin Street is the four-story **Juneau Library**. An observation deck on the top floor provides outstanding vistas of the Gastineau Channel, Douglas Island and the mountains on the western side of the channel. Also by the waterfront is the **USS Juneau Memorial**. On the other side of the dock is **Marine Park**, a pleasant place to admire the views from ground level. Continue on Franklin, bearing left after two blocks onto Front Street. This is the center of the downtown shopping district. Notice that most streets are covered to protect residents and visitors from the frequent rain. Many large murals are painted on the sides of buildings, a common feature in towns throughout both the Inside Passage and the Alaskan interior.

Keep to the right on Front Street as it leads into Seward Street and take the latter for two blocks to Third Street. One block farther at Third and Main streets is the **Windfall Fisherman statue**. This beautiful bronze sculpture is a full-size depiction of a brown bear that has just captured a large fish. The statue serves as a dramatic foreground for the **Alaska State Capitol**, which is a block north at Main and Fourth streets. The structure isn't particularly impressive as state capitols go, but some interesting sculptures and paintings on display in the main lobby show various aspects of Alaskan culture and industry. If you wish, you can take a half-hour guided tour. You might also want to take a look at the State Office Building one block west with its totem pole, pipe organ and more. There's a good view from the eighth-floor terrace. Concerts are sometimes held here.

Walk around the Seward Street side of the capitol to Fifth Street and turn right, proceeding for two blocks until you reach Gold Street and the **St. Nicholas Orthodox Church**, ☎ (907) 586-1023. Funds from Russia were used to construct this octagon-shaped structure in the 1880s, even though control of Alaska had passed to the Americans more than 20 years earlier. There still was a need to serve the sizable Russian Orthodox community that had developed among the Tlingit Indians. The interior of the church is simple, filled with many interesting and beautiful icons. Having admired the church, head back on Fifth. A little beyond Main Street, Fifth will end at a staircase that leads down a cliff, across a bridge leading through a park-like area and, finally, to Willoughby Street. (Handicapped individuals can reach the bottom by going to the State Office Building on Fourth Street and taking an elevator down.) Proceed on Willoughby for a short distance to Whittier and turn left. You'll soon arrive at the **Alaska State Museum**, 395 Whittier Street, ☎ (907) 465-2901. This excellent facility, housed in a modern building, traces the natural and cultural history of the state from prehistoric times to the present in several different galleries. The highlight of the collection is an exhibit featuring a bald eagle nesting in a tree and a brown bear with cub. The two-story exhibit is seen from every side as you ascend or descend a gentle ramp that surrounds it. An 80-foot mural of Alaskan scenery adorns one wall. *Open daily, 8:30 am to 5 pm, $$.*

Now head down Whittier towards the waterfront. At Egan Drive, turn left, passing the large Centennial Hall/Forest Service Information Center, and walk until you get back to Franklin Street and the dock. By now it should be lunch time and your cruise ship will provide the most convenient place to eat. The afternoon will be devoted to additional sightseeing, but I'd like to offer some alternative points of interest for those who are fast sightseers or might prefer them to the sights already suggested.

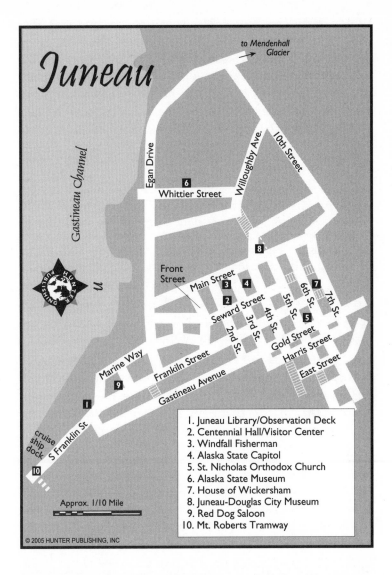

© 2005 HUNTER PUBLISHING, INC

1. Juneau Library/Observation Deck
2. Centennial Hall/Visitor Center
3. Windfall Fisherman
4. Alaska State Capitol
5. St. Nicholas Orthodox Church
6. Alaska State Museum
7. House of Wickersham
8. Juneau-Douglas City Museum
9. Red Dog Saloon
10. Mt. Roberts Tramway

Juneau-Douglas City Museum, Fourth & Main streets, ☎ (907) 586-3572, has mildly interesting exhibits concentrating on the city's early days as a gold mining camp. *Open daily, 9 am to 5 pm (from 10 am on weekends), $.*

House of Wickersham, 213 Seventh Street, ☎ (907) 586-9001. The one-time residence of a noted Alaskan, James Wickersham – a judge, statesman and historian. Built just before the turn of the 20th century, it provides a fine view of the city and Gastineau Channel and houses Wickersham's outstanding collection of Native American crafts. *Open daily except Wednesday, 10 am to noon and 1 pm to 5 pm, $.*

Macaulay Salmon Hatchery, 2697 Channel Drive, ☎ (907) 463-4810. This is a typical hatchery operation. Because Juneau has so many other things to offer, it is not a necessary stop. The hatchery has a number of aquarium tanks that will interest small children. *Open daily, 10 am to 6 pm (till 5 pm on weekends), $.*

Red Dog Saloon, Franklin Street, a couple of blocks from the dock, ☎ (907) 463-3777, is one of Alaska's most famous taverns. Whether or not you care to have a drink, it's worthwhile stopping here just to take a look at the odd assortment of "Alaskarama" that covers almost every inch of wall space.

Lady Lou Revue, in the historic Elks Hall at 109 S. Franklin Street, ☎ (907) 586-3686, is a 90-minute revue in the tradition of shows that once entertained gold prospectors (but now done in a manner that's suitable for children). It's reasonably entertaining, but unless you really go for this sort of thing, your time in Juneau is better spent elsewhere.

Alaska Brewing Company 5429 Shaune Drive, ☎ (907) 780-5866, has the usual combination of free tour and free samples. In this case, the manufacturer claims that their recipe for their local brew, called Alaskan Amber, goes back to the days of the Gold Rush.

Now it's time for the afternoon sightseeing. The first activity is still in Juneau and is a short walk south of the cruise ship dock. **The Mount Roberts Tramway**, 490 S. Franklin Street, ☎ (888) 461-8726, will whisk you in six minutes from just above sea level to 2,000 feet above the city. In addition to the outstanding view, there's a restaurant, gift shop, an interpretive film titled *Seeing Daylight* that describes Tlingit culture, a nature center (including bald eagles from the Juneau Raptor Center), exhibits on native heritage, and plenty of hiking trails of varying difficulty. This can either be a short visit (under a half-hour for the round-trip ride and some time to take in the view at the top) or can take a couple of hours, allowing you to explore the trails. You can also hike to the top of Mt. Roberts from here, as described in the *Sports & Recreation* section. *Open daily, $$$$.*

Twelve miles north of downtown via the Egan Highway (Alaska State Highway 7) is the most famous of Juneau's attractions, **Mendenhall Glacier**. This is one of the most accessible glaciers in the state and its size is most impressive, despite the fact that it has generally been receding for almost 260 years! A modern visitor center, ☎ (907) 789-0097, introduces you to the world of glaciers in general and to Mendenhall in particular. *Visitor Center is open daily, 8 am-6 pm, $ for Visitor Center only.* There is an outstanding view of the glacier from the large observation area. (When the center was built in 1962, the edge of the glacier was right outside). An easy paved trail of less than a half-mile takes you to the best points for viewing and photographing the glacier. Several other trails, including a nature trail, range from a half-mile to about four miles in length and explore the surrounding area. The glacier itself, seen from across Mendenhall Lake, begins 13 miles away in the Juneau Icefield. The front of Mendenhall is 1½ miles across and about 100 feet high. You'll see chunks of ice floating in the lake and hear a loud waterfall gushing from Nugget Creek. Chances are that the vivid blue color of Mendenhall will catch your attention.

CLEAN UP YOUR GLACIERS PLEASE

Many visitors are surprised by the "dirty" look of glaciers, including Mendenhall. But it is not dirt that you see, but rather rock and other debris that has been carried down the mountain and slowly been ground up by the moving river of ice. Alaskans will simply smile pleasantly if you tell them to clean up their glaciers! So avoid the embarrassment and, having now learned about the cause of the "dirt," chat with a local about the transportation abilities of glaciers. By the end of your visit to Mendenhall, you'll definitely have a far better understanding of how glaciers affect the landscape.

Near the visitor center is a viewing platform where you can watch spawning salmon between mid-July and mid-September. Give yourself at least an hour to visit Mendenhall, more if you plan to do a lot of trail exploration. If you don't go the excursion route to see Mendenhall (and there are a variety of different excursions ranging from just the glacier to all-day trips in and around Juneau) it is best to either rent a car or take the bus that leaves from near the cruise ship terminal. Cars cost only $20 for the day, so even two people can probably save money by driving on their own. Taxis are also available, but the cost is very high. The drive to Mendenhall passes along the Gastineau Channel and then Favorite Channel and Auke Bay. The scenery is pleasant and you may catch a glimpse of whales that frequent the area. Also along the route at Milepost 23 is the small but picturesque Shrine of St. Terese. It's on a tiny island connected to the mainland by a causeway.

On the way back into Juneau just off Highway 7 is the **Glacier Gardens Rainforest Adventure**, 7600 Glacier Highway, ☎ (907) 790-3377, an interesting experience that begins with a shuttle ride up the slope of pretty Thunder Mountain. You'll pass through botanical gardens and a real Alaskan rainforest. A stop is made at an overlook almost 600 feet above sea level and you can get a fantastic view of the Mendenhall Valley and the Chilkat Mountains. Figure at least an hour for your visit. *Open daily, $3.*

As the three attractions I've selected for the afternoon will take a minimum of four hours using a rental car (longer if other methods are used), be sure that you make your ship's departure time. Alternately, rearrange the morning and afternoon to accommodate all of these.

Shore excursions are numerous in the major Alaskan ports and Juneau is no exception. You can see all of the sights just described on city tours. A slew of excursions go to Mendenhall Glacier, and many combine a glacier visit with other sightseeing activities. Flightseeing by fixed wing aircraft, seaplane or helicopter is available to the Juneau Icefield. There are also jet boat tours and scenic day cruises to nearby fjords that can't be reached by big cruise ships. Other available tours include a traditional salmon bake luncheon, panning for gold, visits to former gold mines and the ever-popular whale-watching cruises. A good percentage of Juneau excursions are more sport- or recreation-oriented, so check the section below for even more options.

Shopping

Shopping in Juneau is concentrated along Front Street, a couple of blocks off Franklin and on South Franklin Street itself, right near the cruise ship terminal, so it's really convenient for carrying packages! There are all types of stores, from clothing to souvenirs both cheap and expensive, including some that are uniquely Alaskan. Probably one of the most interesting aspects of shopping in this area is the historic nature of almost every building along this stretch of real estate.

The best places for Native Alaskan crafts are **Raven's Journey**, 439 S. Franklin, where you'll find an excellent selection of carvings, dolls, jewelry and masks, among many other items; **Caribou Crossings**, 497 S. Franklin; and the **Fireweed Shop**, 469 S. Franklin. Juneau is one of several locations in Alaska where you can shop for authentic Russian crafts, including dolls, lacquered boxes and items made from Baltic amber. The best place for this is the **House of Russia**, 389. S. Franklin.

If it is art you seek, the best choices are **Juneau Artists Gallery**, 175 S. Franklin, or **Annie Kaill's Gallery**, 244 Front Street. All types of well-made Alaskan clothing, much of it with unique Alaskan designs, can be found at **Galligaskins**, 219 S. Franklin. As if you won't be eating enough on the ship, a lot of visitors like to bring home samples of Alaskan fish and seafood, smoked so it won't spoil. **Taku Smokeries**, 550 S. Franklin, will ship anywhere if you don't want to take it yourself.

Sports & Recreation

Sea kayaking and **canoeing** are favorite sports in Juneau. Either you can rent your own equipment or take guided kayak tours around the Juneau area all the way up to Mendenhall Glacier. One-stop shopping for do-it-yourselfers can be done at **Alaska Boat & Kayak**, 11521 Glacier Highway. Those going the guided route should try **Alaska Discovery**, 5310 Glacier Highway. Remember that it's still easier to arrange a shore excursion via your ship. **Sportfishing** isn't quite as outstanding in the immediate vicinity of Juneau as in other parts of Southeast Alaska, but it isn't bad by any means. Again, shore excursions are the most convenient way to do this.

Hiking is a splendid way to explore the area and get great views of the city and fjords. The trail to Mount Roberts begins from just past the intersection of Sixth and East streets. By hiking, you avoid paying the hefty tramway fare, but the hike involves some exertion and requires a couple of hours to complete. Mendenhall Glacier has several trails. These include the East Glacier Loop, with a great glacier view around midway; the West Glacier Trail, which climbs to above the glacier and provides outstanding views; and the Nugget Creek Trail. The Perseverance Trail isn't far from downtown (take Sixth Street to Gold Street which will become Basin Road; the trailhead is at the end of this dirt road). The trail links with a larger hiking system as it skirts Granite Creek in an area of ex-gold mines.

NOTE: *If you plan to hike any of these trails, it's a good idea to get maps from the visitor center.*

The lure of striking it rich makes **gold panning** a popular activity. Although we haven't heard of anyone finding their fortune this way recently, dedicated panners shouldn't have too much trouble finding a few small flecks of gold if they look in the right places. The Visitor Information Center can direct you to locations that offer the best chances.

Finally, the Alaskan panhandle isn't known for its **golfing** opportunities, but Juneau does boast the nine-hole **Mendenhall Golf Course**, 2101 Industrial Blvd. It isn't anything to talk about, but should do nicely if you are really in need of a golf fix. The surrounding scenery is the best part of the course.

Everything mentioned so far can also be arranged as a shore excursion, and there are some activities that are best done via this route. These include horseback riding, adventure hiking, sportfishing, fly & fish (that is, you'll be flown to a great spot for fishing), kayaking, and all on-glacier activities. The latter include not only guided glacier walks, but also things like dog sledding. In almost all cases you have to get to these activities by air. It is almost impossible to find any shore excursion by air that costs under $200 and prices up to about $350 are not uncommon for these types of adventures in the Juneau area.

Ketchikan

The local chamber of commerce proudly proclaims that "Alaska begins in Ketchikan," and it's geographically correct to say so. After you cross the Canadian border, Ketchikan will be the first stop. The town has also designated itself the "Salmon Capital of the World," based not only on its origins as a cannery town back in 1887, but because that industry is still of great importance to the local economy. Even though Ketchikan has a population of under 8,000, it is one of the state's 10 largest communities, which tells you something about the size of the other cities! Ketchikan's surrounding mountains are a lush green due to the tremendous amount of rainfall in this area. In fact, it's the local populace that has been credited with coining the phrase "liquid sunshine" to describe water falling from the sky. They also invented the term "Ketchikan Sneakers," referring to the high yellow rubber boots often worn in Alaska. Obviously, Ketchikaners have a great sense of humor that includes being able to laugh at their own plight. They poke even more fun at the heavy rainfall totals by prominently displaying a tall rain gauge outside the Visitors Bureau. Annual rainfall is a staggering 160 inches!

Arrival

The cruise ship pier is on Front Street in the heart of downtown. Even very large ships can tie up here. The only possibility of having to use a tender is if there are more than three ships in town at the same time, which shouldn't happen.

Tourism Information Office

The **Ketchikan Convention & Visitors Bureau**, 131 Front Street, Ketchikan, AK 99901, ☎ (800) 770-3300, www.visit-ketchikan.com, is right by the cruise ship pier. It will provide you with an excellent walking tour map. Another valuable source of information is the branch office of the **Alaska Public Lands Information Center** at 50 Main Street (inside the Southeast Alaska Discovery Center), ☎ (907) 228-6220, one block inland from Front Street.

Getting Around

The greater Ketchikan area runs for about 31 miles along the pretty Tongass Narrows, with downtown stretching for the surprisingly long distance of three miles. Like many other towns along the Inside Passage, Ketchikan is long and very narrow – often only a few blocks wide. This is because the coastal mountains along the Alaskan panhandle start almost at the shore. Roads are often carved into the surrounding hills and many "streets" are staircases, rather than thoroughfares for auto traffic. Using this to your advantage, you can often get good views of the Narrows, harbor and mountains from the highest points along these streets. All of the sights in town are close enough to walk to and the journey to them makes for a pleasant stroll (if it isn't raining too hard). Some of the outlying attractions are too far for foot power, but you can either take a taxi ($2.25 for the first drop of the meter and then only $1.10 per mile). Taxi drivers will also rent themselves out for guided tours, but I think it's better to sign up for a shore excursion. Limited local bus service is also available at prices that are considerably less than taking a taxi.

One-Day Sightseeing Tour

From the cruise ship pier, walk south on Front Street to Mill, turn left and proceed one block to Main, where you'll reach the large **Southeast Alaska Discovery Center**, 50 Main Street, ☎ (907) 228-6220. This excellent facility is devoted to the rainforest environment of Southeast Alaska, and you can experience it here without getting wet. The lobby has three totem poles and salmon suspended from the ceiling. There's also a multi-media show and an office of the Alaska Public

Lands Information Center. You and your children could spend up to an hour here without getting fidgety. *Open daily, 8:30 am to 5 pm, $$.*

Now walk back north on Main until you get to Dock Street. Turn to the right. Although most of the downtown streets are rather tacky affairs, lined on both sides with souvenir shops, this street looks like something from an Old Western movie that has been mistakenly transported to Alaska. The **Tongass Historical Museum**, 629 Dock Street, ☎ (907) 225-5600, features interesting displays that will acquaint you with the various native tribes and their culture, as well as local history. *Open daily, 8 am to 5 pm, $.*

After leaving the museum, continue walking on Dock, which will bear into Stedman Street. Follow Stedman for a few blocks until it reaches **Creek Street**. This famous street is actually a boardwalk built on pilings above Ketchikan Creek. The buildings in this area are also supported by pilings. The city fathers designated Creek Street as the Red Light District in 1903, a status it held for 50 years. Now, most of the colorful wooden buildings are restaurants or shops that cater to thousands of visitors annually. The first house you will come across is **Dolly's House**, home of Ketchikan's most famous Madam for many years. It is furnished as it was during the years of her residence and provides an interesting glimpse into Creek Street's very colorful and rowdy past. *Open daily, $.* As you continue walking along Creek Street be sure to lean over the boardwalk railing now and then to gaze at both locals and tourists kayaking down Ketchikan Creek. It's a colorful sight. Beyond Creek Street is the **Married Man's Trail** (so-called because it provided an inconspicuous way into the Red Light District), which has nice views of the creek. A side trail leads to the Cape Fox Lodge and has a panoramic overlook. But there's an easier way to get to the views, so keep reading.

Adjacent to Creek Street there is a small red incline railway car that will take you up the hill to the **Westmark Cape Fox**

Ketchikan

n

CITY PARK

1. Visitors Center
2. Tongass Historical Museum
3. Dolly's House
4. Incline
5. Deer Mountain Hatchery
6. Totem Heritage Center
7. Return of the Eagle
8. Thomas Basin
9. Southeast Alaska Discovery Center

Approx. 2/10 Mile

© 2005 HUNTER PUBLISHING, INC

Lodge for about a buck. It saves a lot of uphill walking and provides spectacular views of the town and harbor. The lodge features viewing decks that offer a bird's-eye view of your cruise ship and any others that happen to be in port. What is most striking about this picture is how the huge vessels dwarf everything in town – and remember, Ketchikan is one of the larger towns that you'll be visiting! Leave the Westmark Lodge from the opposite side of the tram and walk down Venetia Avenue into Park Avenue. Turn right and follow Park for a few blocks to the **Deer Mountain Tribal Hatchery & Eagle Center**, 1158 Salmon Road, ☎ (907) 222-6760. The hatchery has fine exhibits describing the varieties of salmon and their life cycles. You can also observe some of the ponds where more than 300,000 king and coho salmon, along with trout, are raised each year to ensure adequate supplies for fishermen. Baked salmon samples are offered. An enclosed area on the grounds contains several bald eagles. *Open daily, 8 am to 4:30 pm, $$ for guided tours.* Adjacent to the Deer Mountain facility is the **Totem Heritage Center**, 601 Deermont Street, ☎ (907) 225-5900. Although it's in the city, the center sits on the edge of Ketchikan's rainforest and has a lovely nature trail. It's best known for its collection of authentic 19th-century totem poles (that is, they were not carved for the benefit of tourists like many you'll see all over Alaska). Local native artisans display their carving skills. *Open daily, 8 am to 5 pm, $.*

Return to the waterfront via Deermont Street and then Stedman, following the harbor. Along the way you'll pass the 70 x 120-foot **Return of the Eagle mural**, drawn by local artists and representing the renewal of the earth as depicted in Native Alaskan beliefs. A block later is Thomas Basin, the marina where hundreds of boats belonging to Ketchikan's residents are moored. (In a place like Ketchikan it's more important to own a boat than a car.) In a few blocks you'll be back at the cruise ship pier. The preceding tour, at a leisurely pace, will take between four and five hours.

All of Ketchikan's major in-town sights are along the route just described. Some organized city tours add a visit to **Totem Bight State Historic Park**, 10 miles north of town. It has a Tlingit tribal clan house in addition to some totem poles. However, as long as you visit the Totem Heritage Center, or if you're going to be stopping in Sitka where a national historic park offers an outstanding display of totems, don't feel as though you are missing out on anything by touring independently and omitting the state park. On the other hand, if you're renting a car, Totem Bight is an easy drive up the North Tongass Highway. Allow about 1¼ hours for the round-trip, plus sightseeing time. *Open daily; donations.* A better idea if you're driving is to visit **Saxman Native Village**, ☎ (907) 225-4846, about three miles south of Ketchikan on the South Tongass Highway. Here you'll observe and learn about the Tlingit, an important Native American culture. Several hundred Tlingits actually live at the village. It's a very worthwhile stop for those who are especially interested in learning about these cultures. If you don't have a car, you can reach Saxman by inexpensive city bus or by a more expensive cab ride. *Open daily. Admission to the village is free; $$$$ for guided tours.*

One last attraction that might interest visitors is the **Great Alaskan Lumberjack Show**, Spruce Mill Way, behind the Discovery Center, ☎ (888) 320-9049. This unusual form of entertainment displays the skills of lumberjacks, including pole climbing, sawing and the like. It's more fun than you might imagine. Three shows are held daily when ships are in town; call for the exact schedule. *$$$$.*

Just about all of Ketchikan's "do-it-yourself" sights described above are available via a shore excursion, but let's take a look at some of the more interesting activities that can't be done easily independently. The combination float plane and boat ride to the nearby **Misty Fjords** is expensive but is a fabulous trip. If your cruise ship is one of the few that includes the fjords in its itinerary, then this trip probably won't be offered, nor is it really necessary. In fact, it would be unwise to fork over the more than $250 usually charged per person because much of the area you've already seen. For those who haven't cruised in the fjord, there is gorgeous scenery and the experience can be wonderful. However, given the cost of flightseing, you should be aware that the experience could be vitiated by poor visibility and other weather conditions which are frequently far less than ideal. Therefore, an even better (and less costly idea) is to tour Misty Fjords by high-speed catamaran. **Goldbelt Alaska Cruises**, ☎ (800) 228-1905, has a 6½-hour trip departing from Ketchikan for about $150. I haven't seen many cruise lines offer this option, perhaps because it is so long that it makes viewing other places nearly impossible. But for those who appreciate nature, it could be a better option than in-town touring. Certainly, for those who have been to Ketchikan on a previous cruise, it's a great idea.

Among other worthwhile excursions are the jet boat ride to beautiful **Salmon Falls**. During the summer hundreds of salmon can be seen in the creek. Many other tours on the water are available and include kayaking to area sights or sea tours of surrounding areas via excursion boats. Turning towards the land, excursions include explorations of the rainforest and surrounding areas by jeep "safari." The cruise lines offer about two dozen different shore excursions in Ketchikan. But, again, many of them are combinations of some of the basic trips mentioned here, or are recreation-oriented.

Shopping

I've already alluded to the endless number of souvenir places in downtown. You should be able to find whatever kind of junk you're looking for. Somewhat nicer is the **Spruce Mill Development** on Mill Street. Designed to resemble a fish cannery from the late 1920s, the shops here sell goods that range from cheap to upscale. There are also restaurants if you don't want to go back to your ship for lunch. The **AlaskaMade Gallery**, 123 Stedman, is the best place in Ketchikan to purchase native works of art. And lovers of smoked and canned seafood and fish products won't go hungry if they stop into **Salmon Etc.** They have two stores, one at 10 Creek Street and the other at 322 Mission Street.

Sports & Recreation

Kayaking on the Ketchikan Creek is perhaps the most popular recreational pursuit among visitors. While you won't see that much more from the water than you will from the boardwalk, there's little doubt that it is a fun experience. Trips can be arranged through your shore excursion office or with **Southeast Exposure**, 515 Water Street, ☎ (800) 287-1607. In addition to renting equipment, they run 2½-hour guided kayak tours of the waterfront and Creek Street.

Sportfishing is excellent in the waters near Ketchikan. Trips will be available through your ship, or you can get information about the various operators at the Visitors Bureau and plan independently. But for water lovers, here's an unusual adventure − snorkeling! Ketchikan is perhaps the only place in Alaska where you can actually pursue this sport. You'll don a special thick wetsuit to keep you warm and take a plunge into crystal-clear mountain waters for a first-hand look at the abundant marine flora and fauna.

When it comes to land-based recreation, **hiking** and **biking** are the top choices. There are many hiking trails in the area surrounding town, but you don't even have to go that far. The 2½-mile Deer Mountain Trail begins at Fair Street just southeast of City Park. It climbs to an elevation of more than 3,000 feet and provides stunning vistas. Bicycle trails are also numerous, with the most popular going along the water to Saxman Village. Another bike trail heads along North Tongass Highway to Ward Lake, where you'll find an abundance of hiking trails. Southeast Exposure (above) rents bikes. Guided bike riding trips through your shore excursion office are an easier way to do some pedal-pushing.

Sitka

One of the more attractive communities in Southeast Alaska (and one of the largest, with a population of nearly 9,000), Sitka has always been important because of its location. It provides access not only to the Inside Passage, but to the Pacific Ocean as well. It was for this reason that the Russian Alexander Baranov chose the site as the capital of Russia's Alaskan settlement in 1804. He named it New Archangel. The Russian encroachment soon brought them into conflict with the local natives – the Tlingits (more about that when we get to Sitka National Historical Park). Even today Sitka preserves the greatest evidence of Russian influence of any place in Alaska and the Native American input is also felt strongly here. Set amid a maze of hundreds of islands surrounded by mountains, Sitka is a charming and interesting place to visit. It's a worthwhile part of any cruise that stops here.

Arrival

The port facilities aren't able to handle large ships. All cruise vessels will weigh anchor in the sizable outer harbor and passengers are brought to shore by a brief tender ride. Once on the dock you'll be practically in the heart of everything there is to see in town.

Tourism Information Office

Advance information can be obtained from the **Sitka Convention & Visitors Bureau**, 303 Lincoln Street, PO Box 1226, Sitka, AK 99835, ☎ (907) 747-5940, www.sitka.org. On arrival, you can get information near the tender pier inside the Centennial Building. The office is open whenever cruise ships are in town.

Getting Around

In-town sightseeing is concentrated in a compact area and the best way to get around is on foot. The farthest sights are only a little more than a mile in either direction from the tender pier. If you find yourself tiring, hop into a taxi; the fares won't be very high because of the small distances involved. Better yet is to use the **Transit Shuttle**, Sitka's summer bus service designed with cruise ship passengers in mind. For a daily fare of $7 it connects most of the important sights on its loop through town. It runs frequently. There is no need to rent a car because the road system outside of Sitka doesn't go far nor does it lead to any places of interest. There are worthwhile places to visit outside of Sitka, but they must be reached by boat and your best bet is to take a ship-sponsored shore excursion.

One-Day Sightseeing Tour

Adjacent to the tender pier is the **Harrigan Centennial Building** and the **Isabel Miller Museum**, ☎ (907) 747-6455. The large Centennial Building is the scene of many events in town, including the ever-popular performances by Russian dancers (more about this later). The museum focuses on local history, including that of the Native population. A highlight is the eight-square-foot diorama of Sitka as it appeared in 1867 at the time Alaska transferred hands from Russia to the United States. *Open daily, 8 am to 5 pm; donations.*

A short walk to the north of the Centennial Building on Harbor Drive is the town square (actually a circle) in the middle of which is **St. Michael's Cathedral**. This beautiful onion-domed structure was built in 1966 to replace the original 1848 church that was destroyed by a fire. It is the foremost example of Russian church architecture in North America. A large number of Tlingits are still members of the Orthodox congregation and the cathedral houses numerous beautiful icons and religious artifacts.

After visiting the cathedral continue west on Lincoln Street, Sitka's main thoroughfare which is lined with shops of every type. Soon you'll reach a staircase that will take you to **Castle Hill**, location of the once stately home of Alexander Baronov, head of the Russian-American Trading Company that ruled Alaska for so many years. It was here that the transfer of sovereignty from Russia to the United States took place after William Seward's purchase of the Alaska Territory. Although the castle itself is long gone, the site contains numerous cannons and flags that represent the nations that have ruled over Alaska. Its prime hilltop setting affords visitors a beautiful view of the entire Sitka area, including Mt. Edgecumbe, a 3,000-foot volcanic mountain. At the base of Castle Hill on the north side of Lincoln Street is the **Sitka Pioneer Home**. Established in 1913 to house aging "sourdoughs" (individuals who came to Alaska to find their fortune and were now veterans of Alaska), the large building is still home to a number of people. A large 16-foot-high statue commemorates the prospectors on the spacious and attractive front lawn of the home. Opposite is **Totem Square**. In addition to several totems (including an unusual one with the double-headed eagle of Czarist Russia) are three anchors believed to be from 19th-century British ships. Just a block or so north of here are the remains of a large Russian fort. Only one of the wooden blockhouses is still intact.

After you've finished with this side of downtown, proceed in the other direction on Lincoln Street, going past the cathedral until you reach the **Russian Bishop's House**, 501 Lincoln Street, ☎ (907) 747-0110. This is now part of the Sitka National Historic Park, though it is physically separate from the rest of the park. The building is the largest remaining Russian-built structure in Alaska and has been nicely restored to its appearance of the 1850s. At that time it was home to the in-

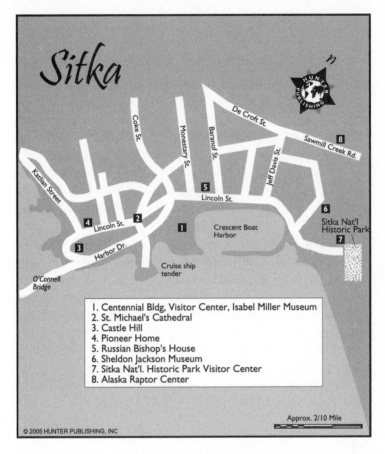

1. Centennial Bldg, Visitor Center, Isabel Miller Museum
2. St. Michael's Cathedral
3. Castle Hill
4. Pioneer Home
5. Russian Bishop's House
6. Sheldon Jackson Museum
7. Sitka Nat'l. Historic Park Visitor Center
8. Alaska Raptor Center

Approx. 2/10 Mile

© 2005 HUNTER PUBLISHING, INC

fluential Bishop of the Russian Orthodox Church in Alaska and, thus, is rather elaborate. Exhibits explain the role of the church in Sitka's Russian days. You can also observe a small portion of the original walls and foundations in some rooms and learn more about the excellent job of restoration that has been done. *Open daily, 9 am to 5 pm, $.* Continue once again down Lincoln Street and you'll soon come to the campus of Sheldon Jackson College and the excellent **Sheldon Jackson Museum**, 104 College Drive, ☎ (907) 747-8981. This museum, housed in a large circular building, has one of the most comprehensive collections of artifacts and exhibits devoted exclusively to the history and culture of Alaska's native peoples, including Inuit (Eskimo), Aleut, Haida, Tlingit and Athabascan cultures. *Open daily except holidays, 9 am to 5 pm, $.*

Just a short walk on Lincoln past the museum is the Visitor Center and entrance to the main section of **Sitka National Historic Park**. Situated about a mile from the tender docking area, the lovely and now serene park documents the 1804 battle fought between the Russians and Tlingits for control of the area. With the Russian victory, the Tlingits no longer presented a threat to Russian domination of Alaska. Nearly two miles of well-maintained pathways lead through lush wooded areas. Scattered along the main walk (with a few more at the Visitor Center) are a total of 28 colorful totem poles. Their location amid the tranquil forest significantly enhances their aesthetic appeal. The ones currently on display are exact replicas of the original carvings that have long since deteriorated with the passage of time. Although the totems represent various native groups from almost every part of Southeastern Alaska, with the majority being from the Tlingit or Haida cultures, none of them came from the Sitka area itself. The Visitor Center has demonstrations of traditional crafts. *Visitor Center open daily, 8 am to 5 pm, $ for Visitor Center only.*

One of Sitka's newer attractions is the **Alaska Raptor Center**, 1101 Sawmill Creek Road, ☎ (800) 643-9425, located on the way to or from the national historic park. Turn off Lincoln onto Jeff Davis Street and walk alongside the college campus to DeGroff Street. Make a right there and then bear right into Sawmill Creek Road. Covering about 17 acres in a beautiful natural setting, the center helps care for about 200 injured birds of prey every year. At any one time there are usually two dozen birds in care, including eagles, falcons, owls and ravens. You'll see interesting exhibits and demonstrations and can hike along an easy nature trail. The center can be toured individually or through a guided tour. *Open daily except Saturday, 8 am to 4 pm, $$$.*

A walking tour of Sitka as described above will take approximately five hours. If you don't walk the full two miles at Sitka National Historical Park and if you take a cab or shuttle bus to and from the Raptor Center, you can probably do it in about four hours. The range of optional tours in Sitka isn't as great as in some other ports of call, but some of them are very interesting and should be included in your visit, time permitting. Many of the best tours take only a few hours, which still allows you to see the sights in town. If you take one or more of the longer tours, then it will probably be necessary to eliminate some of the suggested itinerary.

A couple of entertainment experiences will interest many visitors. The best known are the **Russian New Archangel Dancers**, who perform traditional dances in colorful costumes in the Centennial Building's large hall. Their shows usually coincide with times that cruise ships are in port. As such, the dances will almost inevitably be one of the shore excursions offered and this is usually the easiest way to see them. It also assures that a seat will be available, something you can't always count on if you wait until your arrival and show up on your own. Performances last about a half-hour. Many excursions do other things besides going to the show. If you have time on your own and want to make reservations in advance, you can do so by calling ☎ (907) 747-6774. A completely different type of dance performance is available at the **Tribal Community House** on Katlian Street, along the waterfront near the Pioneer Home. Here, the Sheet'ka Kwaan Naa Kahadi Native Dancers will delight you with their colorful presentation. Interested visitors should contact the Sitka Convention & Visitors Bureau at ☎ 907-757-5940.

Sea Life Discovery Tours, 221 Harbor Drive, ☎ (877) 966-2301, is reputed to be the only semi-submersible boat ride in Alaska. Glass windows are below the water level, but part of the vessel always remains above water. The boat is equipped with underwater cameras whose images are enlarged and viewed on screens. $$$$.

If you happen to be visiting Sitka during the month of June, you'll be here for the three-week **Sitka Summer Music Festival**, a major event held in Centennial Hall. The featured performances are in the evening (but you're probably gone by then) and tickets are hard to come by. However, afternoon rehearsals are easier to get into.

Of the four major Alaskan ports in this chapter, Sitka has the fewest shore excursions. However, the list is still quite extensive and many are truly first-rate. The major activities are easiest to arrange through the ship's shore excursion desk. Tours to Sitka National Historic Park are also always available and this is a good option if you want to avoid the walk there. Sightseeing excursions include wildlife tours by land and by sea. The day cruise to Silver Bay and a local fish hatchery is a scenic trip and there's a high probability of seeing a variety of wildlife, including eagles and even bears.

Shopping

Shopping opportunities in Sitka are surprisingly limited, concentrated between the 200 and 400 blocks of Lincoln Street. This is the town's main shopping drag and stores for residents and tourists line both sides. The **Sitka Rose Gallery** is among the best of a handful of art galleries and native craft shops.

Sports & Recreation

There's great **fishing** in the waters around Sitka and trips can be arranged through the shore excursion office of your ship. **Kayaking**, also a shore excursion option, can be undertaken by independent travelers. There are numerous operators, but the best known are **Alaska Travel Adventures**, ☎ (800)

478-0052, and **Baidarka Boats**, 320 Seward Street, ☎ (907) 747-8996.

There are many **hiking** trails in the forests and mountains that surround Sitka. Most of them are very long, require a certain amount of skill, and aren't easily accessed. If you're interested in the challenge, head to the Visitors Bureau in Centennial Hall for information and maps. Somewhat less difficult are the hiking trips done on shore excursions, which include transportation to the trailhead. Most ships also offer a variety of **biking** excursions.

TOTEM POLES

By now you've likely seen many totem poles, but do you really know what's behind them? Totem poles are much more than mere decorative pieces that the Tlingit and Haida created in their spare time. They have their origin in the animistic religion of these tribes, which had a strong emphasis on the nature of man and his relationship with other animals as well as natural forces. As the Tlingit and Haida had no written language, totem poles provided a means of story-telling; each figure on a totem pole was part of a larger story. The totem could be a record of tribal history (both real and imagined) or it could simply be a genealogical record of a family or clan. The latter type of totem pole typically was placed outside a house and usually displayed a family crest based on either an eagle or raven. In addition, specialized totems were created for specific purposes. For example, a mortuary pole actually contained a compartment where the deceased's ashes could be interred; the person's life was the subject of the outer carvings. Perhaps the most unusual totem was a type that served as a means of punishment. If a person shamed a tribe or clan he or she would, according to tribal custom, have to repay the debt. A totem would be placed by their home and had to remain standing until the debt had been satisfied.

Totem poles vary greatly in size. They are almost always carved from cedar trees. After the careful carving process was done, the poles were painted. The Tlingit and Haida used all natural pigments. Two of the more common ones were salmon eggs and the mineral hematite. When you see your next totem pole up close, think about how much it meant to the Tlingit and Haida way of life.

Skagway

Skagway is, without a doubt, one of the most colorful towns you're likely to visit anywhere. Born in the days of the 1898 Klondike Gold Rush, it was a wild town of over 20,000, populated by prospectors, working girls, gamblers, thieves and criminals of every type. There were more than 80 saloons and probably as many houses of ill repute. Among the most notorious of the town's residents was Jefferson "Soapy" Smith, whose end came in a famous shoot-out. The excesses of Skagway at the turn of the century can almost be excused because the prospectors faced an arduous journey over the Klondike. Many would never return and few found the fortune they came to seek. This history is faithfully re-created today in a town that seems to have been left exactly as it was almost a hundred years ago. In fact, the streets are still boardwalks and many of the buildings have false fronts like a movie set. Still the "Gateway to the Klondike," only about 900 people make Skagway their home today. (Almost every major cruise ship that comes into town will be carrying more than twice as many visitors.) Fortunately, the people of Skagway today are not of the same ilk as many of the town's former residents. Tourism provides the livelihood for most. You'll be pleased to learn that Skagway's location makes its weather considerably better than in other towns of the Inside Passage. Sunshine can almost be considered common here during the summer months. And, as you read in the Lynn Canal section, the cruise to and from Skagway is a scenic delight.

Arrival

The cruise ship dock is at the southeastern end of town on an extension of 2nd Avenue. It is walking distance into the main part of town, but there are taxis and buses if you're feeling lazy. The bus, which travels as far as 8th Avenue, costs only a buck.

Tourism Information Office

For advance planning purposes you should contact the **Skagway Convention & Visitors Bureau**, PO Box 1029, Skagway, AK 98840, ☎ (888) 762-1898 (recorded information) or (907) 983-2854, www.skagway.org. Information when you're in town is available inside the Arctic Brotherhood Hall (Broadway between 2nd and 3rd avenues), as well as at the Klondike Gold Rush National Historic Park Visitor Center.

Getting Around

Sightseeing in Skagway is remarkably easy because the entire town is only five blocks wide and about 25 short blocks long. Once you walk (or ride) in on 2nd Avenue from the dock you'll be in the middle of town. Broadway is the principal thoroughfare and the place where most of the attractions are located. A few sights are also just to the north of town. For anything that you feel isn't in walking distance, you can take a taxi or a bus, a line of which runs north as far as 23rd Avenue ($2). There are many activities and sights beyond Skagway that just about everyone will want to see (and most port calls allow you enough time to do so). To get to these places, renting a car is a wise option because there is a good road system leading out of Skagway to many interesting points.

One-Day Sightseeing Tour

Your first stop should be at what is the most famous (and most photographed) structure in town, the **Arctic Brotherhood Hall**, Broadway between 2nd and 3rd avenues. The front of the building is faced with more than 20,000 pieces of driftwood that were gathered from nearby beaches and the building houses the Visitors Bureau. The **Klondike Gold Rush National Historic Park Visitor Center**, Broadway and 2nd Avenue, ☎ (907) 983-2921, is another important stop that should be made early in your walking tour. Although much of Skagway itself and scenic areas to the north are part of the historic park (as is an area to the south of downtown Seattle at the other end of the Klondike Gold Rush story), the visitor center will provide you with a good understanding of the short but tumultuous Gold Rush era. Brochures describing many of the historic buildings on Broadway are available here. As you walk along the boardwalks (cars ride along semi-paved or dirt streets), you'll feel as if you have traveled back in time. The colorful buildings have been faithfully restored to their original appearance. Other reminders of the past range from turn-of-the-century buses and taxis (that you can ride if you want to save some shoe leather) to the town's former saloons that now house restaurants or pubs on the first floor. Peering out from the windows on the second floor are mannequins of seductively clad "painted ladies" encouraging prospectors to come up for a visit. Candles behind a red glass cover burn throughout the day to let you know what used to occupy these premises. It's little things like these and the dummy gold-panning prospector sitting on a bench that add fun to the to Gold Rush-era atmosphere that permeates Skagway. If you want to learn more about the history of that time, head on

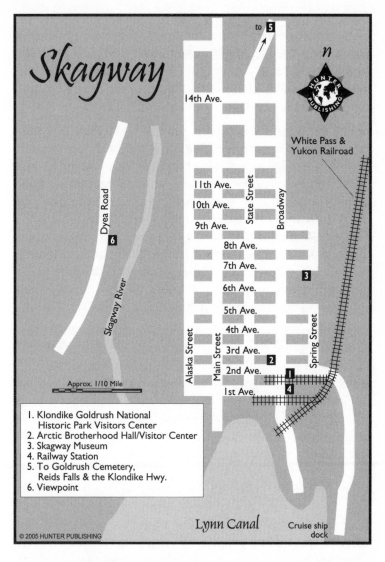

Skagway

to 5

n

HUNTER PUBLISHING

14th Ave.

White Pass & Yukon Railroad

Dyea Road

6

Skagway River

11th Ave.

State Street

Broadway

10th Ave.

9th Ave.

8th Ave.

7th Ave.

3

6th Ave.

5th Ave.

4th Ave.

Alaska Street

Main Street

3rd Ave.

Spring Street

2nd Ave.

2

1

4

1st Ave.

Approx. 1/10 Mile

1. Klondike Goldrush National
   Historic Park Visitors Center
2. Arctic Brotherhood Hall/Visitor Center
3. Skagway Museum
4. Railway Station
5. To Goldrush Cemetery,
   Reids Falls & the Klondike Hwy.
6. Viewpoint

Lynn Canal

Cruise ship dock

© 2005 HUNTER PUBLISHING

over to the **Skagway Museum**, 7th Avenue & Spring Street in the McCabe Building, ☎ (907) 983-2420, which has some interesting artifacts and exhibits. *Open weekdays, 9 am to 5 pm, and weekends, 1 to 4 pm, $.*

One other place to consider seeing is **Corrington's Museum of Alaskan History**, behind an ivory shop on Broadway at 5th Avenue, ☎ (907) 983-2579. This free attraction (they hope you buy something in the shop) is really misnamed. It houses a collection of 40 pieces of hand-carved walrus tusks, more commonly known as scrimshaw.

Entertaining performances are provided throughout the summer season at the **Days of '98 Show With Soapy Smith**, in the Eagle's Hall at Broadway and 6th Avenue, ☎ (907) 983-2545. This is one of the most popular attractions and is a part of many optional shore excursions; you can also see it on your own. Show times are daily at 10:30 am, 2:30 pm and 8 pm (if your ship is staying for a part of the evening). Although it has a can-can act and somewhat bawdy behavior, the show is suitable for all ages. $$$. There is gambling for adults every evening at 7 pm but it doesn't use real money. Hey, look at it this way – you can't lose anything if it's fake!

All of these in-town sights and shows should take only about three hours of your time. So let's head a bit farther afield. A half-mile north of town (via State Street following signs) is the **Gold Rush Cemetery**. Here, amid a real graveyard that will remind you of a scene from a horror-film spoof, are the remains of the town's famous and infamous residents. These include "Soapy" Smith and Frank Reid, the unfortunate man selected by the townspeople to bring Smith to justice. Both died in a gunfight more famous in Alaska than the shoot-out at the O.K. Corral. Much of the cemetery is in a state of chaos and the graves are not generally attended to, but that, too, adds to the ambiance. A short trail leads from behind the cemetery to **Reid's Falls** (hidden from view when you're in the cemetery, but just follow the sound of rushing waters). Allow about a half-hour to visit this area, including getting to and from town (longer if you're walking).

There's little doubt that the big attraction for many visitors to Skagway is the chance to take a ride on the famous **White**

Pass & Yukon Route Railroad, leaving from the depot on 2nd Avenue between Broadway and Spring, ☎ (800) 343-7373, www.wpyr.com. Half- and full-day narrated excursions travel over the narrow-gauge line that was built in around 1900 to transport prospectors on the first leg of their journey into the Klondike region. The trip is a lot more comfortable today, but you'll be seeing much the same thing the prospectors did – a spectacular narrow river valley surrounded by towering mountains on either side and a gorge filled with wonderful waterfalls. The train carries you over frightening wooden trestles, through tunnels and over deep and very narrow ravines. The journey is considered by train buffs to be one of the most scenic train rides in all of North America. *Frequent departures daily, $$$$.*

While no one who takes this exciting train trip is likely to be the least bit disappointed, it still isn't, in my opinion, the best way to see the area. It travels only as far as the White Pass (the border with Canada), where you have the option to continue into the Yukon via motor coach. With an adult fare exceeding $80 ($40 for children), you will find that renting a car in Skagway and taking the 130-mile round-trip to Carcross in the Yukon Territory is less expensive and just as worthwhile. Taking into account how much time you have in port and whether or not you do the sights in Skagway, you might even be able to travel the additional 65 miles round-trip from Carcross to Whitehorse, the capital of the Yukon Territory. Although it's not likely you'll be stopped at the border, you should remember to bring all of your identification documents with you.

If you elect to drive, your journey begins at the north end of Skagway at the Klondike Highway. The most scenic portion of this route is between Skagway and Carcross. The first 14 miles (to the Canadian border) are on the opposite side of the gorge from the railroad. There are several overlooks on this well-paved road that offer a chance to admire the scenery and even to watch the trains going by. Once you've entered the Yukon, the road traverses an area that resembles a moonscape before reaching a beautiful mountain wilderness with green glacial lakes, towering peaks and gloriously colorful wildflowers. Again, there are pull-outs at some of the most scenic spots. The town of Carcross isn't much to look at, but it does have a couple of interesting attractions and is also a good place for lunch (this trip will definitely require having lunch away from your ship). The **Carcross Desert**, just north of town, is reputedly the world's smallest and signs detail the story as to why this desert developed in a region that is usually a lush green from considerable rainfall. In brief, a retreating glacier left an area devoid of vegetation. Local wind patterns continue to blow away seeds. As a result, the area has remained sandy and barren. **Caribou Crossing Trading Post**, just north of town on the Klondike Highway, ☎ (867) 821-4055, is a re-created frontier town that will be of interest to children. There's a small petting zoo. The post also has a fine collection of stuffed specimens of bears and other large animals native to the area. The surrounding grounds cover 30 acres containing native animals and plants and offer splendid views of Lake Bennett and the surrounding mountains. *Open daily, 8:30 am to 6 pm, $$.*

Being able to go beyond the White Pass is only one advantage of having a car in Skagway. Once you get back to Skagway from your Yukon journey you can also cross the bridge at the north end of town that leads to the **Dyea Road**. At the end of this road, nine miles farther, is the beginning of the **Chilkoot Trail**, a three-day hike into the Yukon. Obviously, as a cruise ship passenger you won't be doing the trail, but there are several places along Dyea Road where you can stop for panoramic views of the town, the docks and snow-capped mountains in every direction, and the northern end of the Lynn Canal. You can also drive to the Gold Rush Cemetery and Reid's Falls instead of taking a long walk or using public transportation. In any event, allow about four hours for the complete round-trip self-guiding excursion to Carcross.

A final possibility, especially if you have previously visited here, is to take a trip to **Haines** (either on your own or via a shore excursion). For details, see the town listing in the *Less-Visited Ports* section, page 207. Some shore excursions visit Haines Bald Eagle Preserve but, unfortunately, the summer cruise season isn't the best time of the year to do so.

Speaking of shore excursions, Skagway has a whole bunch of others to tempt you. One of the most dramatic is a flightseeing adventure to **Glacier Bay**. This can be an especially worthwhile trip if your cruise doesn't actually sail to Glacier Bay. While there's nothing like it from sea level, an aerial view does present a different perspective and it's certainly better than not seeing it at all. Again, as in all Alaskan flightseeing trips, weather can be a major impediment. Other trips include jet boating; various wildlife tours by sea, land and air; visits to some of the nearby historic Gold Rush era towns (now mostly abandoned) with or without a salmon bake; and jeep trips into the interior. The White Pass Railroad trip is also made, more often than not, as a shore excursion. Those who want to save a little money and don't need the thrill of riding on a historic railroad to appreciate the scenery can opt to take a van tour as far as the White Pass. There are sometimes longer excursions available by road.

Shopping

There's nothing unusual or especially noteworthy about shopping in Skagway. On the other hand, you won't find any lack of souvenir and other shops selling just about everything you can imagine all along Broadway. Since almost every store is in an historic building, that aspect of the shopping can be more rewarding than the actual buying experience.

Sports & Recreation

Horseback riding, bicycling, hiking, fishing and **kayaking** are the usual pursuits. These can be accessed through local operators and rental facilities, but are easiest to plan as a shore excursion. Kayaking is a fun experience even for the most inexperienced boater. Kayaks are extremely stable and are easy to paddle.

An unusual and enjoyable excursion is with **Alaska Sled Dog Adventures**, ☎ (907) 983-3990, which offers 2½-hour trips on wheeled sleds pulled by Alaskan huskies. The trip ends across the river in Dyea. Sled dog trips on real sleds are also an option, but these will involve flying to a location with suitable conditions and will be much more expensive.

There are many **hiking** trails in the area, but most are long and arduous. One that does begin in the city is the AB Mountain Trail, a 5½-mile walk leading to the 5,100-foot summit. It takes an entire day and is quite steep. Lastly, **mountain climbing** opportunities abound for the real adventurer. You can partake in a climb either on your own or as part of a guided trip.

Less-Visited Ports

The ports and scenic cruising locations discussed up to this point comprise the overwhelming majority of places that are currently visited by the big ships of the major cruise lines. However, if you are traveling on a small ship or via the Alaska Marine Highway System, then there are numerous other ports of call. Because only a small number of people will opt for this method of travel, the port descriptions will be more limited. Only ports situated along the Inside Passage and Alaska's southern coast are included. Thus, even though you might find a small ship line that goes to Nome, for example, you won't find it here. Note that the majority of these ports are never called on by the big ships. They can be reached only by AMHS or small ship lines. Some, however, can be reached by road before or after your cruise.

Cordova

In a beautiful setting on the shores of beautiful Prince William Sound and in the shadow of Mount Eyak, it's too bad that the majority of visitors to Alaska will never get to see Cordova, a small fishing town of about 2,600 people. Among its places of interest are the **Cordova Museum** (exhibits on local history) and the **Prince William Sound Science Center**, which has a small collection mostly dedicated to the 1989 *Exxon Valdez* oil spill and aftermath. The **Cordova Fisherman's Memorial** can be found at the small-boat harbor (it's only small in the types of boats it can handle; as far as size goes, it is one of the largest facilities of its type in Alaska). Finally, some of the local fish canneries are willing to give tours if enough people are interested, and the surrounding mountains are a hiker's paradise.

> **Visitor Information:** Cordova Chamber of Commerce, PO Box 99, Cordova, AK 99574; ☎ (907) 424-7260, www.cordovachamber.com. For information when you get to town their office is on 1st Street (also called Main Street) at the corner of Council Avenue.

Haines

Pretty Haines sits on a small peninsula formed by the Chilkat River and the Lynn Canal. Although lots of people never heard of it, Haines actually has more than twice as many residents as better-known Skagway.

A walking tour of the town can include the **Sheldon Museum** (not to be confused with the Sheldon Jackson Museum in Sitka), which has native artifacts and items relating to the history of Haines; the remains of **Fort William Henry Seward** (south end of town), now devoted to the arts and crafts and dancing of the Tlingit and Chilkat tribes; and the **Tsirku Canning Company**, an old salmon cannery.

Chilkat Bald Eagle Preserve, less than 20 miles from town, is a major migratory area. However, the best time to visit is between October and March, and very few birds are likely to be seen during the summer. Just for fun, you can take a four-hour float trip through the scenic waterways of the preserve and surrounding areas.

If you're here during the middle of August, you'll be able to enjoy the colorful five-day **Southeast Alaska State Fair** in Haines.

Those who've already seen Skagway and are returning to Alaska can use a port call in Skagway to get to Haines. The **Chilkat Cruises Fast Ferry**, ☎ (888) 766-2103, provides a quick and convenient way to get from one to the other. There are several departures in either direction each day, so it should fit into your available time without a problem. The sleek catamarans make the trip in just 35 minutes. The dock in Skagway is just to the east of the cruise ship docks and it lets you off practically in the heart of downtown Haines.

> **Visitor Information:** Haines Convention & Visitors Bureau, 122 Second Avenue, PO Box 530, Haines, AK 99827; ☎ (800) 458-3579, www.haines.ak.us. In town, there's a visitor center at the corner of Willard Street and 2nd Avenue.

Homer

In the old days when cruise ships actually sailed around the Kenai Peninsula and docked in Anchorage itself, you could find itineraries that paid a port call at Homer. Not so today, although Homer can easily be visited as part of a trip through the Kenai Peninsula from Seward or Anchorage.

The small town of Homer is still primarily a fishing community, although it has become somewhat of an artist colony as well. It sits perched below a long bluff that rises more than 1,000 feet. An even more prominent geographical feature is **Homer Spit**, a narrow strip of land extending out into Kachemak Bay for five miles. Driving out onto the Spit will reward you with wonderful views of the sea as well as the bluff.

The main attraction in town is the **Pratt Museum**, which houses a reasonably good collection of Native Alaskan artifacts with an emphasis on the Inuit culture. It also has excellent exhibits on marine life. Several art galleries scattered throughout town (especially along Pioneer Avenue around Main Street) display the works of the artists who make Homer their home for at least part of the year.

A ride up along **Skyline Drive**, which traverses the top of the bluffs for several miles above town, will reward the visitor with excellent views of the Spit, town, Kachemak Bay and some of the glaciers coming off nearby Harding Icefield. Splendid wildflowers grow along the bluff's top during the summer. A good tour, especially for wildlife enthusiasts, is a short boat trip to the **Gull Island Rookery**. In summer, these three small, rocky islands are almost entirely covered with birds, with more than 15,000 coming to nest. It's unlikely that you'll see a larger concentration of birds anywhere else in your Alaska trip. In addition to gulls, there are cormorants, colorful puffins and many other species. Contact **Homer Ocean**

Charters, ☎ (800) 426-6l2. Trips leave daily at noon and return at 3:30 pm.

> **Visitor Information:** Homer Chamber of Commerce, PO Box 54l, Homer, AK 99603, ☎ (907) 235-7740, www.homeralaska.org.

Kodiak

Kodiak is an isolated town even by Alaskan standards, located at the northern tip of Kodiak Island some 75 miles south of the Kenai Peninsula. Despite that, it has more than 6,000 residents and an economic robustness that comes from its status as a major commercial fishing port. A former Russian settlement, Kodiak retains examples of architecture from that era, including the onion-domed **Holy Resurrection Russian Orthodox Church** and the **Baranov Museum**, a home that was used by the Baranov Trading Company as a warehouse.

Fort Abercrombie State Historical Park is on a rocky headland about four miles from town. The fort was built for defensive purposes in World War II and its scenic setting and war-era remains make for an interesting little excursion.

The Kodiak Alutiiq Dancers perform ancient rituals in an authentic underground earthen hut in the Alutiiq Museum, 2l5 Mission Road. The traditions expressed in the dances go back more than a millennium.

The town of Kodiak can be used as a jumping-off point to explore the natural wonders of Kodiak Island. Wildlife tours are especially popular.

> **Visitor Information:** Kodiak Island Convention & Visitors Bureau, l00-AAA Marine Way, Suite 200, Kodiak, AK 996l5, ☎ (800) 789-4782, www.kodiak.org.

Petersburg

A cannery town on Mitkof Island along the Inside Passage, about halfway between Ketchikan and Juneau, Petersburg was founded by a Norwegian immigrant. Even today the colorful wooden buildings make Petersburg reminiscent of a small, picturesque Norwegian fjord town. In fact, the town is lovingly referred to as "Little Norway." The town's **Clausen Memorial Museum** has exhibits devoted to the fishing and canning industries, as well as Tlingit artifacts. Boat trips from Petersburg are a popular way to spend your time visiting. These include whale-watching trips on Frederick Sound or longer rides to the magnificent Le Conte Glacier. The latter can also be reached by plane and helicopter tours.

> **Visitor Information:** Petersburg Visitor Information Center, PO Box 649, Petersburg, AK 99833, ☎ (866) 484-4700, www.petersburg.org. In town, a small visitor center can be found at the intersection of 1st and Fram streets.

Prince Rupert (British Columbia)

The founder of Prince Rupert envisioned it as a place that would someday rival Vancouver as a major Canadian west coast port. It never made it that far, but it is a big commercial shipping point. Visited by some Norwegian Cruise Line, Celebrity and Silversea itineraries, Prince Rupert has made an impressive impact on the Alaskan cruise scene considering that no cruise ships visited here just a few years ago. The city fathers have big plans to make it a major port of call on Alaskan itineraries. Whether they'll ultimately be successful in that endeavor remains to be seen but they have, to their credit, already completed the first phase of a port expansion designed to lure the major players in the Alaskan market. The Northland

Cruise Ship Terminal opened in 2004 and can accommodate the largest ships. Like an adjacent smaller terminal that still handles explorer-type vessels, the terminal is conveniently located right on the edge of downtown.

The native heritage of Prince Rupert, which is perched on pretty Chatham Sound only about 40 miles south of the border with Alaska, is represented by the Tsimpsean and Haida cultures. Totem poles grace many of the city's parks, including **Roosevelt Park** (which has wonderful views of the sea) and the beautiful terraces of the **Sunken Gardens**. Prince Rupert emerged when a railroad was built leading to it and this era is chronicled inside the **Kwinitsa Railway Station**. The city's most important point of interest is the fine **Museum of Northern British Columbia**. Exhibits portray the native cultures, their meeting with Europeans and industries important in the development of Prince Rupert and the surrounding area.

Just outside the city at **Oliver Lake Provincial Park** you'll encounter pines that have been twisted into weird shapes by forces of nature. Going farther inland, **Trans-Canada Highway 16** between Prince Rupert and Terrace (one-way distance of just under 90 miles) is a highly scenic corridor through the mountains along the broad Skeena River. Several provincial parks are on the route. Areas along the Skeena are known for their great tidal variations which produce such phenomena as "reversing rapids" that are more frequently associated with many towns in Canada's Atlantic provinces.

> **Visitor Information:** Prince Rupert Visitor Information Center, 215 Cow Bay Road, Suite 100, Box 22063, Prince Rupert, BC, Canada V8J 3S1, ☎ (800) 667-1994, www.tourismprincerupert. com.

Valdez

It's too bad that more ships don't visit Valdez because it's in such a beautiful spot on the shores of Prince William Sound. Called "Little Switzerland" because of the ring of mountains and snow-capped peaks that surround it, the alpine environment is quite appealing. Many cruise ships visiting College Fjord and the Sound get awfully close, but they just don't spend the time in port. Valdez is known today as the southern terminus of the Alaska oil pipeline and the home of a vast terminal that loads the oil onto huge tankers. Unfortunately, due to security concerns, the fascinating pipeline terminal tours are no longer given. You can, however, view films about the terminal operations.

The town itself is rather drab as compared to its stunning surroundings. You can visit the **US Coast Guard's Vessel Traffic Center** and the **Valdez Museum & Historical Archive**, which has interesting pictures of Valdez before and after the devastating 1964 earthquake. (The current town actually lies a few miles from the abandoned original site.) It also has information on the *Exxon Valdez* oil spill.

The **Salmon Spawning View Point** over the Crooked Creek about a half-mile from town makes an interesting stop in July and August when the creek is crowded with salmon desperately attempting to make their way upstream. At times it's hard to see the water! Sadly, most of the salmon will die making the trip.

Most people who get to Valdez will spend their time outside of town in the gorgeous surroundings. There are a number of ways to do this. Rafting trips through **Keystone Canyon** are highly popular and include a visit to 900-foot **Bridal Veil Falls** and the smaller but no less beautiful **Horsetail Falls**. **Worthington Glacier**, reached by road, is one of Alaska's most accessible. This large retreating glacier is about 30 miles from Valdez. You can get very close to the base of the glacier.

A number of boat and air tours to some of the more scenic surrounding areas are also available from town.

Since you probably won't be calling on Valdez via ship, you should keep in mind that it is possible to get here by car from Anchorage. Take the Glenn Highway (State Highway 1) north to Glenallen and then the Richardson Highway (State Highway 4) south to Valdez. The total one-way distance is approximately 295 miles and all the roads are good. Another option is to take the ferry from Whittier. Either way makes for a nice trip of about three days, possibly more if you're adventurous enough to drive the rough and unpaved road that leads into the heart of the Wrangell-St. Elias National Park & Preserve.

> **Visitor Information:** Valdez Convention & Visitors Bureau, Box 1603, Valdez, AK 99686, ☎ (800) 770-5954, www.valdezalaska.org.

Victoria (British Columbia)

The provincial capital is located on Vancouver Island, the largest island on the Pacific Coast. The actual city of Vancouver is on the nearby mainland, which may be somewhat confusing to the geographically uninitiated. The city is filled with marvelous attractions but, since it's a relatively rare port of call, we review it only briefly in this book. Certainly, a day isn't enough time to see all that the area has to offer.

It has been said that Victoria offers more of an "old English" atmosphere than anyplace outside of England. This is reflected in the Victorian-era streetlights with hanging baskets that adorn major streets, and by the time-honored tradition of afternoon tea at the Fairmont Empress Hotel that faces the inner harbor. The hotel's ornate interior is worth a visit.

The many downtown attractions are all in a compact area and include the stately provincial **Parliament**, with its beautiful grounds and statue of Queen Victoria. You might get the chance to see the building gloriously illuminated at night as many cruise ships that do call on Victoria do so in the evening. Adjacent is the **Royal British Columbia Museum** with many exhibits on the human and natural history of the province, including life-like dioramas of wildlife and native villages. **The Undersea Gardens** are in a structure resembling a submarine that allows you to look through windows into the harbor and see a variety of colorful marine life. There are also feeding demonstrations.

Other in-town attractions include **Miniature World**, the **Royal London Wax Museum** and a number of historic homes and pretty parks and gardens. However, when it comes to gardens, the highlight of a trip to Victoria is 12 miles north in Brentwood, where the famous **Butchart Gardens** occupy the site of a former rock quarry. They have evolved into one of the most stunning gardens in the world, with dazzling colors and imaginative displays. The gardens are illuminated at night and sometimes there's evening entertainment and fireworks. **Victoria Butterfly Gardens** are adjacent to Butchart and the two make a great combination.

Shore excursions are limited in Victoria because, as mentioned, many visits are in the evening. But with so many things to see in town, they aren't really necessary. However, you may find excursions that explore the nearby interior of Vancouver Island, the largest island off the western coast of North America (not that you could see a large part of the island in a day-trip). It is approximately 286 miles from north to south and has an average width of more than 50 miles. The entire island is mountainous and heavily forested, with a rugged and highly indented coastline, especially on the more remote Pacific side. Its natural beauty has served as an incentive for other communities to try and lure some of the cruise ship traf-

fic. One such town is Campbell River, about halfway up the island from Victoria. Although they haven't gotten any
commitment from cruise lines as yet, don't be surprised to see
it as a future port of call.

Victoria and Vancouver Island are so fascinating that you
should consider visiting them even if your cruise ship doesn't.
The island can be reached by frequent car-carrying ferry service from Vancouver, or by fast passenger boat from Seattle. It
makes an ideal overnight trip or two-night getaway before or
after your cruise.

> **Visitor Information:** Tourism Victoria Infor-
> mation Centre, 812 Wharf Street, Victoria BC,
> Canada V8W 1T3, ☎ (250) 953-2033, www.
> tourism- victoria.com.

Wrangell

This fishing and lumbering town of about 2,500 hearty and
rather independent souls enjoys a pleasant setting on the scenic Zimovia Strait. The town is at the northern end of the island of the same name. A channel of the Inside Passage
separates it from the nearby mainland. The town has a strong
Russian influence dating back to its founding in 1834. Because
it isn't visited by many large ships (and few small ones),
Wrangell isn't commercialized and hasn't changed its ways to
accommodate visitors. That's a big part of its allure to those
who do venture here.

The major points of interest downtown are the chronicle of
the town's history at the **Wrangell Museum**, which was
built in 1906 and once served as a schoolhouse; and the four
totem poles in **Kiksadi Totem Park**. A little bit away from
the town center and reached by a small bridge is **Chief
Shakes Island**, where the Shakes Community House displays various items made by the local native Alaskan tribe.

There are even more totem poles here than at Kiksadi. This spot also provides an excellent view of the harbor. The island is named for a former chieftain whose grave is back across the bridge. Two totem poles depicting killer whales stand guard at the entrance to the grave site. Petroglyphs carved into the rocks by tribes can be seen at the island's northern end.

Other ways to pass the time in Wrangell include fishing expeditions and boat tours that navigate the narrow passages between the many offshore islands. Right now, the only major cruise line calling on Wrangell is Norwegian.

> **Visitor Information:** Wrangell Convention & Visitors Bureau, PO Box 1350, Wrangell, AK 99929, ☎ (800) 367-9745, www.wrangell.com. In town, a small visitor center is near the dock on Outer Drive.

Beyond the Cruise

Many Inside Passage cruise passengers will, no doubt, extend their trips by visiting their gateway city and surrounding area. Since these places aren't in Alaska, they are beyond the scope of this book except for the brief outlines provided in the information on ports of embarkation. On the other hand, a majority of passengers who take the Gulf of Alaska itinerary will combine it with some sightseeing in Anchorage and beyond. Denali National Park is one of the favorite destinations. You can do the land portion of your trip either before or after the cruise, depending upon your point of departure.

Just about every place described in this chapter can be seen as part of the cruise lines' formal cruise tour programs. All can also be done on your own via a variety of methods. The purpose of this chapter is to inform you about these places so that you can plan either an independent journey or choose a cruise tour that visits the spots you are most interested in seeing. The format for describing most of the important destinations beyond the cruise will be similar to that used in the previous chapter for ports of call, with some of the less important places receiving less attention.

The Best Way to Explore

Before I start to describe the myriad land attractions, I believe it is necessary to first devote considerably more attention to two important aspects of visiting the interior. These are the Alaska Railroad and cruise tour options.

The Alaska Railroad

The Alaska Railroad, ☎ (800) 544-0552, www.alaskarailroad.com (fares, schedules, etc.), operates 470 miles of mainline track between Seward and Fairbanks. Major stops along the way include Anchorage and Denali National Park. As you learned in the ports of embarkation section, the Alaska Railroad also provides service between Whittier and Anchorage. Cruise tours make big use of the Alaska Railroad and almost always have their own special cars so it's like a continuation of your cruise with some of your fellow passengers. Princess Cruises has an entire train (with locomotive) and simply uses the Alaska Railroad right of way on some trips. For individual travelers, the train is a good option. Although it doesn't have the flexibility of driving into the interior, it does save a lot of driving miles and allows you to relax while you soak up the scenery along the way. If you're doing the popular Anchorage-Denali-Fairbanks interior tour, then you can take the train up to Fairbanks and fly home from there. Although the airfare will be higher from Fairbanks, it can be mostly offset by the money you save by traveling just one way, and by the almost inevitable additional hotel night in Anchorage. Although cruise lines will make a big deal about the fact that their cars are specially designed observation cars with panoramic windows, don't think you can't enjoy the view just as well from the regular Alaska Railroad cars. So, if you think that the Alaska Railroad is right for you, it isn't a necessity to go the cruise tour route. Independent travelers make excellent use of the rails in Alaska.

Cruise Tour Itineraries

It wasn't that long ago when a couple of cruise lines first started offering Alaskan interior tours before or after a Gulf of

Alaska cruise. It used to be limited to the two biggest players in Alaska – Holland America and Princess – and although they still have the biggest tour operations, almost every major cruise line going to Alaska will offer at least some cruise tour packages. Just as the variety of lines and ships cruising to Alaska has increased dramatically, so too has the selection of cruise tours. Long gone are the days when an Alaskan cruise tour meant only an Alaska Railroad trip from Anchorage (or Seward) to Denali National Park and then on to Fairbanks for your flight home. Today, options are almost endless. Let's take a closer look.

Both Holland America and Princess offer more than two dozen cruise tour itineraries. Even after allowing for similarities in most of them, it's a big choice. Royal Caribbean has about 20 tours, while Carnival and Celebrity have fewer options. At press time, Norwegian was the only major line not offering cruise tours. This was because through 2004 it offered only Inside Passage cruises. No doubt this will change soon as NCL are scheduled to inaugurate their first Gulf of Alaska itineraries in 2005.

The land portion of a cruise tour generally ranges from three and eight nights, although Holland America does have a few options that are as long as 11 nights. However, it is most common for a cruise tour to last four or five nights. A typical cruise tour costs about $200 per person, per night, which is usually considerably higher than your nightly cruise fare. And the cruise tours are not all-inclusive, meaning you are on your own for meals. Read itineraries carefully to see exactly what is provided – rates customarily include all accommodations, transportation and sightseeing. Princess and Holland America generally arrange the land tours with overnights in locations where they have their own hotels (Princess Lodges or Westmark Hotels). Other cruise lines stay at places of comparable quality.

Beyond the Cruise

Using a combination of bus, train and air to get from one place to another, cruise tours can take you to many different destinations in Alaska and Canada's Yukon Territory. It is still most common for them to visit Anchorage, Denali National Park and Fairbanks, perhaps with one or two other stops along that route. It is common for one part of the trip to be via the Alaska Railroad from either Anchorage or Seward. Princess also has interior tours leaving directly from the port of Whittier on their own trains. These can actually bypass Anchorage altogether and can be a good option for those want to see the scenery of Alaska and aren't particularly interested in visiting the towns and cities. But not all Princess trains are their own. They offer trips on the *Midnight Sun Express*, which has their passenger cars attached to an Alaska Railroad locomotive. Holland America, Royal Caribbean and other lines have a similar setup, all with catchy names on their special rail cars, such as the *Wilderness Express* or *McKinley Explorer*. Which brings us to another point about train travel on cruise tours. All cruise lines transport their rail passengers in specially designed cars that maximize the view with large windows and glass domes. Admittedly, these are somewhat better than the plain vanilla cars on regular runs of the Alaska Railroad, but whether they're worth the extra price you'll be paying on a cruise tour is another matter. Prices vary by cruise line, but can be several hundred dollars more than booking independently.

Among the other destinations that you will be able to find in cruise tour packages are Seward and the wildlife-rich Kenai Fjords National Park; the fabulously beautiful Wrangell-St. Elias National Park; and some interior towns such as Eagle and Tok. You can also get into the Arctic region of Alaska. Possible tour stops on these itineraries can include Prudhoe Bay, Kotzebue and Nome (the latter two destinations always involve flying, while Prudhoe Bay usually requires flying in one direction). Another Arctic destination is the beautiful and remote Gates of the Arctic National Park & Preserve (with stops at the Anaktuvak Pass and overnight in one of the tiny communities of Coldfoot or Wiseman). You can even opt to take a tour that visits the Yukon Territory. Destinations here include Beaver City, Dawson City, Whitehorse and the Kluane National Park. Kluane borders on Alaska and is home to five of the seven highest mountain peaks in North America. (One is shared with Alaska's Wrangell-St. Elias and the other two are in Denali.) Some Yukon tours include a scenic day cruise on the Yukon River.

With one exception, the trips listed above are limited to cruises with a Gulf of Alaska itinerary since Anchorage, via the ports of Whittier and Seward, is the gateway to the interior. As such, these cruise tours can be done either before or after the cruise portion of your trip. So, does that mean that people who choose an Inside Passage cruises can't do an Alaskan land tour? Not entirely. First, one big exception. Holland America has several land tours that depart from Skagway and go through the Yukon into Alaska or start in Alaska and end in Skagway. The only problem with these packages is that the cruise portion of your trip is only a three- or four-night affair (depending upon the direction of the cruise) to or from Vancouver. I don't know about you, but short cruises, although highly enjoyable, always leave me wanting more. On the other hand, if you're more interested in seeing the interior and you have a limited amount of time and budget, this could be a way for you to get what you want and still have at least some cruising experience. More commonly, Inside Passage cruises offer land tours to the Canadian Rockies, rather than somewhere in Alaska. These four- to six-night tours cover the beautiful mountain scenery between Calgary, Alberta and Vancouver and typically visit several of the outstanding Canadian Rocky Mountain national parks, such as Banff, Jasper, Yoho and Kootenay. Although these can be entirely motorcoach tours, it is common for at least part of the trip to be by Canada's VIA rail. This may not be Alaska, but there is

Beyond the Cruise

no doubt that it does give you the chance to see some of the most breathtaking scenery in the world.

Destinations

Anchorage

With a population of about 270,000, Anchorage is home to almost 42% of all Alaskans! The city itself isn't what most people would expect from Alaska. Its downtown has a modern skyline and, for the most part, looks much like any American city of comparable size. It's the commercial, cultural and recreational capital of the state and has more people working in government than the capital city of Juneau.

As you've already learned, there's hardly a place in Alaska that doesn't have a scenic setting and Anchorage is no exception. At the head of the 220-mile Cook Inlet, Anchorage sits where the inlet splits into two arms, called the Knik and Turnagain. The latter was named by Captain James Cook when he reached the end and found that he could proceed no farther, forcing him to "turn again." The downtown area sits atop a bluff looking out on the Knik Arm and part of the Cook Inlet. Compared to most places in Alaska, Anchorage has a surprisingly mild climate. This is a result of the many tall mountains that ring the city and protect it from the wrath of Alaska's worst climatic conditions. Settlement began in 1915 when construction of the Alaska Railroad to then-larger Fairbanks began. It didn't take long for it to become Alaska's premier city. But Easter Sunday in 1964 saw one of the most powerful earthquakes in recorded history and it did extensive damage to downtown. However, the spirit of Anchorage's people wasn't daunted and they quickly repaired and rebuilt the city to ever-new heights.

Today, construction requirements are much more stringent and, hopefully, any future acts of Mother Nature will have less severe impact.

Arrival

Refer back to the information in the *Ports of Embarkation* section for details on transferring from the city and airport to the cruise ship or vice-versa.

Tourism Information Office

There are two excellent sources of information. The first is the **Anchorage Convention & Visitors Bureau**, 524 W. 4th Avenue, Anchorage, AK 99501. Its famous **Log Cabin Visitor Center** is the place to go once in town, ☎ (800) 478-1255, www.anchorage.net. Another good place (especially once you get to Anchorage) is the nearby **Alaska Public Lands Information Center** at 605 W. 4th Avenue, ☎ (907) 271-2737.

Getting Around

Anchorage, especially downtown, is a very easy city when it comes to finding your way around. Downtown is a neat grid pattern, with numbered avenues running east to west and lettered streets running north to south. There's a good city bus system called the "**People Mover**." Buses run weekdays from 6 am until 10 pm, with more limited service on weekends and holidays. Regular fares are $1.50 for adults (35¢ for seniors), but a $3 all-day pass is the cheapest way to travel. Passes are sold on the buses; exact fare is required. Most of the 17 routes originate at the People Mover Transit Center at 6th Avenue and G Street. Information on routes is available at the Transit Center or you can call ☎ (907) 343-6543. **Taxis** are not too expensive compared to many cities, with rates being $2 for the initial drop plus $2 per mile. It is not common practice to hail taxis on the street. Instead, call one of the major companies for pick-up: **Yellow Cab**, ☎ (907) 272-2422; **Anchorage Taxi Cab**, ☎ (907) 245-2207; or **Checker**, ☎ (907) 276-1234.

Although Anchorage is quite spread out, most of the important visitor attractions are clustered within walking distance of one another in the compact downtown area. For traveling to attractions in the outlying areas, there's no substitute for a car. As in any large city, Anchorage has parking and traffic problems but, for the most part, any congestion will seem quite manageable compared to that of most urban areas in the Lower 48, especially if you avoid downtown during weekday rush hours.

One-Day Sightseeing Tour

The most logical place to begin your tour of Anchorage is at 4th Avenue and F Street, at the **Log Cabin Visitor Center**. The cabin itself is an odd but pretty sight, sitting as it does in the middle of a modern city. In summer it's bedecked with hanging flower baskets and the surrounding grounds are picturesque. Anchorage calls itself the "Crossroads of the World" and outside the cabin is a wooden signpost showing the direction and air mileage to places all around the globe. It's a noted picture-taking spot. On the side of the building, directly across F Street from the Visitor Center, is a mural of Alaskan scenes. You've already discovered in other ports that murals are common in Alaska, but nowhere will you find more in quantity, variety and size than in Anchorage. Some of the other better murals that are close by include one in the State Historical Museum at 4th and F Streets (an impressive 160 feet long); another depicting the route of the Iditarod Dog Sled Race is at 4th and D Street; and murals in the form of wool tapestries showing scenes of Alaskan history are in the National Bank of Alaska Building at 4th and E Street. Across from the Log Cabin is the Alaska Public Lands Information Center. In the former Federal Building, the center has, besides useful visitor information, interesting exhibits on the geology and wildlife of lands owned by the federal and state governments. This represents a sizable portion of the state and includes almost all of the most scenic areas. *Open daily, 9 am to 5 pm.* Speaking of the famous Iditarod race, you should check out the starting point at 4th Avenue and D Street. A large bronze sculpture of a sled dog graces the area. The turreted building on the corner is unique in Alaska.

Walk north on E Street until 3rd and turn right, proceeding one more block where you will find the **Earthquake Buttress Area**. During the 1964 earthquake a large chunk of the bluff gave way at this point, dropping more than 20 feet. It has been filled with gravel to stabilize the area. At 2nd and E is the **Alaska State Monument**, which features a bust of Dwight Eisenhower, President of the United States at the time of Alaska's admission into the Union. From here it's a short walk to C Street where a left turn soon bears into the Port Access Road. Just across the bridge is the **Ship Creek Viewpoint**, a busy salmon spawning area in mid- to late summer. Just beneath the bluff you can see the **Alaska Railroad Depot**. If you're heading to the interior of Alaska via the Alaska Railroad you don't have to make a special trip to see it now, but if you're going to be journeying by car or not going beyond Anchorage, then consider taking a short detour now in order to explore the very ornate interior of this historic structure. On the grounds outside is an actual locomotive used to build the Panama Canal before it arrived in Alaska to begin freight service operations.

Anchorage has a number of unique sculptures dispersed throughout downtown. The first of these is the **Last Blue Whale Statue** on L Street between 3rd and 4th. This somewhat abstract work is sculpted in fiberglass and rises above the second story of the building behind it. At the western end of 3rd Avenue is **Resolution Park** and its **Captain Cook Monument**. The park is a pleasant place to view the Cook In-

227

let and mountains beyond ,as well as a nice spot to take a rest from your walking tour amid benches and flowers.

Head right for one block on 5th Avenue until you reach M Street. Turn right at this junction. The **Oscar Anderson House Museum**, 420 M Street, ☎ (907) 274-2336, built in 1915, was home to one of Anchorage's early residents and businessmen. The Anderson family figured prominently in the commercial development of the city. The house has been refurbished and is furnished in period style. A number of other historic homes are concentrated in this part of town; you can pick up information about them at the Anderson House. *Open weekdays, noon to 5 pm, $.* You are now at the walking tour's farthest point from the center of downtown, so let's head back toward the center. On K Street between 4th and 5th is the **Three Ships Sculpture**, which depicts the voyage of discovery led by Captain Cook. **The Imaginarium**, 737 W. 5th Avenue at G Street, ☎ (907) 276-3179, is a hands-on science discovery center that is interesting for all ages, but especially for children. *Open Mon-Sat, 10 am to 6 pm, Sun, noon to 5 pm), $$.*

At the corner of 6th and C Street is the fascinating **Wolf Song of Alaska**, ☎ (907) 274-9653. The large exhibit will bring you into a face-to-face encounter with wild Alaskan wolves. Although the museum traces many myths and legends associated with wolves, the emphasis is on the history of the animal and its surprising relationship with humans. A worthwhile and surprisingly entertaining and educational stop for both adults and children. *Open weekdays, 11 am to 6 pm; Saturday, 10 am to 5 pm; Sunday, noon until 5 pm; $.*

> NOTE: *Wolf Song has plans to develop an approximately 200-acre wolf observation facility somewhere within a 75-mile radius of Anchorage. Your donations at Wolf Song of Alaska will help this become a reality.*

Anchorage

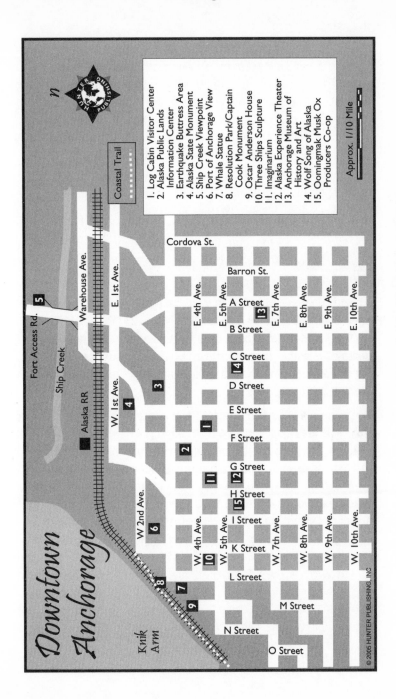

Downtown Anchorage

Knik Arm

Coastal Trail

1. Log Cabin Visitor Center
2. Alaska Public Lands Information Center
3. Earthquake Buttress Area
4. Alaska State Monument
5. Ship Creek Viewpoint
6. Port of Anchorage View
7. Whale Statue
8. Resolution Park/Captain Cook Monument
9. Oscar Anderson House
10. Three Ships Sculpture
11. Imaginarium
12. Alaska Experience Theater
13. Anchorage Museum of History and Art
14. Wolf Song of Alaska
15. Oomingmak Musk Ox Producers Co-op

Approx. 1/10 Mile

Fort Access Rd.
Ship Creek
Warehouse Ave.
Alaska RR
Cordova St.
Barron St.
A Street
B Street
C Street
D Street
E Street
F Street
G Street
H Street
I Street
K Street
L Street
M Street
N Street
O Street

E. 1st Ave.
E. 4th Ave.
E. 5th Ave.
E. 7th Ave.
E. 8th Ave.
E. 9th Ave.
E. 10th Ave.

W. 1st Ave.
W. 2nd Ave.
W. 4th Ave.
W. 5th Ave.
W. 7th Ave.
W. 8th Ave.
W. 9th Ave.
W. 10th Ave.

© 2005 HUNTER PUBLISHING, INC

A few blocks away at 621 W. 6th at F Street is the **Alaska Center for the Performing Arts**, ☎ (907) 242-4291, with two different IMAX films being shown daily. The films feature the natural scenery and wildlife of the state and are always technically excellent and visually stunning. Call for schedules and ticket information. Another possibility for IMAX lovers is the **Alaska Experience Theater**,705 W. 6th at G Street, ☎ (907) 276-3730. The film here, called *Alaska, the Great Land*, is similar to those shown at the arts center. The Alaska Experience also has an interesting exhibit on the great Alaskan Earthquake. *Open daily, 9 am to 9 pm, $$$ for combined movie and exhibit or $$ for each.* It doesn't make much sense to visit both of these attractions unless you're really into this sort of thing.

Go to 7th Avenue and head east until you reach the **Anchorage Museum of History & Art**, 121 W. 7th Avenue, ☎ (907) 343-4326. This a very large facility covering many aspects of Alaskan history and the native cultures of the state. Big dioramas in the Alaska Gallery are of special interest. *Open daily, 9 am to 6 pm, $$.*

The time is takes to complete the preceding portion of your tour will vary based on your walking pace and how long you spend at the two major museums (Imaginarium and Museum of History & Art). The minimum time, including one IMAX film, should be approximately four hours, but it could be as much as six. That means you should still have a couple of hours to take in one of the most interesting attractions in Anchorage. The **Alaska Native Heritage Center**, 8800 Heritage Center Drive, ☎ (800) 315-6608, is about 3½ miles from downtown via the Glenn Highway (go to the Muldoon Road exit, then head north to Heritage Drive). You can get there by bus, but a taxi is the easiest way if you don't have your own set of wheels. The center covers almost 30 acres of wooded grounds and it does an excellent job of informing visitors about Alaska's various native cultures. Authentic tribal homes represent five different native "villages" built around a pond and tribe members conduct daily activities. There is also a program of entertainment with visitors being encouraged to participate. The admission price is rather high, but it is worth it, especially if you have children. The educational experience will be one they remember for a long time. *Open daily, 9 am to 6 pm, $$$$.*

Trolley & Coach Tours

If you have a very limited amount of time in Anchorage and no car, then you should consider taking one of the various one- to three-hour tours offered by **Anchorage Trolley Tours**, ☎ (907) 276-5603, and **Gray Line of Alaska**, ☎ (800) 478-6388. Information on these and other tours is available at the Log Cabin Visitor Center.

Additional Sights for Longer Stays

Since so many people who wind up or begin their cruise in Anchorage will be exploring other parts of Alaska, it's possible that you may want to devote more than a day to seeing the city. Or, you may simply find some of the places in the suggested tour not to be of interest. Either way, here are some additional places to consider.

Alaska Aviation Heritage Museum, 4721 Aircraft Drive, ☎ (907) 248-5325. Located near the airport on the south shore of Lake Hood, the museum has almost 30 vintage aircraft, most of which were in service in Alaska during the 1930s and are quite rare. The museum helps explain the relationship of aircraft to the development of Alaska, something that is of more importance here than in most places. Visitors can also see restoration work in process. *Open daily except Tuesday, 10 am to 6 pm, $$.*

Beyond the Cruise

Alaska Zoo, 10 miles south of downtown via Seward Highway (State Highway 1) and then east on O'Malley Road. This isn't one of the world's great zoos, but it isn't shabby either and is of special interest because of its emphasis on Arctic and Alaskan animals, including Siberian tigers, snow leopards, bears and yaks. You'll want to spend a couple of hours here if you have small children. *Open daily, 9 am to 6 pm, $$$.*

Chugach State Park covers a broad swath of land on Anchorage's eastern edge and is a good place to do some nearby scenic touring close to the city. It is reachable from the south side via the Seward Highway and from the north side by the Glenn Highway. **Eagle River Nature Center** within the park (take Eagle River Road from the Glenn Highway) is an easily accessible spot with nice hiking opportunities and wildlife viewing. Nearby is a one-mile walk through a deep canyon to Thunderbird Falls. Depending on your interests and level of activity, a visit to Chugach can be for an hour or two or a whole day. An extensive system of trails leads into the park's interior, including access to many of its 50 glaciers. For further information on the park contact the Alaska Department of Natural Resources at ☎ (907) 269-8400. Option 1 will give you recorded information on the park. Or you can access their website at www.dnr.state.ak.us/parks/units/chugach.

Earthquake Park, west of downtown at the end of Northern Lights Blvd, provides good views of Cook Inlet and downtown, backed by the beautiful Chugach Mountains. For those of you who love long walks, the Tony Knowles Coastal Trail runs through the park and extends all the way to downtown.

Elmendorf Air Force Base no longer gives regular tours because of security concerns, but they still usually have an open house with air shows and other events. It is generally held at the end of June. There's also a small wildlife museum that's open regardless of whether any public events are scheduled. Call ☎ (907) 552-7469 for information.

H2Oasis Water Park, 11030 Chelea Street, ☎ (800) 426-2747, is Alaska's only water recreation park. It's a good facility if you like this sort of thing. No doubt it will be a welcome stop if you have little ones in tow.

Finally, if you aren't taking a cruise tour and are not planning a long interior trip on your own but want to see some of the state's greatest scenery, you can make Anchorage your base and see the sights via a series of day-trips. These include day cruises, bus tours, helicopter tours and flightseeing. Operators include the cost of transportation from Anchorage to the departure point when it is outside the city, and prices can range from $30 to more than $250, depending on the length of the tour and the mode of travel (air tours are, of course, the most expensive). A complete list of operators and itinerary information is available at the Log Cabin Visitor Center.

Shopping

As Alaska's largest city, Anchorage is also the place where you'll find the greatest variety of shops. Downtown contains a number of large modern malls and there are even more scattered throughout the city. However, if you came to Alaska to shop, chances are you'll be looking for handicrafts. Among the best places in Anchorage to buy native crafts are the **Taheta Art & Culture Co-op**, 5th and A and the **Oomingmak Musk Ox Producers Co-op**, 604 H Street, ☎ (907) 272-9225. The former has a wide variety of handicrafts and makes an interesting place to visit, while the latter features scarves and other items of qiviut for sale at good prices. A free exhibit will familiarize you with how qiviut is made from Arctic musk ox wool. The wool is eight times warmer than sheep's wool, even though it is the same weight, and is soft that you absolutely have to touch it. Although fur garments are a controversial item these days, there are still many people who like them. If you are interested, then head for the **Alaska Fur Exchange**, Old Seward Highway and Tudor Road, which also has a large selection of native-made arts and crafts. Be aware that many people in Alaska (and that probably includes a majority of native Alaskans) don't mind the use of fur for coats and other luxury items. So, if you're against fur, don't make a big show of it when in Alaska. A wide selection of authentic carvings, jewelry and other items is available at **Alaska Unique**, 3601 Minnesota Drive.

If you're looking for a gift package of Alaskan seafood to send to someone back home, check out **10th & M Seafoods**, with the main store at 1020 M Street and a branch at 301 Muldoon Road. **Grizzly Junction**, 5225 Juneau Street, has a great selection of wild berry jams and other products. They also have free factory tours and some exhibits.

I don't usually feel a great need to recommend places for more mundane mall shopping, but since you don't find these Meccas of retail commerce in small Alaskan towns, you might need a shopping fix by the time you get to Anchorage. The **5th Avenue Mall** (intersection of A Street) or the less centrally located **Diamond Center** (Diamond Boulevard and Old Seward Highway) are the biggest. The former has Nordstrom's among its department stores. More unusual is the **Saturday Market**, 3rd & E, where you can purchase native crafts and foods from May through September, but only on Saturday.

For art galleries try **Artique**, 314 G Street, or the **Decker-Morris Gallery**, 621 W. 6th. Both of these focus on Alaskan artists, although not necessarily native Alaskans. **The Downtown Alaska Glass Gallery**, 423 G Street, has high quality works. Places featuring arts and crafts of the local native groups are scattered around downtown and include **Arctic Rose Galleries**, 420 L Street. However, I prefer **One People** or **Tundra Arts**, both at 425 D Street. Of course, the **Alaska Native Heritage Center, Oomingman** and **10th & M Seafoods**, all mentioned in the sightseeing section, are also great places for native arts. Surprisingly, the very best of all might be the Auxiliary Craft Shops inside the **Alaska Native Medical Center**, off Tudor Road at 4135 Diplomacy Drive (west of downtown and south of the Alaska Pacific University campus). Besides having a great selection of goods at reasonable prices, the shop boasts a first-rate exhibit of native Alaskan arts and crafts. If you're looking for Russian crafts, pop into **Lanette's Fine Art & Russian Crafts**, 345 E Street, or the **Russian Gift Shop "Alesksandr Baranof"** at 321 W. 5th Avenue. Finally, if you want an authentic, locally produced knife known as an ulu (great for cooks), then head on over to the **Ulu Factory**, 211 W. Ship Creek Avenue.

Sports & Recreation

Walkers, hikers and **cyclists** will love the extensive (covering 120 miles) system of trails in this area that includes the popular Tony Knowles Coastal Trail, a paved and easy 11-mile route. This trail is probably the best place for visitors to get some exercise, whether by foot or by bike. You can rent a bike at **Downtown Bicycle Rentals** at 245 W. 5th Avenue. The Coastal Trail ends at Kincaid Park, where you'll find another trail system, this one covering more than 40 miles. The park is situated at the point where Turnagain Arm meets Cook Inlet. In the southeastern part of Anchorage is **Flattop Mountain**, a great place for people to try out a simple mountain climb. The 3,500-foot summit affords stunning vistas on a clear day.

Kayaking isn't as popular here as it is in the Southeast, but there are good opportunities for the sport on the many lakes and lagoons throughout the metropolitan area. Contact **Alaska Sea Kayakers/Alaska Outdoor Adventures**, ☎ (877) 472-2534. **Fishing**, too, is a possibility in area lakes such as Jewel, University and Eklutna. You can also fish in the Ship Creek if you don't want to venture far from town. For **rafting** you'll have to go a little farther afield. The nearest rafting experiences are in Girdwood, off the road that leads to Whittier or the Kenai Peninsula.

Beyond the Cruise

Anchorage has a few golf courses. Two nine-hole courses are the municipally run (and, therefore, less expensive) Russian Jack Springs and the private Tanglewood Lakes Golf Club. The latter is south of the city. The 18-hole course of choice is the Anchorage Golf Course at 3651 O'Malley Road.

South from Anchorage to the Kenai Peninsula

For those who wish to do a little touring on their own after finishing Anchorage, the nearby Kenai (pronounced KEEN-eye) Peninsula makes a great destination. If you do all of the towns and other sights in the suggested agenda it will take a minimum of three days and probably four. Depending on how many boat tours, flightseeing trips and other special trips you make, it could be considerably longer. Also consider basing yourself in Anchorage and doing a series of day-trips; some of the sights are quite close to the city.

Tourism Information Offices

For information on destinations including Homer, Kenai, Seldovia, Seward and Soldotna, among others, contact the **Kenai Peninsula Visitors Bureau** at ☎ (800) 535-3624, www.kenaipeninsula.org. Other places that can offer valuable services include:

Kenai Fjords National Park, Superintendent KFNP, PO Box 1727, Seward, AK 99664, ☎ (907) 224-3175, www. nps.gov/kefj.

Kenai Convention & Visitors Bureau (town info), 11471 Kenai Spur Highway, Kenai, AK 99611, www.visitkenai.com.

Seward Chamber of Commerce & Visitors Bureau, PO Box 749, Seward, AK 99664, ☎ (907) 224-3046, www. sewardak.org.

Soldotna Chamber of Commerce & Visitor Information Center, 44790 Sterling Highway, Soldotna, AK 99669, www. soldatnachamber.com.

Getting Around

Although the Alaska Railroad travels between Anchorage and Seward and there is some local bus service, a car is the only way to adequately explore the Kenai Peninsula. There are various tour operators in Anchorage who will take you to different points of interest on the peninsula, but none has a comprehensive tour, and doing it through a number of tours will become a very expensive proposition. Via car from Anchorage, the main route is the Seward Highway, Alaska State Highway 1. The road eventually splits, with the Seward Highway becoming Alaska State Highway 9 for its final leg into Seward. Alaska Highway 1 itself continues as the Sterling Highway and visits a number of communities before ending in Homer. Some back-tracking is necessary because there is no direct road connection between Seward and Homer. The mileage chart below will give you a better picture of what's involved. All of the roads are good.

KENAI PENINSULA MILEAGE CHART						
	Anchorage	Kenai	Homer	Seward	Soldotna	Whittier
Anchorage		157	221	128	146	53
Kenai	157		86	11	11	112
Homer	221	86		75	75	176
Seward	128	103	167		92	83
Soldotna	136	11	75	92		101
Whittier	53	112	176	83	101	

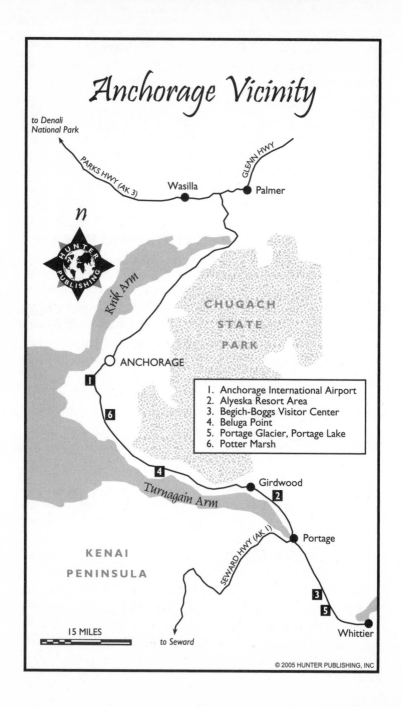

Anchorage Vicinity

to Denali
National Park

PARKS HWY (AK 3)

GLENN HWY

Wasilla   Palmer

n

HUNTER PUBLISHING

Knik Arm

CHUGACH

STATE

PARK

ANCHORAGE

1. Anchorage International Airport
2. Alyeska Resort Area
3. Begich-Boggs Visitor Center
4. Beluga Point
5. Portage Glacier, Portage Lake
6. Potter Marsh

1

6

4

Turnagain Arm

Girdwood

2

SEWARD HWY (AK 1)

Portage

KENAI

PENINSULA

3

5

15 MILES

to Seward

Whittier

© 2005 HUNTER PUBLISHING, INC

Touring

When it comes to natural beauty near Anchorage, the majority of the best sights are south of the city, either on the Kenai Peninsula or to the southeast in the Chugach Mountains (and national forest of the same name). The Seward Highway has been designated as a National Scenic Byway because of the remarkable panorama it affords from end to end. The initial part of the route from Anchorage parallels the Alaska Railroad along Turnagain Arm. This excellent road is sometimes down at the water level, but frequently climbs the lower slopes of the mountains that hug the coast. A number of attractions can be found by traveling just a short distance off the main road, and the highway itself is certainly a primary attraction. Between Anchorage and Portage Glacier it contains more than 30 scenic pullouts, some of which have trails that lead up into the mountains for even more dramatic views. However, you should be aware that most of the paths are steep and strenuous. Details on trails can be obtained from the Supervisor of the Chugach State Park.

A few miles south of Anchorage is the first major point of interest, Anchorage Coastal Wildlife Refuge, more commonly known as **Potter Marsh Waterfowl Refuge**. It's right off the highway on a broad coastal marsh set in front of picturesque mountains. A long boardwalk traverses the entire area, giving visitors an opportunity to view almost a hundred different bird species as well as salmon and other fish in the shallow waterways of the marsh.

Soon after the refuge begins one of the most scenic sections of the Seward Highway where the pullouts follow one after the other. Among the best of these is **Beluga Point**, where white beluga whales are commonly spotted during the summer months. Tidal bores often occur here; consult Anchorage newspapers for tide times. **Windy Point** and **Falls Creek** also provide great views of mountains and sea, but are best

Beyond the Cruise

known as places where you're likely to see Dall sheep clinging to the lower slopes. Stop to get a closer look, but don't approach these horned animals – they're wild and might be frightened into charging you in self-defense.

A little beyond the small town of Girdwood is a short cutoff road leading to the year-round **Alyeska Resort**, one of the most elaborate hotel and resort complexes in the state. During the summer you can take a tramway to 2,300 feet for an unforgettable view of Turnagain Arm surrounded by lofty peaks. There are other activities at Alyeska, including carriage rides and hiking trails. Fees are charged for all visitor facilities. Gold panning is popular in the nearby Crow Creek Mine. Alyeska is only 2½ miles off of Highway 1 and a total distance of just 40 miles from the city.

Back on the main road is another well-placed pullout, this one for the **Explorer Glacier Viewpoint**. Continuing along Seward Highway you'll soon reach another side road, this one extending for five miles to what has become Alaska's most heavily visited attraction, **Portage Glacier Recreation Area**. This outstanding scenic attraction quickly fills a few hours of your time. The highlight is Portage Glacier itself, a five-mile-long and mile-wide ice floe so close to you that it's called a "drive-in" glacier. It sits on Portage Lake and can be viewed from along a lakeside walkway or by taking a boat ride on the MV *Ptarmigan*, ☎ (907) 277-5581, *departures daily at 10:30 am, noon, 1:30, 3 and 4 pm, $$$$*. Also not to be missed is the **Begigh-Boggs Visitor Center**, ☎ (907) 783-2326, which describes in detail the history of Portage Glacier and the surrounding area. A walk-through model of a glacier is inside the building and there are both inside and outside observation areas. *$ for film presentation only*. Other parts of the recreation area have lovely waterfalls cascading down sheer mountain slopes and there are several hiking trails of varying lengths and difficulty. One of the easiest trails is the one-mile route to the base of Byron Glacier, a hanging-type glacier (as opposed to Portage, which is a tidewater glacier).

> NOTE: *If you don't want to rent a car, various boat and combination land/sea tours of the Portage Glacier area are available. Make inquiry at the Log Cabin Visitor Center and review brochures from several different tour operators.*

Shortly after Portage Glacier comes the junction for the road to Whittier. Until 2000 the only way to get to Whittier on land was by train. Then they decided to put a one-lane road through the tunnel that connects to Whittier. So, you can now drive through the tunnel (the toll is $12), but if you take this detour expect delays because of the one-way nature of the road. You can skip Whittier on this excursion if your ship arrived at the Whittier port because there isn't really much to see in the town. The setting of Whittier, which has fewer than 2,000 residents, is the best part. If your ship came into Seward you might then consider a side-trip to Whittier. The town is a good place to take a half- or full-day boat tour on Prince William Sound. However, ask what you're going to see as much of this will duplicate what you might have seen or will see from your cruise ship.

Seward

Continue south on the Seward Highway (now Alaska Highway 9). Like many Alaskan communities, there isn't that much to see in Seward itself, but the town serves as a gateway to areas of extraordinary beauty and havens for wildlife. Seward was established fairly early, in 1902, because of its year-round ice-free waters. It was determined that the site would be a good place for the beginning of the Alaska Railroad, a status that it still holds today. Located on Resurrection Bay, Seward is home to about 3,000 people. Mount Marathon provides a 3,000-foot backdrop to the town; you can climb to the top without too much difficulty. In fact, a yearly marathon race begins and ends at the summit.

Getting Around

You can easily navigate most of the sights in Seward on foot. However, if you want to save some shoe leather or explore some of the points of interest to the north of downtown, then the **Seward Trolley** is a convenient way to get around. It operates every day during the cruise season from 10 am until 7 pm. Fares are inexpensive, but purchase an all-day pass if you plan to use the trolley more than a couple of times.

Sightseeing

Those taking a walking tour of the small downtown area should begin at the **Visitor Information Center**, housed in an old Alaska Railroad car at 2nd Avenue and Madison Street. Two blocks southwest at 336 3rd Avenue (corner of Jefferson Street) is the **Seward Historical Society Museum**, ☎ (907) 224-3902, which contains exhibits on local history and has a small collection of native crafts. *Open daily, 9 am to 5 pm, $.*

Clearly, Seward's major attraction is the excellent **Alaska Sealife Center**, ☎ (800) 224-2525, at the very beginning (or end, depending on how you look at it) of the Seward Highway at Milepost 0. The 115,000-square-foot marine science center re-creates the natural habitats of native species, including sea lions and puffins. Many exhibits are dedicated to the preservation of the environment. Guided tours that give you a look behind the scenes are available. Allow a minimum of 90 minutes (without the guided tour) to see everything the center has to offer. *Open daily, 8 am to 8 pm, $$$, additional $$ for guided tours.*

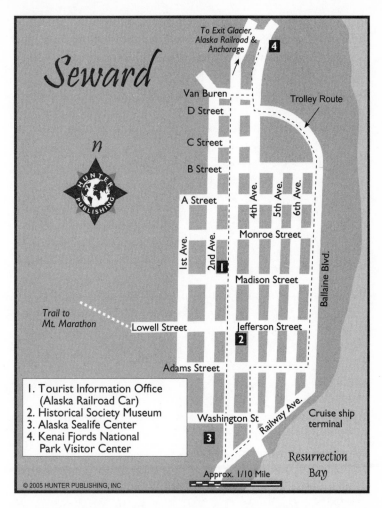

Seward

To Exit Glacier,
Alaska Railroad &
Anchorage

4

Van Buren
D Street

Trolley Route

C Street

B Street

4th Ave.
5th Ave.
6th Ave.

A Street

1st Ave.
2nd Ave.

Monroe Street

1

Madison Street

Ballaine Blvd.

Trail to
Mt. Marathon

Lowell Street

Jefferson Street

2

Adams Street

1. Tourist Information Office
   (Alaska Railroad Car)
2. Historical Society Museum
3. Alaska Sealife Center
4. Kenai Fjords National
   Park Visitor Center

Washington St

Railway Ave.

Cruise ship
terminal

3

Resurrection
Bay

Approx. 1/10 Mile

© 2005 HUNTER PUBLISHING, INC

Beyond the Cruise

The main sights in the surrounding area are all connected with magnificent **Kenai Fjords National Park**. The largest section of the park stretches along the coast south of Seward. As there are no roads into this part (and the best scenery is along the coast), the way to see it is via a boat tour. These tours last anywhere from four to eight hours and explore the coast and some of the many inlets in Kenai Fjords. Views of some of the eight glaciers leading off the vast Harding Icefield are common and you'll also see a wide variety of the marine wildlife that is so abundant in this area. Much of the wildlife is seen on and around the small offshore islands that comprise the Alaska Maritime National Wildlife Refuge. The Chiswell Islands, in particular, are teeming with sea lions. It seems as if they're just waiting for you to come by and look at them. Whales are also frequently spotted. You can opt to flightsee over the fjords. While this method doesn't give you close-ups of the beautiful coastline or wildlife, it does take you over the 700-square-mile Harding Icefield. Either way (or both) makes a wonderful excursion. Among the many tour operators are **Kenai Coastal Tours**, ☎ (800) 770-9119; **Renown Charters & Tours**, ☎ (800) 655-3806; **Major Marine Tours**, ☎ (800) 764-7300; **Scenic Mountain Air**, ☎ (907) 288-3646; and **Kenai Fjords Tours**, ☎ (877) 258-6877. The latter is part of the larger Alaska Heritage Tours organization that operates Prince William Sound Cruises and also has hotels in Seward and Talkeetna, so that they can offer complete packages. Most boat operators have several options regarding the length. Sea tours cost from $35 to $125, while flightseeing excursions can range up to about $225, depending on the itinerary. Reservations are suggested for all tours.

A few miles north of town is **Exit Glacier**, the only part of Kenai Fjords National Park that can be reached by road. From the parking area it is a nice easy stroll over paved paths to the very foot of the glacier. Of all the glaciers you can visit in Alaska, this is very likely the one you'll get closest to. Depending on conditions, the Park Rangers might allow you to get within several feet of the glacier's face. Numerous waterfalls on the side of the glacier make it a very picturesque scene. A hiking trail leads to excellent viewing points above the glacier.

> NOTE: *Exit Glacier is more than 60,000 years old. Although it may retreat as much as two feet a day during the summer, it's been advancing*

for the most part since the early 1990s, sometimes at an average rate of up to 70 feet per year.

If you can spare 90 minutes, here's something that is fun, exciting and very Alaskan! **Ididaride Summer Sled Dog Tours**, Old Exit Glacier Road, ☎ (800) 478-3139, will take you on a two-mile journey through Box Canyon on a wheeled sled pulled by a dog team. You also get to tour the dog kennel, play with the husky puppies and see a training demonstration. The sled ride is captained by an experienced rider from the famed Iditarod Sled Race. Notice the play on the name: I Did A Ride. Get it? *Open daily, 9 am to 7 pm, $$$$.* For those who prefer more of the real thing (that is, a sled ride on snow and ice), **Goodwin Glacier Dog Sled Tours**, ☎ (888) 989-8239, at Seward Airport on the Seward Highway, will fly you by helicopter onto the nearby Goodwin Glacier where you'll take a 2½-mile sled trip. Wildlife is almost always seen during the flight. Glacier hikes and other sightseeing options are also available. *Operates daily except Sunday, 8 am to 6 pm. Single adult fare, $360; family of four, $1,200.* The complete adventure takes about two hours.

Soldotna & Kenai

After visiting Seward you'll have to reverse your route by driving back north on the Seward Highway to the junction of Highway 1. Take Highway 1 (the Sterling Highway) southbound until the town of Soldotna. This small community is the headquarters for the two million-acre **Kenai National Wildlife Refuge**, known for its populations of Dall sheep, bears and eagles, but especially its large numbers of moose. The Visitor Center is on Ski Hill Road, ☎ (907) 262-7021. Many recreational tours from easy to adventurous can be booked in Soldotna.

Off the main road from Soldotna via the Kenai Spur Road is the town of Kenai, an 18th-century Russian settlement that still has a Russian Orthodox Church. The town's visitor center on the Kenai Spur Highway can put you in touch with trip outfitters of all kinds and also give you information on picking berries, a popular activity in summertime. **The Kenai Visitors & Cultural Center**, 11471 Kenai Spur Highway, ☎ (907) 283-1991, has a collection of native art, Russian artifacts and several good exhibits on the area's abundant wildlife. *Open weekdays, 9 am to 8 pm, and weekends, 11 am to 7 pm, $.*

After getting back to Soldotna, continue south on the Sterling Highway until you reach the end of the line in Homer. The sights of Homer are described on page 209.

The Interior

Heading to Denali National Park

Before getting started on seeing the interior, I'll briefly address the two main methods for visiting these vast regions of Alaska – by guided tour and on your own. Guided tours can most easily be arranged as a continuation of your cruise with a complete cruise tour as was explained earlier. You can also arrange land tours separately, which will probably wind up being less expensive than a cruise tour but will lack the continuity between the two portions of your trip. Most guided tours use a combination of motor coach and the Alaska Railroad, although air travel is sometimes incorporated. If this part of your vacation is arranged by the cruise lines, you get to stay in special domed train cars that offer a better view of the scenery. Although this section will address seeing the interior as if you are doing it on your own, it can be used to help you select the cruise tour that most matches your interests. This is because the variety of cruise tours, which was once limited primarily to Denali National Park and Fairbanks, is now so great that you have to make a decision as to what you want to see.

If you're going to be driving, car rentals are available throughout Alaska and are especially easy to find in Anchorage. You can bring the car back there, although one-way rentals to Fairbanks are also common. The one-way distance from Anchorage to Denali National Park is 240 miles and it's another 125 miles if you continue to Fairbanks. All of this is via Alaska State Highway 3, a well-paved and maintained road that won't present any special driving problems during the summer. The road is also known as the George Parks Highway. Many people find it more fun to take the Alaska Railroad one way and drive the other. This may be especially good advice if you have small children who might find it less necessary to say "are we there yet?" on a train than they would cramped up in a car!

Should you decide to take the Alaska Railroad for all or part of your journey, it is wise to have advance reservations. Call them at ☎ (800) 544-0552 or book online at www. alaskarailroad.com. Their ticket office and Anchorage depot is at 411 West 1st Avenue, ☎ (907) 458-6025.

The area between Anchorage and Denali National Park is sparsely populated. But there are a few towns and you're never that far from civilization, so finding a place to have lunch or fill the car up with gas doesn't present a problem. Although some of the larger towns may have a motel or two, standards are generally a bit below those found in other parts of Alaska and elsewhere in the United States. Simplicity is the rule of thumb. As the drive to Denali takes less than one day (even with a few sightseeing stops), you should plan on staying overnight in or near the park itself. For the most part it's a very pleasant and scenic ride.

Beyond the Cruise

Among the towns you'll be passing through or near to are **Wasilla**, **Willow** and **Talkeetna**. Wasilla and Talkeetna each have a museum focusing on the local history and a collection of native artifacts. Wasilla's **Museum of Alaska Transportation & Industry**, Milepost 47, ☎ (907) 376-1211, is one of the more interesting possible stops along the way. *Open daily, 10 am to 6 pm, $$.* In the vicinity of Wasilla (and most other towns along the route) there are state parks or wilderness areas with opportunities for hiking. Most trails, however, are primitive or difficult and are generally a few miles off the main road. Many travelers who are simply extending their cruise will not have time for this type of exploration. If you do, the towns all have visitor information centers that will be glad to give you advice and directions on these out-of-the-way places.

A few miles north of Wasilla is the town of Willow. While there isn't anything of great appeal in town, you might be interested in knowing that Willow gained some notoriety back in the 1970s when it was selected to be the site of a new state capital to replace Juneau. Many people, both then and now, felt that the capital should be more centrally located within the state and closer to the population center of Anchorage. The issue resurfaces from time to time, but it doesn't look as if Willow is ever going to become home to the state house.

Talkeetna is 14 miles off the George Parks Highway via a good side road beginning at Milepost 98.7. A mining community established just after the turn of the 20th century, Talkeetna maintains the same atmosphere today – mainly dirt roads through a town of some 400 log cabins. The **Talkeetna Historical Society Museum** is housed in four old buildings, including a school. It's just out of town; follow the signs. You can get a map here that will guide you on a walking tour through the town's historic buildings, many of which have been restored. The **Museum of Northern Adventure**, on Main Street, ☎ (907) 733-3999, features taxidermy specimens of big game among its other interesting exhibits. *Open daily, 10 am to 6 pm, $.* Talkeetna is also a base for numerous air tour operators that fly over Denali and other scenic highlights.

Once you're back on the Parks Highway heading north, the scenery starts to become even more impressive. The road will have a number of pullouts for admiring the scenery, so do take advantage of them. Denali State Park is a largely undeveloped wilderness area to the south of Denali National Park. The very best scenery of the entire route is on this portion of the highway. From Denali State Park you'll have an excellent distant view of Mt. McKinley (weather permitting) and many other peaks, as well as the glaciers on the mountain's southern slope. The **Glacier Overlook** at Milepost 135.2 is an especially good place to stop for a stretch and take in the view. The interior of the state park has many trails, but they're rather difficult and only for the experienced hiker.

Denali National Park & Preserve

For a park map and other information, contact the Superintendent, Denali National Park & Preserve, PO Box 9, Denali Park, AK 99755, ☎ (907) 683-2294, www.nps.gov/dena.

Denali is one of America's largest national parks, covering a mind-boggling six million acres. It was established in 1917 as McKinley National Park, named for its single most prominent feature, one of the world's tallest peaks at 20,320 feet. In some ways, it is the highest peak because the surrounding terrain is generally not at a great altitude. McKinley soars some 18,000 feet higher than the immediately surrounding landscape. Denali is known as much for its diverse wildlife as for the "High One," which is the English translation of the Native Alaskan term for the mountain. The most common of the larger animals found here are the almost 3,000 caribou, 2,500 Dall sheep, 2,000 moose, 2,000 wolves and about 500 grizzly and black bears. There are dozens of other species found within the park, but those mentioned are the result of a survey of park visitors and were spotted by more than 80% of respondents. So, you have an excellent chance of seeing wildlife. Denali also covers a number of different environmental zones, including taiga (far northern forests of coniferous trees) and tundra (nearly flat and treeless plains).

For those making the journey from Anchorage by train, the Alaska Railroad has a station right in the park within walking distance of lodging, restaurants and the Visitor Access Center. Daily service is available from Anchorage and Fairbanks during the summer. Although most of the park is inaccessible to those who are not hiking into the backcountry, there is a single road that extends for 97 miles into the park. However, only the first 14 miles to the Savage River are open to general traffic. Beyond that point, the only access is either by shuttle bus or authorized tour bus. This is because the unpaved road could not handle greater levels of traffic and, even if it could, officials are doing what they can so as not to damage the pristine environment. There is an exception which allows campers with reservations (difficult to obtain) at the Teklanika campground to pass.

Touring Options

Let's first look at the shuttle bus method of exploring Denali. These buses aren't luxury touring vehicles. In fact, some are little more than old-fashioned school buses and aren't very comfortable for a long ride on a rather bumpy road. But, then again, this is the wilderness and a little "roughing" it never hurt anyone. Nor are they tour buses – that is, no narration is provided. Drivers will, however, usually stop to allow picture taking. In addition to scheduled stops for pick-up and drop-off of passengers, stops are made at approximately 1½-hour intervals at restroom facilities. (Once you get on the bus there are virtually no facilities in the park, so bring food, warm

clothing and insect repellent along with you.) You can disembark at any of the stops and board another bus on a space-
available basis. It's getting on the bus in the first place that requires a little advance planning or a lot of patience. Over half
the seats on each bus departing the Visitor Access Center are
held on a reservation basis. The cost ranges from $18-31 per
day, depending on how far into the park you travel. Multi-day
passes are available at a somewhat reduced cost. There is an
additional $4 registration fee and you also have to pay the
park admission fee, $10. Reservations can be made by calling
☎ (800) 622-7275 or you can reserve online at www.reserve-
denali.com. The park's website has a link to the reservation
site. The remainder of seats can be reserved only in person at
the Visitor Access Center up to two days in advance on a first-
come, first-served basis. If you arrive without a reservation,
sign up as soon as you get here. During the summer, it is not
uncommon to find few or no seats available for the day you arrive. For those arriving with fixed hotel reservations and a limited amount of time, this system probably means not being
able to stay around long enough to get on a bus. The key is to
reserve in advance. If you plan on spending several days in the
area, this isn't a big deal; you could do other things in Denali
for a day or visit Fairbanks and be back in Denali in time for
your scheduled departure.

Guided tours on more comfortable buses (with lunch or snack
provided, depending on the length of the tour) are offered
twice daily, usually at 6 am and 3 pm (always confirm the time
when you book your reservation). These tours last from four
to eight hours and cost between $40 and $80 per person. They
don't go as far into the park as the shuttles do, but they do allow you to visit the highlights in greater comfort. Advance
reservations are almost a necessity since these tours also fill
up very quickly, often with cruise passengers on escorted
tours. Information and reservations for these trips can be arranged through **Tundra Wildlife Tours and Natural History Tour**, ☎ (800) 276-7234. You can also reserve online at

the same website as for the shuttle buses. Shorter tours go only as far as Savage River so, if you have your own car, they don't accomplish much except providing you with some professional narration. On the other hand, longer guided tours travel on the part of the road closed to private vehicles and you'll be seeing much that you couldn't otherwise experience.

Sights & Attractions

Mt. McKinley first becomes visible from the park road at Milepost 9.4. The capricious weather in Denali often obscures part or all of the mountain for long periods of time. The summit itself is obscured by clouds approximately three-fourths of the time during the summer months. In fact, there is no guarantee that you'll see Mt. McKinley at all during your visit. If you're lucky enough to get a clear day, then the view of the distant perennially white peak is a sight that, alone, is worth the trip from Anchorage. Even better views are afforded from various points farther along the road, all in the area where private vehicles are not allowed.

The **Riley Creek area** near the park entrance is the hub for all activities and services. Here you'll find several lodging facilities and restaurants (advance reservations for rooms are an absolute must). A number of trails leave from the Visitor Access Center area. These include Horseshoe Lake Trail (.75 of a mile), Morino Loop Trail (1.5 miles) and Rock Creek Trail (2.3 miles). All are relatively easy. Horseshoe Lake Trail leads to a bluff overlooking a picturesque lake and the Nenana River. Rock Creek Trail leads to the dog kennels (more about that in a few moments). There are several more difficult trails in the area if you're looking for a challenge.

As a wilderness area, Denali is very isolated, especially during the winter. Supplies to remote portions of the park and more than an occasional rescue mission must be done by dog-sled, just as in the *Sgt. Preston* TV shows of days long ago! The park maintains its own dog teams, which are housed in kennels a couple of miles from the visitor center. **Sled-dog demonstrations** are given by park rangers daily at 10 am, 2 pm and 4 pm from June through August only. You can get to the kennel area by car, trail or free shuttle bus from the Access Center. The rangers will tell you all about the dogs, show you how they're hitched up and take them for a short spin around the complex. It's a most interesting and rewarding experience for all. You can visit the dogs at any time throughout the day.

Some other activities begin outside the park. Two **raft trip** operators offer scenic float trips and whitewater adventures through a narrow canyon on the Nenana River. Rafting is a popular activity, with trips ranging from two hours to a full day. Reservations are strongly recommended. At Milepost 238, **Alaska Raft Adventures**, ☎ (800) 276-7234, offers trips at 8 am, noon, 1:30 pm and 6 pm. A half-mile north of the park entrance is **Denali Raft Adventures**, ☎ (888) 683-2234, with trips at 7:30 am, 9 am, 10 am, 12:30 pm, 3 pm and 6:30 pm. A number of flightseeing trips are also available. **Denali Flightseeing** is the largest operator, ☎ (800) 843-1947.

Fairbanks

Despite the fact that Fairbanks is officially Alaska's second-largest city, it retains a strong frontier-style atmosphere and its downtown streets are lined with log structures. In most ways, Fairbanks is much more "Alaskan" than Anchorage and that alone makes it worthwhile to venture this far north. Fairbanks and its residents proudly reflect their mining community origins. A trading post existed on the city site as early as 1901. It likely would have faded into oblivion if not for the discovery of gold about a year later. The gold boom didn't last that long, but the completion of the Alaska Highway and the development of several military installations ensured that

Fairbanks wouldn't become a ghost town. More recently, the Alaska oil pipeline gave another economic boost to the city. It's less than 400 miles to Prudhoe Bay from Fairbanks, almost a hop, skip and a jump by Alaska standards!

Arrival

If coming by car you'll simply continue on the George Parks Highway from Denali. The road changes names to the Mitchell Expressway as it skirts the south side of Fairbanks. Get off at Airport Way and drive east for about 3½ miles to Cushman Street. A left turn there will bring you right into downtown. Those taking the Alaska Railroad will arrive at the depot, conveniently located near downtown, just across the bridge that traverses the Chena River.

Tourism Information Office

The two best sources of information on Fairbanks and the surrounding area are the **Alaska Public Lands Information Center**, 250 Cushman Street, ☎ (907) 456-0527; and the **Fairbanks Visitor Information Center**, 550 First Avenue, ☎ (800) 327-5774, www.explorefairbanks.com. The visitor center is a log cabin, like the one in Anchorage. It is just off of Cushman Street.

Getting Around

Downtown, if you can call it that, consists of a few blocks on either side of the main thoroughfare (Cushman Street) stretching from 1st through 12th avenues. This area is best explored on foot, not because of any traffic problems, but simply to get a better feel for what it's like. The rest of the city is, considering its size, rather spread out and occupies a peninsula formed by the Chena River and the wider and island-dotted Tanana River. Additional areas to the north of the Chena are also within Fairbanks' city limits. The adjacent communities of Ester, Fox and North Pole all comprise greater Fairbanks. Almost all of the area's attractions are outside the downtown core and a car is the only suitable way of getting around. Although taxis are available, riding them to sightsee could become prohibitively expensive. The limited local public bus system doesn't get to all of the important visitor attractions.

Sightseeing

Because you aren't limited to a single day in any place on the land portion of your Alaskan visit, this isn't a one-day highlight tour but a more comprehensive guide to what the area has to offer.

Either of the two information centers listed above is a good place to begin a walking tour of downtown. There are displays about Alaskan wildlife in the Public Lands Information Center. Although there aren't a lot of specific attractions downtown, it's worth taking a walk around in order to experience the quaint look and feel of the city. One place that is worth stopping into is the **Fairbanks Ice Museum**, 500 2nd Avenue, ☎ (907) 451-8222, in an historic old theater building. The museum displays ice sculptures by local residents. Films demonstrate ice-carving techniques (but you might already have seen that on your cruise). *Open daily, 10 am to 9 pm, $$.*

The University of Alaska campus is home to the fine **Museum of the North** at 907 Yukon Drive, ☎ (907) 474-7505. Take Airport Way west to University Avenue and turn north. This is one of the finest museums in the state and houses a large and interesting collection of items related to Alaska's natural and cultural history, including the wild days of the Gold Rush era. *Open daily, 9 am to 5 pm (till 7 pm June through August), $.* Guided walking tours of the campus depart from the museum and last about two hours. *Tour given weekdays except on holidays, 10 am.* A number of specialty tours are also offered, including the Arctic Region Supercomputer, an Arctic research center and others. Tour times vary; ☎ (907) 474-7581 for in-

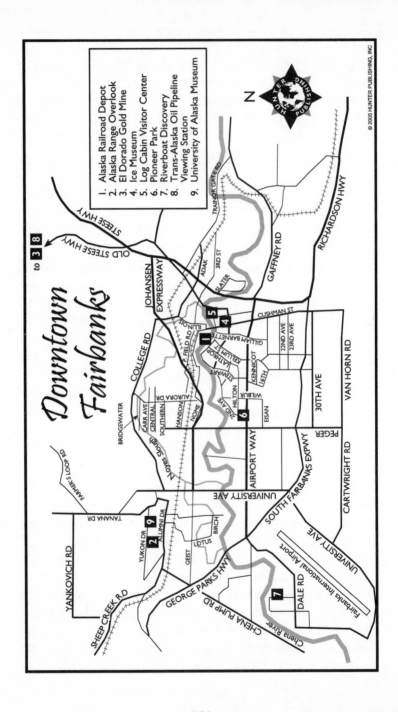

Downtown Fairbanks

1. Alaska Railroad Depot
2. Alaska Range Overlook
3. El Dorado Gold Mine
4. Ice Museum
5. Log Cabin Visitor Center
6. Pioneer Park
7. Riverboat Discovery
8. Trans-Alaska Oil Pipeline Viewing Station
9. University of Alaska Museum

formation. Be sure that you don't leave the campus area until you've taken a good look from the Alaska Range Overlook (on Yukon Drive just past the museum). Here you'll have a fabulous view, weather permitting, of the Three Sisters (Mt. Hayes, Hess and Deborah, which range in altitude from over 12,000 feet to almost 14,000 feet.). On really clear days you can even see Mt. McKinley, but this isn't that common.

Excursions from Fairbanks

A few short excursions from Fairbanks are worthwhile ways to spend some time. Many involve aspects of Fairbanks' days as a gold-mining community. Nine miles north on the Elliott Highway (Alaska State Highway 2) is the **El Dorado Gold Mine**, ☎ (866) 479-6673. You'll be able to enter the mine via an old train to see how the operations work, but El Dorado has one unique offering – the train goes through a permafrost tunnel. You can also pan for gold. The entire tour takes about two hours, without panning. *Tours daily at 9:45 am and 3 pm (3 pm only on Saturday), $$$$.* Reservations are required.

Somewhat closer to town is the **Riverboat Discovery**, ☎ (866) 479-6673, departing from 1975 Discovery Drive, off of Airport Way, ☎ (907) 679-6673. This 3½-hour journey on the Chena and Tanana rivers offers an excellent opportunity to see wildlife. A stop is made at the Chena Indian village. Informative guides provide an interesting narrative throughout the trip. *Departures daily at 8:45 am and 2 pm, $$$$.*

North of Fairbanks via the Old Steese Highway (Alaska State Highway 6) to Goldstream Road is **Gold Dredge #8**, ☎ (907) 457-6058. The five-deck ship towers more than 250 feet and dates from 1928. Interesting 90-minute tours are offered and afterwards you can pan for gold to your heart's content. While this is an interesting stop, I feel it is somewhat overpriced. *Open daily, 9:30 am to 3:30 pm, $$$$.* And while you're on Goldstream Road, take it for a short ride to a spot overlooking a section of the Alaska Pipeline. You may find that viewing a small section of the pipeline doesn't allow for proper appreciation of the massive scope of the pipeline project. However, you'll still probably agree that the small detour was worth it.

The next attraction is the neighboring town of Ester, five miles west of Fairbanks via the George Parks Highway (although the road markers will indicate south). Here you'll find the **Ester Gold Camp**, ☎ (800) 676-6925, site of a 1904 gold mining community of the Fairbanks Exploration Company. It operated until as recently as 1958, much longer than most of the other area gold operations. Two shows here cover completely different but uniquely Alaskan topics. The "Photosymphony" (not recommended for small children) is a multi-media recreation of the phenomenon of the *aurora borealis*, more commonly known as the Northern Lights, while "Service with a Smile" is a musical revue about the Gold Rush era. The name refers to the poet Robert Service, who wrote "The Shooting of Dan McGrew." Part of the fun of this 1½-hour show is the setting. You'll watch the performance in a relic-filled saloon with floors covered in sawdust. The camp has a restaurant and gift shop. *The camp is open at all times; the Northern Lights show is given nightly at 6:45 pm and 7:45 pm, $$; Service with a Smile is shown nightly at 9 pm, with an additional 7 pm performance Wednesday through Saturday during July, $$$.* Reservations are suggested.

Additional Sights for Longer Stays

Alaska Salmon Bake & Palace Theatre & Saloon, 3175 College Road, ☎ (800) 354-7274, offers an evening of dining and entertainment. The comedy show is really funny. *Dinner served nightly beginning at 5 pm; comedy show at 8:15 pm, $$$$.*

Creamer's Field, 1300 College Road in nearby Lemeta, is a nice area of nature trails that run through a variety of terrain, including wetlands. Numerous waterfowl and other birds can be seen and, with only a little bit of luck, you'll catch sight of some moose. The site was once a dairy and the original farmhouse is now the preserve's visitor center. *Open daily.*

Pioneer Park, Airport Way and Peger Road, ☎ (907) 459-1199. With a pretty setting by the Chena River, this large area encompasses a number of interesting aspects of Fairbanks' history. There are native villages, mining displays, cultural museums, an Alaska Railroad car used by President Harding, and a river sternwheeler. You can even take part in an authentic salmon bake. A number of historic buildings have been moved here from other places. This is a good destination for adults and children. A visit here can take anywhere from an hour to a half-day. *Open daily, 11 am to 9 pm; no admission, but $-$$ for some individual features.*

Chena Hot Springs. This is a lengthy side-trip. Head north from Fairbanks on Highway 2 for five miles to the Chena Hot Springs Road. After 57 miles on the latter you'll be in the highly scenic Chena River State Recreation Area. Many people come here to experience the natural hot springs, which have a temperature of 156 degrees. The water is so hot that it actually has to be cooled before people can use it. It is the most well known of Alaska's nearly 125 geothermal areas.

Santa Claus House, 101 St. Nicholas Drive, in the nearby town of North Pole, ☎ (800) 588-4078, is where you can get an original letter from Santa along with a deed to one-square-inch of the North Pole! Could any child resist this? There's also a great selection of souvenirs and collectibles featuring Christmas and Alaskan themes. Reindeer are also on the premises. *Open daily.*

The Arctic. As Fairbanks has the distinction of being the nearest city of any size to the far northern reaches of Alaska, it is the starting point for guided tours into the Arctic. There are a number of reliable operators offering tours of a half-day up to a week. They use a combination of road and air. You can get information at Fairbanks' visitor center; however, some good places to start are the **Northern Alaska Tour Company**, ☎ (800) 474-1986; **Trans Arctic Circle Treks**, ☎ (800) 336-8735; or **Arctic Outfitters**, ☎ (907) 474-3530. And, for all you Arctic fans, here's a trivia question:

Q: What is the Arctic Circle?

A: It's the imaginary line of latitude where the sun never sets on the summer solstice and doesn't rise on the winter solstice.

THE AURORA BOREALIS

The *Aurora Borealis*, more commonly known as the Northern Lights, is one of nature's most unusual and beautiful phenomena. The scientific explanation of why this occurs and how is quite complicated and I don't pretend to understand it very well. But almost everyone is interested in seeing it. The aurora is a wonderful display of rapidly shifting patterns and columns of flashing lights. Most of the time, they are either whitish or green, but on occasion they'll be a bright red. At its best, the aurora will dazzle you as it lights up the sky in an uncountable number of shapes.

While the *Aurora Borealis* can occur anywhere north of about the 60th parallel of latitude, it is much more frequently seen in the far northern reaches, such as Alaska. However, even in Alaska there are great variations. Fairbanks happens to be among the very best places in the world to view the Aurora yet, not too far north (where it should theoretically be even better), the conditions are not as good. In Fairbanks, the Northern Lights put on their show about 243 days out of the year. However, the long summer nights interfere with viewing for most of the summer. Therefore, the best time for cruise passengers to see it is from late August through the end of the cruise season. Unfortunately, unlike some other phenomena, it can't be predicted with any great accuracy. You can get the "forecast" at www.gi.alaska.edu. Even then, you don't know beforehand if it's going to be a so-so performance or a spectacular one to remember for a lifetime. It's all just a matter of being in the right place at the right time. Hope you see a good one!

Shopping

Those who travel to shop won't find a great deal in Fairbanks. A few places that you might try for native Alaskan arts and crafts are the **Arctic Travelers Gift Shop**, 201 Cushman Street; the **Craft Market**, 401 5th Avenue; **Raven Mad**, 535 2nd Avenue; and **Beads & Things**, 537 2nd Avenue. They are all close to one another, as is most of the downtown shopping. Although not in the category of native art, jewelry hunters will likely find something nice at **Judie Gumm Designs**, 3600 Main Street in nearby Ester. Ms. Gumm creates original and unique jewelry based on various Alaskan themes. For more jewelry (not only the Alaskan variety) try **Taylor's Gold-N-Stones**, 357-B Airport Way. Looking for that stuffed animal to put on your wall so you can tell your friends that you bagged it? Then the place to go is **King's Interior Taxidermy**, 3200 N. Athena Circle, in North Pole. They also have cold-weather clothing and a great selection of teddy bears. Speaking of clothing, since Fairbanks winters are so cold, you would be correct in assuming that it was here that native Alaskans came up with some of the best outer clothing for keeping warm. *Kuspuks*, women's parkas made from the skins of various animals, can be bought at various clothing stores downtown. They're expensive, but if you live in a cold climate, it will be well worth the price.

Sports & Recreation

The major outdoor activities are **kayaking** or **canoeing** on the many area rivers, including the Chena, Tanana and Chaanika. **Fishing** opportunities are abundant and there are numerous excursions lasting anywhere from a day to a week. The visitor information center can put you in touch with outfitters. The most northerly 18-hole **golf** course in North America is Fairbanks' North Star Golf Club.

The Matanuska Valley, Palmer

The attractions in this last section are much closer to Anchorage than Denali or Fairbanks, but I've included them separately because they are all located off the direct northbound route from Anchorage. You have the option of doing them on the way to or from Anchorage, on a separate trip, or as daytrips from Anchorage. The valley can also be seen on the way to Valdez if you're heading that way.

The pretty Matanuska Valley, surrounded by the impressive peaks of the Chugach and Talkeetna mountains, is centered around the town of Palmer on the Glenn Highway (Alaska State Highway 1). You reach it by branching off the main Anchorage-to-Fairbanks road just before the town of Wasilla. From there it is only a short ride into Palmer.

There are many farms in the Matanuska Valley. Due to the unusual summer growing conditions (up to 20 hours of sunshine daily), vegetables sometimes reach enormous sizes. Seventy-pound cabbages are not unusual – and you thought they grew things big in Texas! Few farms are visible from the Glenn Highway, but you can get information and a good local area map at the Visitor Information Center in Palmer if you want to drive the back roads and track down the farms. Giant vegetables are always on display in the attractive garden outside the Visitor

Center, Valley Way near Fireweed, ☎ (907) 745-2880, which is easily found along the main road through the heart of Palmer. If agriculture is your thing, visit **Matanuska Agricultural Experimental Farm**, seven miles southwest of town, where some of the larger vegetable specimens can be seen.

Palmer is the site of the Alaska State Fairgrounds. However, the most famous town attraction may well be the **Musk Ox Farm**, Milepost 50 on the Glenn Highway, ☎ (907) 745-4151. This allows you to take a guided walk through the farm and come face to face with over a hundred of these large and unhandsome beasts. It's the only domestic herd of musk oxen in the world. You'll learn how their hair, qiviut, is woven into the rich cloth that is so sought after by discriminating shoppers. We previously mentioned how much warmer it is than wool, but another of its qualities is strength. It has 20 times the tensile strength of wool. *Open daily, 10 am to 6 pm, $$.*

A little farther east along the Glenn Highway is a fantastic view of the **Matanuska Glacier**, which measures some 27 miles in length and almost four miles across. A trail here leads to the edge of the glacier.

An approximately 20-mile ride north from Palmer via Hatcher Pass Road will take you to **Independence Mine State Historical Park**. This was once a booming gold mining town and you can visit some of the 15 well-preserved buildings from that time (the 1930s and '40s). The park itself is quite interesting and the surrounding area provides some lovely scenery on the drive to and from town. *Park open daily, 10 am to 7 pm, with somewhat reduced hours before June 15th and after Labor Day; $$ per vehicle; guided tours, $.*

Beyond the Cruise

Index

Index